A General Theory of Economic Process

A General Theory of Economic Process

BY NEIL W. CHAMBERLAIN

Professor of Economics
Graduate School of Business
Columbia University

HARPER & BROTHERS
Publishers   New York

CONTENTS

PREFACE

IN the chapters which follow an effort has been made to fashion a system of concepts which will explain the economic process. Such an effort may appear pretentious when made by one who lays no claim to being a general theoretician but has, instead, maintained a safe specialization in the field of industrial relations. I feel (almost apologetically) a need to explain the existence of this work.

First, for several years at Yale I taught courses in both general theory and labor economics, and in the process acquired an increasing interest in the extent to which the concepts of a specialization (such as industrial relations) could find their partial testing in the search for the parent *general* concept, at a higher level of abstraction, as well as the extent to which the concepts of general theory might suggest their more narrowly applied counterparts in a field of specialization.

Second, in my own work in industrial relations I had reached a stage where the significance of my further research appeared to depend on the relevance of union-management relationships to economic activity generally, requiring a larger theoretical framework in which to cast the specialized studies. There were, however, several respects in which current theory seemed deficient for this purpose, and my only recourse was to accept the challenge. This is the result.

Among the respects in which present theory appears remiss are these. It excludes certain types of relationships which affect the allocation of scarce resources, most notably political relationships. The micro and macro aspects have been difficult to join within an integrated theoretical framework in which fluctuations in aggregate income as well as the allocation of income are explainable with the same set of concepts. Maximization as the motivation behind economic behavior has become less and less satisfactory but has not found an adequate replacement. I do believe that the present effort makes some advances on at least these problems. To the extent it succeeds, it may stimulate others to follow lines of inquiry which are, in any event, already becoming quite evident in the literature. To the extent it fails, it may nevertheless serve its purpose by encouraging some reflection on the reasons for its failure.

N. W. CHAMBERLAIN

New York, N. Y.
January, 1955

A General Theory of Economic Process

CHAPTER 1

Individual and Culture: Micro and Macro

IN analyzing any economy one must achieve an understanding of its culture. The only admitted exception to this rule is in the case of the advisory approach of those who, like Professor Frank Knight, define the study of economics as the study of economizing. For them, principles of economizing can be laid down which are applicable to any society or culture. Their system is a description or prescription of how "economic men" in any cultural setting would or should behave. "Economic man" is considered as an abstract rule of conduct rather than a concept of human behavior. Except for this approach, however, economists cannot escape the fact that the economic relationships of a society will reflect the cultural background of that society. Its games, system of law, patterns of courtship and family life, methods of instruction, techniques of warfare, processes of government will all help to influence the character of the economic relationships. Consequently, just as we find cultural diversity, so we find economic diversity.

It would be erroneous to conclude, however, that economic relationships are only a resultant of other kinds of relationships. It might equally be said that the religious, political, familial, educational, and other social patterns of a group are in part a reflection of economic relationships. The economy must then be viewed as

1

in part determined by, in part determining the whole social system. The wants of a people and the means for reducing the gap between wants and satisfaction condition and are conditioned by the kind of a society in which people live, the nature of the organized repetitive responses to which they conform.

If a culture molds the individual's responses, society becomes an active agent in the economic process. If the structure of competitive and coöperative relationships characterizing a society is determined not simply by the undirected choice of individuals but by culturally directed choices, the culture existing at the moment is integral to economic analysis.

The individual is not simply a resultant of this process, however. He is not a being whose responses are mechanistically predetermined by some larger social organization. Culture does not arise spontaneously or change autonomously. It is itself a resultant of interpersonal relationships, over which the individual has his own measure of influence.

That the individual is not simply a product of his cultural environment is readily demonstrable. It is only the individual (the culture-acquiring child) who can from the start "interpret, evaluate, and modify every culture pattern, subpattern, or assemblage of patterns that it will ever be influenced by. . . . Culture is then not something given but something to be gradually and gropingly discovered. We then see at once that elements of culture that come well within the horizon of awareness of one individual are entirely absent in another individual's landscape."[1] The unique nature and experience of the individual lead him to unique selections and interpretations of all the myriad data surrounding him, lead him to unique associations of ideas resulting in discoveries and creations. These personal contributions in turn influence others and at times may even affect the culture.[2]

---

[1] E. Sapir, "The Emergence of the Concept of Personality in a Study of Cultures," *Journal of Social Psychology*, vol. 5 (1934), p. 414.

[2] ". . . While according to the accepted science of 1901 man's every act was completely determined in advance by the motions and forces of the elemental atoms, the science of 1951 recognizes that there is no complete predetermination

Interpersonal relations are thus culturally influenced, just as the culture is itself individually influenced. Individual behavior cannot be explained without reference to the culture, and culture cannot be explained without reference to the individual. Both views are correct, yet neither is complete without the other.

The Yale philosopher Paul Weiss has admirably expressed this double condition of behavioral explanations.

He who insists that men are free acknowledges that men are more than reservoirs of past conditioning. He allows that they can decide which one of a set of alternatives is to be selected; he grants that they are free to utilize dynamically, in an unconditioned way, whatever it is that conditions them. But he risks losing hold of the truth that men are molded by training and are dated in speech, clothing, work, idea, image, aspiration, fear, and hope. This truth is as important as the other. We should not be satisfied with less than both.

We are free to select any alternative, yet there are reasons for our selecting what we do. We can intend otherwise than we now do, but we do intend as men who are, want, and have undergone specific things. We are neither free from all conditioning nor inexorably bound.[3]

Acceptance of a degree of freedom from determining circumstances comports fully with the modern approach to science as a search for probabilities rather than eternal truths. It is now widely accepted that events are not fully determined but that causation may be attributable to chance, hence explainable statistically as likely, but not logically as inevitable. Here the admission of personal influence over the course of events is one element which puts us

---

of man's actions by physical law. After taking into account all the physical factors introduced through the external world and the physiology of the nervous system, there still remains an area within which man's actions are in principle unpredictable. This means that in terms of physical science, while fifty years ago one saw no possible counterpart in man's actions to his feeling of free choice, now the physical possibility of such a counterpart must be recognized." Arthur H. Compton, "Science and Man's Destiny," an address December 29, 1951, before the American Association for the Advancement of Science as presented in the Phi Beta Kappa *Key Reporter*, February, 1952, p. 2.

[3] Paul Weiss, *Man's Freedom* (New Haven: Yale University Press, 1951), p. 63. This thoughtful book will repay reading in its entirety by those who are interested in the philosophical aspects of the place of the individual in his society.

outside the realm of determinacy. We admit that predictions are only expressions of probabilities. We can seek to narrow the range of indeterminacy which is due to ignorance of the conditioning influences, but there must remain an irreducible element of unpredictability—for which, indeed, we may be thankful since it precludes controlled outcomes by those in authority. "Predictable in general, to be counted on to do certain kinds of things and not others, the full, detailed nature of our actions cannot be known in advance. Reliable, predictable on the whole, we are free in detail, both as biological beings with well-known stable anatomies and appetites and as socially trained men with acquired interests and habits." [4]

The above considerations are relevant to economic analysis. Economic relations, as one category of social relations, are subject to our conclusion concerning the mutually conditioning relationship between individual and culture. In economic analysis, the micro model is built solely on the individual and deals with interpersonal relations only. The macro model, on the other hand, deals with aggregative relations, being similar in this respect to the concept of culture (another aggregate); indeed, macroeconomic relations can be viewed as an aspect of culture dealing with organized repetitive influences on individual economic behavior. The micro and macro relations of economic analysis thus correspond to the individual and culture in sociological theory. And the conclusion that individual and culture are interrelated so that one can be explained only in terms of the other can be transferred to micro and macro economic analysis. Neither can explain economic behavior adequately without the other.

This basic truth is obscured in the micro and macro models which have come down to us. In the concepts of the price analysis, society is simply the locus of individuals, who alone have reality. Economic relationships arise from individual choices, rationally made. While it is true that the competitive mechanism is regarded as controlling the individual, compelling him to given behavior whether he wills it or not, this phenomenon is *not* viewed as a cultural determination

[4] *Ibid.*, p. 7.

of individual behavior; rather, it is regarded as the product of the maximizing nature of the individual himself.[5] Society is conceived as an artificial abstraction, a thing without reality, something which can be identified only as the sum of the individuals who compose it. The individual is the basic unit, the independent variable. It is individual choices which add up to culture patterns. If we study the individual, we thus arrive at a knowledge of society. Since culture patterns are products of individual choice, they are not so much controlling of the individual as controlled by individuals, not so much determining of behavior (including economic behavior) as determined by behavior. On such an approach it appears much less important to analyze culture patterns when one may go more directly to the individuals responsible for them.

It is not accidental that economics books of the nineteenth century (and even of the twentieth) took, for examples of the economic process in its simplest form, the Robinson Crusoe economy—expressive of pure individualism, devoid of social setting.

Macro economics has been less guilty of ignoring interpersonal relations, but the emphasis has nonetheless been unmistakable. Individual behavior is primarily a predeterminable reaction to the movement of impersonal variables like total consumption, total savings, total investment, total income, the total money supply. Interpersonal relationships are not explored, since it is believed that they are in large degree simply reflective of the broad, aggregative movements.

The problem of joining micro and macro relations in a common theoretical model involves a search for the *process* by which one

[5] Of all those in the stream of development of the price system, none recognized the importance of cultural control over the individual so much as Adam Smith. While Smith stressed the economic philosophy of individualism, he nevertheless held relatively advanced notions about the two-way relationship between society and individual. He would have been at home with modern sociologists on this point. His influence in this respect was nullified at the start by the rationalistic approach of Bentham, however. It was largely due to Bentham that economics in its formative years enthroned the individual and ignored his culture. Society and its network of relationships were, basically, nothing more than individuals guided by their independent rational calculation of the balance of pleasure and pain existing in alternative relationships.

influences the other and is in turn influenced. And as soon as it is recognized that micro and macro relations can be joined only in a process, the time factor becomes an important ingredient, as we shall see.

In the pages which follow we shall seek to build a set of concepts producing theoretical explanations which—*prima facie*—appear to have a greater degree of reliability than either the micro or the macro model taken by itself. But reliability must be judged by probability rather than certainty. Out of our analysis should emerge the picture of economic relations always in the process of change—always becoming, with no event predetermined but still not undetermined, a picture of relations which are constantly flowing out of past and present events, but which the past and present do not make inevitable.

CHAPTER 2

"Economic" Aspirations

ECONOMIC activity is purposive. The purpose is necessary to an explanation of the activity. Purpose, moreover, is an attribute of individuals, even though individual purpose is culturally influenced. We should look to the micro models, then, for a clue as to the purpose of economic activity. In such analyses the purpose of economic behavior is construed as the maximizing of consumer gain (which is equivalent to the minimizing of factor effort). We are searching, then, for a conception of economic aspiration which will serve, in our process analysis, the same functions which the maximizing assumption serves in the price analysis.

In the price analysis the minimizing of the pain of labor is considered simply the obverse of the maximizing of the pleasure of consumption. Whether workers will move to the highest-paying jobs (where the required effort is equal) or to the jobs requiring least effort (where pay is equal) makes no difference in the argument, since the maximum and minimum are always relative to each other. Consumption and work serve as these related extremes in the price system. In our discussion, while continuing to treat consumption and work as the two primary categories involving economic aspiration, we shall make no such assumption about their inverse relationship. In our system, then, it will be possible to have job goals which are both competitive and noncompetitive with, and at times virtually independent of, consumption goals.

7

ASPIRATIONS INVOLVING CONSUMPTION

By consumption goals (or aspirations or objectives) we mean to include all goals which involve the use or allocation of scarce resources, irrespective of the motive behind the activity. There is no intent to imply that consumption itself is either the motive or the goal, only that consumption is necessary to the achievement of the motive or goal. This point deserves some emphasis, since there has sometimes been a tendency to identify *certain* objectives or goals as "economic" and then to consider the allocation of scarce resources to achieve these economic goals as constituting the economic problem. Many discussions, indeed, appear to treat consumption itself as the objective of economic activity, and some go further by confining the analysis to personal consumption. The objective of economic activity is never consumption itself, however, but always some purpose which consumption serves. The objective may be religious, political, charitable, scientific, artistic, or anything else, and as long as its achievement affects the allocation of resources we are faced with an economic problem.[1]

This is not a matter of trifling importance. When one considers the enormous range of economic activity which is omitted from the price analysis—all forms of taxation, government transfer payments, other coercively imposed levies on time or money, the distribution of income within the family, and so on—he is led to suspect that such matters are left out because they are considered, in some sense, noneconomically motivated. Once it is agreed that goals, whatever their nature, are relevant to the economic problem whenever they involve the allocation of scarce resources, all such omitted areas become theoretically as significant as the included area of price exchanges for the satisfaction of personal wants.

---

[1] There is thus an economic problem inherent in all human activity, since activity of whatever sort involves a use of time, which is a scarce factor. The relevance of this to economic analysis need not detain us now but will be considered in another chapter.

When we set up consumer goals as one category of economic aspirations, then, we imply nothing more than that goods are wanted in order to achieve a variety of objectives. Nevertheless, the breadth of this category can be more readily shown if we recognize three subcategories of consumer objectives: personal consumption, collective consumption, and vicarious consumption.

PERSONAL CONSUMPTION

By personal consumption is meant that range of activity which is normally identified with consumption itself—the use of goods and services *by* oneself for one's own satisfaction. Attitudes toward personal consumption are culturally conditioned, but by this we mean something more than that the goods and services among which choice is made are themselves cultural products. It is too obvious to require elaboration that the food preferences of a resident of the United States would differ substantially from those of a resident of even nearby Jamaica, for example. The foods demanded by the former may not even be available in the latter location. The Jamaican resident is not likely to have any demand for baked beans, clam chowder, peach pie, griddle cakes, or other dishes common to an American's diet. Similarly the American in his own environment will have no demand for soursop, naseberries, plantain, and chocho. The same observation may be made with respect to clothing, travel, entertainment, housing. The consumption items which individuals prefer are the familiar products of their own society; in most cases these are also the only products generally known or available. This elementary influence of a society's culture on consumption is not disputed by the price analysis. The indifference functions start from this point. A person's indifferences are expressed between the products of his culture. When it is said that culture influences consumption in a manner not adequately described in the theory of competitive price, then, something more is intended.

By cultural influences on consumption we shall here mean the attitudes which the society encourages concerning the personal consumption of goods, in contrast to their use for other purposes (such as religious ceremonies or military conquest) or in contrast to the expenditure of time and effort on nonmaterial satisfactions (such as philosophical contemplation or games or indolence). We shall have to confine our attention to the United States, from limitations of time and space.

American culture has a strong materialistic bias which emphasizes the importance of personal acquisition of goods. Goods are in fact associated with good living. For many Americans the civilizing influence is often identified with the spread of sanitary plumbing and refrigeration, automobiles and radios. These possessions are regarded not only as valuable for their utilities but as somehow expressive of a more desirable way of life, almost a higher stage in the evolution of mankind. Poverty stunts individual development; wealth opens new horizons and permits greater achievement.

This social emphasis on consumption has invested material possessions with special significance. Goods become a means of satisfying even the most basic desires. One spends his income to win acceptance and respect from neighbors, business associates, his social set. As Carl Jonas's fictional character, Jefferson Selleck, remarked: "I would like to say that a great deal of the money which I have spent I have not enjoyed, and have only spent because I had to. A man assumes a certain station in life, a certain picture of himself, and he must live up to it or else pull down his colors." [2] The emphasis may extend into early childhood. "An unsatisfied thirst for love from parents may be expressed in the greedy demand for food, clothes, or other gifts, a pattern that can persist through life." Equally it might be said that parents sometimes attempt to substitute gifts for personal attention, in their relations with their children; the giving of goods is identified with the giving of love. "The goals and self-pictures that men and women try to validate for them-

[2] Carl Jonas, *Jefferson Selleck* (Boston: Little, Brown & Company, 1952), p. 167.

selves and their children are as festooned as a Christmas tree by con-
traptions bought in shops." [3]

This cultural emphasis on the possession of goods cuts across any
class or income distinctions, it is endemic to the society as a whole.
The possession of goods has become an aspiration common to all.
Moreover, it is an aspiration without finite limit. This is not to
imply that American people are forever greedy for more goods. To
say that the culture imposes no limits on a person's consumption
wants is not to attribute to him *insatiable* wants at every moment
of time, as we shall see more clearly later. To say that the culture encourages the acquisition of goods as a means of acquiring position
is not to argue that people generally have no limit to their status
ambitions. It does mean, however, first, that there is a widespread
expectation of improvement in one's material standard of living over
time, and second, that the effort to attain such improvement constitutes a primary goal for most people in our society. We are inclined
to judge the "success" of our society in terms of its ability to supply
greater quantities of goods of superior quality. Over time we expect
a general and continuing income elasticity of demand.

We take this characteristic of our society so much for granted
that we sometimes overlook its significance. The generalized aspiration for more and better goods is the basis for the mass markets
which permit mass production.[4] Although the techniques of mass

[3] The last two quotations are from Ruth P. Mack, "Economics of Consumption,"
in Bernard F. Haley (ed.), *A Survey of Contemporary Economics*, vol. 2 (Chicago: Richard D. Irwin, Inc., 1952), p. 42.

[4] The importance of such generalized aspiration for more consumer goods is
pointed up by the comment of an American agriculturalist stationed in Turkey as
a member of the Joint American Military Mission for Aid to Turkey. "The peasants have all they need for bare subsistence, and they're inclined to be satisfied
with that. We've got to go to work and create a demand for a higher standard
of living before we can make them produce the goods to attain the higher
standard." Quoted by Joseph Wechsberg, in "Letter from Ankara," *New Yorker*,
October 4, 1952, p. 112.

Professor Talcott Parsons writes of the German sociologist, Max Weber, that
he emphatically denied that an endlessly expanding bundle of concrete wants is
the "normal" situation. The "normal" situation was, rather, that acquisitive activities were oriented to a traditionally fixed standard of living, with the "economic

production must exist before a mass market can be established, the conditions permitting the rise of a mass market must preëxist before mass production is economically feasible.

The existence of a mass market carries with it significant conse-quences. Producers find it profitable to take a small per-unit gain on a large number of sales. There is thus continuing pressure to reduce prices to win a larger market. Producers find it profitable to engage in extensive advertising campaigns to establish and then protect their positions as suppliers to the many. Their advertising has as one effect the increasing of the strength of consumer wants, inducing a dissatisfaction with current levels of consumption, fo-menting unrest with current levels of real income, stimulating de-mands for higher wages with which to purchase the advertised goods.[5] Finally, the prevalent disposition to expect more and better goods has created a receptivity to innovations. Under such circum-stances innovation is pressed upon the producer; he is caught, whether he wills it or not, in the process of keeping up with com-petitors in the provision of the new and improved. These results are not attributable solely to cultural attitudes toward consumption, to be sure, but they are partially dependent on such attitudes.

COLLECTIVE CONSUMPTION

Some objectives of resource expenditure can best be gained or can only be gained through joint action. As Professor J. M. Clark

principle" taking the form of satisfaction of these traditional needs with the least possible exertion. According to Weber, it is only in capitalistic cultures that this traditionalism has been broken down on any significant scale. When broken down, "acquisition has been freed from any definite limit and becomes an endless process." Parsons, *The Structure of Social Action* (Glencoe, Ill.: Free Press, 1949), p. 514.

[5] Our society has thus developed the peculiar phenomenon of a dominant group (the business interests) themselves stimulating the mass of wageworkers to be discontented with their material condition. This phenomenon may be contrasted with other societies where an attempt has been or still is made to restrain the wants of the laboring class so that a low scale of real wages will satisfy their wants, both physically and culturally, leaving more wealth to satisfy the more nicely developed tastes of the employing class.

has said, no matter how strong the demand for protection from infectious diseases, the demand cannot be made effective by letting individuals bid for such protection. The objective can be gained only when a public health service is established and empowered to enforce certain health and sanitary standards. A list of the use of resources for collective purposes would be long; it would include, among its major items, all military expenditures, local street lighting, police and fire services, the postal service, the support of all legislative and judicial bodies.

Collective consumption is distinguished from personal consumption by the element of compulsion. Whether or not all are agreed upon the desirability of the objective, each is committed through his membership in some common organization to the objective for which organizational resources are to be expended and shares along with all the others in the consumption undertaken. Collective consumption is thus not something peculiarly associated with government. A large proportion of the expenditures of private clubs and voluntary associations falls in the same category. Such expenditures are undertaken by vote of the membership (or on authority voted by the membership) for a variety of uses by the organization itself, and while individual members may normally resign in protest if they choose, as long as they remain members they are organizationally committed to and personally share in the collective consumption which has been decided upon.

VICARIOUS CONSUMPTION

Personal consumption is the use of resources by oneself for his own satisfaction. Collective consumption is the use of resources by a group for its own satisfaction, where the consumption is shared by all regardless of personal agreement or disagreement with its desirability. Vicarious consumption is the appropriation of resources by an individual or group for use by others.

An example will fix the point. Every year millions of individuals make contributions to the Red Cross. These contributions involve a transfer of title to scarce goods and services; the contributor who himself could have consumed goods and services chooses instead to make it possible for the Red Cross and its beneficiaries to do so. The contributor earns the right to a certain amount of scarce resources by his own economic activity, but instead of using these resources for his own advantage he passes them along to others for a different use. This transfer of purchasing power may give great satisfaction to the contributor, but not because of any consumption of his own. It is the Red Cross and the recipients of its aid who consume the scarce resources, made available by the generosity of others. It is not a *personal* consumption aspiration which leads to this use of resources, even though resources must be consumed to satisfy the giver's objectives. The use of resources which is made is not governed by the individual's goal of a rising standard of living for himself, but by his regard for others, by his conception of the kind of a society in which he would like to live—in this case a society which makes provision for those who are rendered helpless and destitute by unforeseen calamity. The use which is made of resources in the society (such as for Red Cross purposes) is possible only because individuals are motivated by something other than a desire to advance their own consumer satisfaction.

The forms of vicarious consumption which come most readily to mind are public relief and private charity. We should have to include in this category too, however, contributions to public and private schools, to the extent that individuals support the spread of education not because of benefits which they expect to derive but because of benefits accruing to the individuals receiving the education and because of long-run advantages to society as a whole, perhaps long after the contributor is dead. In the same category are contributions to hospitals and to funds for medical and scientific research, the gifts of foundations for artistic and scholarly pursuits by others, the endowment of public parks, and so on.

Involved in all such vicarious satisfaction is an empathy which is similar to Adam Smith's "sympathy." The giver feels himself in the position of the recipient and experiences satisfaction in the contemplated satisfaction of the recipient. Once this quality of empathy which is characteristic of vicarious consumption is brought to our attention, we are then reminded of innumerable additional ways in which this form of consumption crops out in our daily lives. All forms of giving—birthday, Christmas, anniversary, graduation, retirement, Mother's Day, Father's Day, and so on—are examples of vicarious satisfaction. At times, to be sure, other qualities than empathy are involved. Sometimes there is less identification with the recipient than concern for the opinions of others—prestige is sought through pretentious gifts, or group acceptance through customary or expected contributions. Finally, there is sometimes associated with vicarious consumption a notion of justice, as in the case of transfer payments to low-income families, to whom, it may be felt in a vague sort of way, the "system" has been unfair.

Let us conclude this brief examination of consumption objectives by restating the argument which is most important to our analysis. It is sometimes maintained that consumption is the end of all economic activity. It is the use of scarce resources which concerns us, as economists, and use necessarily means consumption. Once we identify the consumption goals of a society, then, it is said, we have identified the only aspirations which interest us as economists. All other aspirations reduce to these.

This line of argument is adequate enough if one focuses his attention on society as a whole, on the aggregative economic performance. In this case it is true that consumption (that is, use) of limited resources, whether in the present or the future, lies behind all economic activity, and the economist, who is interested in the problem of allocating limited resources, can reasonably maintain that he is concerned only with consumption. But as soon as one transfers his attention from the economy as a whole, the aggregative performance, to the complex of competitive and coöperative relationships of which the economy is composed, it is no longer true that consumption is the only motive underlying economic activity. Personal consumption is the objective (in the loose sense previously indicated) of all economic activity taken together, but it is not the objective of all individual economic activity.

Since we are interested in exploring the connection between the micro and the macro relationships, it is necessary for us to admit other aspirations than personal consumption as motivating the economic behavior of individuals. Otherwise we are left in the position of *price* analysts, who are capable of explaining—with the tools which they have inherited or devised—only exchange transactions which are intended to maximize personal consumer satisfaction. The gift or charity contribution or tax payment—even if explained as something advancing personal satisfaction (as what activity is *not* designed to do?)—cannot be incorporated within a supply-and-demand and equilibrium-price framework. If interpersonal economic transactions are to be systematically related, it would appear that the price relationship is incapable of performing that function. And unless we can systematically relate the interpersonal (micro) transactions, we are unlikely to be able to link them with aggregate income flows.

ASPIRATIONS INVOLVING WORK

By lumping together all work as "pain" or "cost," the price analysis has obscured the truth that there are elements of the work process which give satisfaction or, at a minimum, that make some forms of work less burdensome than others. As Professor Knight has suggested, work is not sharply separable from play, and aspects of one are to be found in the other. Unless we are prepared to class play as pain, then, we are scarcely warranted in classifying all work as pain.

The social psychologists now tell us that work serves many purposes and satisfies aspirations in other respects than by providing claims to consumption goods. Without attempting any precise survey of the field, we shall note the more important satisfactions associated with jobs and careers aside from those invoking consumption.

First, there are the "psychic" satisfactions afforded by the nature

of the work in relation to the nature of the individual. Such satisfactions were recognized by all price economists only to be ruled
out as of little significance. The numerous instances known to us
all of individuals who take and retain jobs and careers partly if not
largely because of their satisfaction in the work itself, aside from
the remuneration, raise a doubt as to whether this desire to find
some meaning and significance in one's work, other than that it
provides income, is actually of such little significance that it can be
ignored.

Second, there are the social satisfactions to be found on the job,
in the company of one's fellow workers. The historian Frank
Tannenbaum has argued that this clustering of men around their
work is a persisting phenomenon and that labor unions are largely
explainable as a device to protect the integrity of the work society
against disruption from market forces. Repeated studies of worker
groups and inventories of "job satisfactions" have revealed almost
without exception that workers judge a job as "good" or "bad" in
large part on the strength of its social context—whether it permits
frequent and pleasant interpersonal relations, a result which should
scarcely prove surprising.

Third, there is the prestige to be gained by the nature of one's
calling. Sociologists now express little doubt that the status which
an individual occupied in his society derives in substantial part from
his occupation. The respect which he is accorded in his society depends significantly on the kind of work he does. In this respect the
prestige rating of a job may be considered to have the same kind of
significance as its wage rate in influencing job choice and affecting
job satisfaction. The apparent high correlation between prestige
rankings and pecuniary returns of jobs has led some to question
whether circularity may not be involved, with the prestige accorded
a job determined by its wage or salary rate. While some circularity
is unquestionably present, it is equally apparent that it is not entirely
the same thing which is being measured.[6]

[6] That prestige and pecuniary values of a job do diverge can be shown by reference to job evaluation systems, which rank jobs on the basis of a number of

Fourth, there is the social prestige which accrues from the quality of one's own performance. The job becomes a means by which the individual can distinguish himself from others. He becomes known as the "fastest" operator, the "best" salesman, an "outstanding" actor, a minister "with great drawing power," a mechanic "with all the answers," a "distinguished" professor, and so on. This element is particularly important in the case of those individuals occupying positions of great authority in the economy, as for example the top management of large corporations. Here the wish to distinguish oneself by one's performance can lead to corporate expansion for its own sake, innovation to get the jump on others or prevent their moving ahead of one's own company, price reductions to get the reputation for never being undercut, a jealous protection of one's reputation as a quality producer, and so one. It is not some impersonal organization which is so motivated but individuals in particular jobs, with personal reputations at stake.

These considerations support the view that it is not only the income (consumption) aspects of a job that are important to job-holders, even though these may dominate in many cases, but that other aspirations than wages and salaries (equivalent to goods) govern the choice of jobs and behavior on jobs, affecting the production process. Nevertheless, we must formulate our conclusion carefully to avoid a logical trap.

Work, if the word has any meaning, implies something which is undertaken not for its own sake but for the hope of a reward. Work for its own sake is sport, as the sociologist William Graham Sumner pointed out, and while the two are often related they are not identical. For all the psychic and social satisfactions deriving from work, it is the economic return which gives work its distinctive character.

---

factors, with each factor being scored and the wage rate being determined by the total score given to the job. Some factor ratings are "rewards" or "prizes," thus carrying a prestige significance; this is true of the ratings given for degree of skill or training or degree of responsibility required by the job. Other ratings are in the nature of compensations, however, such as those for dirtiness of the job or unpleasantness of physical surroundings. No prestige value normally attaches to these. One would, then, expect some but not a perfect correlation between prestige value of the job and its wage rate.

Income-remuneration from a job is what gives meaning to the category of work, is all that distinguishes it from play. In this sense, then, abstractly, consumption must be viewed as the end of all production.

But the fact that the *category*, "work," is distinguished from other forms of activity because remuneration attaches to it does not mean that the particular cases making up that category—specific jobs— are valued only in terms of their remuneration. One form of work may be preferred over another form of work even though neither would have been undertaken without remuneration. The quality of one's job becomes important, just as the quality of one's consumption. Work involves personal participation in a social process, and all the nonincome elements of job satisfaction affecting one's psychic and social position become—like consumption—objectives of aspirations, arising out of the production process.

The price system omits from consideration any motivation except the pleasure of consuming and the pain of exertion. But this rules out a large part of purposive activity, where people engaged in some pursuit perceive the means as integral to the end so that the two are really inseparable. Purposive activity then becomes directed to more than eating and getting by with the least effort; activity itself breeds its own wants and satisfactions. The productive activity would have no meaning unless it were directed to consumption, but once so directed it acquires more meaning than consumption alone endows it with, even though the consumption objective dominates.

This consequence is of significance in economic analysis since it affects the production process by conditioning the direction and intensity of effort. It suggests too something which we shall examine more specifically later—that when the element of time is admitted, in which production and consumption are continuous and interacting processes, it becomes difficult to determine which is cause and which effect, which is end and which is means. Continuous interaction makes both production and consumption parts of a single process and gives rise to special interests by the participants on both parts of the process.

Where the nature of the work process precludes the types of nonpecuniary satisfactions that we have observed—where repetitive operations prevent informal personal contact on the job, carry no psychic value in themselves, are granted no significant prestige rating, and offer no opportunity for personal distinction—then it may be that the pecuniary return becomes almost an exclusive consideration and is forced to compensate for the lack of other values in the work process. In the cultural setting wages may thus become the central concern of many workers. But we would be in error to assume that the pecuniary return is the sole aspiration related to work which is of any importance. At least at the level of the leaders, nonpecuniary considerations may be of greater importance, and motivation here is likely to set the pace for the economy as a whole.

As in the case of consumption, so with respect to work aspirations would it be possible to distinguish collective and vicarious objectives. The former are pursued chiefly through labor unions or trade associations, with the decisions of the majority determining the policy which is binding on all. The latter are more frequently the basis for wage and hour laws, factory legislation, safety and health requirements, and so on. We allude to these forms of job objectives not because the subcategories of personal, collective, and vicarious satisfactions are themselves analytically important but in order to suggest the range of actions which are referable to categories of aspirations which are often more narrowly interpreted.

ASPIRATIONS OF CAPITAL SUPPLIERS

In traditional economic analysis the factors of production include not only labor and entrepreneurship but also capital and natural resources. Factors of production, in the sense in which that term is there used, are the impersonal agents of the production process. As such no aspirations can be imputed to them, since aspirations characterize only persons. The only personal agents in the production process are of course those who perform services—workers and entrepreneurs—and it is their aspirations that we have just discussed.

We are left with the question, then, of where in our scheme of analysis there is room for the aspirations of capital suppliers.

We shall lump together in the general category of capital suppliers both those who retain ownership over capital in use, receiving profits, and those who exchange capital for debt, receiving interest. Both are instances of capital supply but under different terms, in one case terms which reduce both risk and return, in the other case terms which increase both risk and possible return.

The view on which we proceed in this analysis is that all "economic" aspirations relate to the two primary categories which have already been analyzed, those involving consumption and those involving work. Capital suppliers, no differently from other individuals, are characterized by these same aspirations. Their use of their capital is directed to achieving one or the other or both.

The use of capital is related to job aspirations when the capital supplier himself makes his career in the business for which he supplies capital (or, vicariously, makes a career for someone who is important to him, such as a son or relative). Capital is related to consumption aspirations when it is employed to obtain a pecuniary return, whose usefulness is ultimately for consumption purposes.

The use of capital to obtain work satisfaction is to be found principally in small businesses, whose owners are its managers and who derive satisfaction from their independence even though the pecuniary return on their invested capital (and on their services) may be less than they could obtain elsewhere. In most other situations capital is supplied in order to obtain an income the value of which lies in the consumption it makes possible.

To argue that "capital" is motivated by profit is to personify an abstract factor of production. In many instances no serious analytical error may be introduced; only an ellipsis may be involved. We should nevertheless be on guard against allowing a manner of expression to obscure the underlying realities.

CHAPTER 3

Comparative Achievement

"ECONOMIC" aspirations in western cultures have no precise limit, as we have seen. People's wants are not so unstructured, however, that they deliver themselves up to continuous pursuit of unattainable (infinite) objectives. Immediate goals are set which become the proximate motivation of behavior, and it is these immediate goals which determine one's satisfaction with his level of achievement at any given time. Similarly, it is usually one's present level of achievement which determines his immediate objective: the worker aspires to be classified in labor grade 5 only after he has reached labor grade 6, the college teacher regards a full professorship as his next advance only after he has become an associate professor. We are interested, then, in what determines one's satisfaction or dissatisfaction with his present level of achievement, a question which when answered likewise reveals a person's proximate objectives.

We live in a world of comparisons, and it is comparison with others that largely determines satisfaction with present levels of achievement. We observe what others are accomplishing around us, and tend to be satisfied or dissatisfied depending on whether we are doing better, as well, or worse. The student with a grade of 100 would lose much of his pleasure if everyone else in his class achieved the same grade. The householder with the unpaved driveway would mind the mud less if his neighbor's drives were not all paved. Wartime rationing and shortages are more readily tolerated because it is known that others are being subjected to the same privations; grumbling quickly develops, however, if word spreads that some are getting more than their share. The president of a corporation is eased out because he has been unable to produce a record of profit that compares favorably with competitors. The salesgirl who is given a 10 percent commission on her sales becomes unhappy when she finds that her friend is allowed 15 percent.

The comparisons in which we are now interested are those which are related to aspirations. Let us consider consumer comparisons first.

CONSUMER COMPARISONS

Certain kinds of products from among those confronting us are so emphasized by our culture that they may be considered *necessitous* purchases. It would be physically possible for individuals in our society to live for a few cents a day by eating large quantities of rice, perhaps topped off with something like inexpensive windfall apples to add variety of taste and food values. Expenditures on food might thus be minimized so that the individual could indulge his "greater" preference for travel or movies or clothing. As a matter of fact, however, no significant number of United States residents would choose such a diet, even though it made possible the satisfaction of "stronger" preferences. A society indoctrinates its members from birth in certain patterns of behavior, including consumption behavior, and most individuals conform without protest to the standards set for them by their culture.

In time, then, a large part of a person's consumption expenditures may become routine and habitual—bought not in contemplation of the satisfaction to be derived from the marginal unit but as a matter of custom. Indeed, certain expenditures may become in the nature of fixed charges upon an individual's income—the premiums of insurance policies, payments on the mortgage, installments on the car, the radio, the television, the refrigerator, other household appliances, Christmas gift savings, telephone, gas and electric bills, taxes. On these expenditures there is frequently no choice. Once the original decision has been made to purchase the house, to install the telephone, to lay aside one dollar a week for next Christmas's presents, allocations for these items out of income allow little discretion.[1] Yet the list of such fixed expenditures may run much longer. The expenses of operating a car, of educating children, even of food and clothing consumption, may be *relatively* unalterable, to the extent that they involve habitual behavior or customary expectation. The culture of the community tends to fix behavior and expectation along lines which are difficult to resist. Even in the case of major expenditures—as for a house, a car, or an appliance—recent research suggests that the decision most consumers face is not whether to buy such goods but when to buy them.

This is not to suggest that the individual reacts like an automaton to his culture, buying whatever products are taken up by the people in his community. It does imply that the culture acts as an important determinant of consumer choice—not simply in providing certain types of goods for purchase but in accustoming individuals to their purchase, building up subconscious expectations of purchase long before the formal decision is made. How many boys growing up in the United States entertain any doubt that they will some day own their own car? Similarly, "Preliminary investigations appear to show that the major question, most commonly raised, is not whether a car or a refrigerator should be bought or a life insurance policy or savings bond should be contracted for. It is the timing of money outlays that represents the most usual problem of choice. A family needs a refrigerator; the need is psychologically real and possibilities to buy are given; should the refrigerator be bought 'now' or later? Should the purchase of a house, a car, a fur coat, or a man's suit be made or postponed?" [2]

A people's culture establishes the general nature of the demand for goods at a particular time, according to this view. Obviously,

---

[1] Professor George Katona has developed this line of thought most convincingly in his *Psychological Analysis of Economic Behavior* (New York: McGraw-Hill Book Co., Inc., 1951), especially p. 111.

[2] *Ibid.*, p. 111.

however, all people in a society do not and cannot buy the same products, if only for reasons of differing incomes. Within our culture, however, the principal difference between the standard of living of one family and that of another family is a difference in the quality of the goods which they buy. Both live in houses, both wear functionally the same clothing, both eat foods dictated by their culture, both are likely to drive cars, own an icebox or refrigerator, some kind of heating apparatus and cooking stove, and so on. The quality differences between their choices may be great—as great as between a 20-year-old used Ford and a current model Cadillac, for example. Nevertheless, substantially the same wants are being satisfied but with differing degrees of technical or aesthetic satisfaction.[3] Moreover, the differences in the quality of these substitute goods is rather generally appreciated throughout the society. If numbers of people were asked to rank substitute goods (let us say, all makes of automobiles, or the style and construction of houses, or real estate locations, or types of clothing) in order of quality preference, it is more than likely that there would be a high degree of consensus as to the hierarchy in such product lines. In addition to the consumer's decision as to when to buy, he thus faces another important decision—what quality of goods to buy to meet culturally determined needs.

This quality decision is much less a matter of independent individual decision than we sometimes believe. Each individual tends to identify himself with a particular social group or class of people—certain customary associates, whether of work, recreation, profession, community residence, or some other nexus, most of whom live within roughly the same income range. His identification of himself with such a social group tends to mold his quality decisions for him. In social sets one must generally conform to the customs and standards of the group, whether the group is at the upper or lower end of the income spectrum. In workingmen's circles, the individual

[3] The analysis here has been developed by James Duesenberry in his *Income, Saving, and the Theory of Consumer Behavior* (Cambridge: Harvard University Press, 1949).

who drove a patched up Model A Ford would find himself uncomfortable and self-conscious on this score—at least his wife would impart such a feeling to him. The rising young lawyer who sought entrance into some of the better clubs—a desire itself indicative of quality choice—would be likely to be uneasy and unhappy over the fact that he lived in a flat in a run-down section of town, to which he would have to invite those friends whom he sought to cultivate. The examples here could be multiplied almost without limit.

Individuals accordingly tend to develop *patterns* of consumption or general standards of living reflecting the social grouping with which they class themselves and the general income level characteristic of such a group. These relative social and income levels are associated, with rough correspondence, with an appropriate band on the quality spectrum of those goods which we have called cultural necessities. Thus the quality level of one's habitual purchases of food and clothing, his major purchases of home, car, and appliances, are determined by his social identification and his income. There is, of course, considerable latitude for individual discretion. Nevertheless, the discretion is confined to narrower limits than we often imagine. We can best appreciate the limitations of consumer freedom under which we live, by virtue of these social patterns of conduct to which we conform, when in the face of personal adversity we try to reduce our budgets. There seem to be no expenditures which can be eliminated without serious damage to the standard of living to which we have become accustomed and which others have become accustomed to associate with us. We assume certain stations in life which have materialistic trappings that give us our identity, as the uniform identifies the army officer.

This determination of the quality choices of an individual by his socioeconomic position requires some further explanation to avoid misunderstanding and to facilitate later analysis. It is to be underscored that there is no suggestion here of any sumptuary conventions decreeing that people of such and such a "class" ought not to buy goods appropriate only to other "classes." Such lines have been and still are drawn in some other cultures, but they are foreign to that of the United States. Here, on the contrary, individuals have been encouraged to improve their material positions, and "rags to riches" is a phrase embodying not scorn but approval.

When we picture individuals as being placed somewhere on a quality spectrum of the goods we might label cultural necessities, a placement which, within a range, tends to determine the quality (price) choices which they make, we have another explanation for such behavior. We are assuming that within a culturally cohesive group people will tend to develop common patterns of consumption, tending to the same quality levels of goods and services. These common consumption patterns may not require the same level of expenditures nor arise out of identical levels of income. Differences in income will, however, be compensated for by differences in saving, by differences in the carefulness with which the budget is managed, by differences in quantities purchased (fewer new suits, less meat, a house heated at 68° instead of 70°, a one-week vacation instead of two, and so on). There will be quality differences in purchases, too, but only within a range. Steaks may be sirloin instead of tenderloin, but beef liver will not appear on the table. A Bond suit instead of a Kuppenheimer may be purchased, but not a cut-rate model which is known only for its cheapness. Rent may be shaved by moving to a new location, but only in a neighborhood that is consonant with one's social position.

Individuals within the group (however the group is defined— by work, by neighborhood, by consanguinity, by nationality of origin) will be subject to pressure to maintain a standard of living which is characteristic of the group and outward evidence of affiliation with it, a standard of living which is based on the quality of goods consumed, the placement on the quality spectrum. If goods of lesser quality are purchased, one's social position is threatened, since the material aspects of that position identify it to the outside world. (An individual who lives in a shack cannot expect to maintain his place in a socioeconomic group whose standards dictate a more reputable if nonetheless modest dwelling.) If goods of higher quality are purchased, the more lavish expenditure in one direction must be compensated for by reduced expenditures (poorer quality) in another direction, again threatening one's position in the group.[4]

For dissatisfaction with one's plane of living to arise, then, there must generally be differences between the quality of the goods which one consumes and the quality standards of others in the group with which one regularly associates and with which he identifies himself. How do such disparities arise within the group? There are a number of possibilities.

First, social classes in the United States are fluid. To a marked extent they tend to follow lines of economic function rather than of heredity. By ability and exertion an individual can advance without legal or cultural hindrance some distance up the social (and income) ladder. In any social group there tend to be certain individuals who are more successful in ascending the promotional ladder than are others in that group. These individuals begin to dissociate themselves from the present circle of friends and associate more and more frequently with those in the social group into which they are hopeful of moving. (The ones with lesser upward mobility will later say, "I knew Bill when . . .") During this stage of transition, the upwardly mobile individuals will begin to purchase the quality of goods associated with the social group to which they aspire; these may become the superior goods with which their present circle comes into frequent contact.

[4] There has been some argument as to whether absolute income levels are more important than consumer comparisons in determining how much of a person's income will be spent on consumption goods. The view adopted here is that both are important. Absolute levels of income are important as a permissive factor, and in a society like ours, where personal consumption is stressed, we may reasonably expect an upward pressure on expenditures as income rises. This is not disputed, however, when we add that pressures on consumption expenditures are also generated by comparisons of the sort discussed in the text, and that such pressures account for disproportionate expenditures out of income as individuals attempt to maintain position with some social group. We are all aware of the phenomenon of social pressure on individuals to maintain the material aspects of social position —pressures which in some instances have been so great as to lead respected citizens to acts of theft, embezzlement, and forgery. Indeed, even equiproportionate expenditures out of incomes of given magnitude still require explanation, which the notion of consumer comparisons supplies.

Second, because the culture so generally emphasizes the importance of consumption, as we have already seen, the things one buys constitute an important method of winning prestige and respect; they are evidence of one's personal advancement, the symbol of achievement. There is thus some inducement for a substantial portion of any income increases to be spent on higher-quality goods, even though one entertains no expectation of breaking away from his customary associates. The cultural emphasis on individual accomplishment, and on consumption as the mark of accomplishment, fosters an intent not simply to keep up with the consumption standards of one's associates but to help set the standards. The advertising profession is ready at hand to assist slow imaginations in devising ways to accomplish such an objective. A cigarette with a fancy filter, a late-style dress, a prize-winning rosebush, a new car, alterations to the house—these may be ways of establishing one's leadership in his circle. Where one's consumption habits exceed those of his associates, there is social pressure on the latter to catch up. "Keeping up with the Joneses" is a most revealing description of American consumer habits.

The cultural emphasis on consumption has almost guaranteed that consumer standards (quality levels) should become a thing of competition. Because consumption stands for so much in our society, relative consumption standings become almost as much a matter of competition, on the home front, as relative business standings do on the commercial and industrial front. Comparisons of one's standard of living with those of his customary associates—customary in terms of frequency of contact—set up strong coercive pressures not only to match but also to exceed performance. We thus establish the sequence that rising income for any within a group is likely to be translated into some improvement in consumption, which creates a new and higher standard of comparison for at least some within the group.

Third, we would generally be in error to assume that individuals were members of only one social group. Many individuals are mem-

bers of several socially integrated groups—work, church, neighborhood, for example—and such individual crossing of subcultural lines
may introduce into one group standards from other groups.

Fourth, while it is true that social position tends to fix the quality
band of the consumers' goods spectrum in which a person operates,
the quality band is broad enough to tolerate considerable variation.
It may be thought of as a kind of "normal curve" with a modal
emphasis. But the existence of dispersion within a broad quality
band means that there can be frequent contact, even within one's
own social circle, with superior goods. Over time, as other individuals respond to the frequency of such contact and themselves
adjust their consumer demands upward, the expectations of the
group as a whole may be raised. The "normal curve" shifts to the
right, up the quality scale.

Professor Duesenberry summarizes the argument as follows:
"Consumption expenditures of a particular consumer will have
to rise until the frequency of contact with superior goods is reduced
to a certain level. This level of frequency has to be sufficiently low to
permit resistance to all impulses to increase expenditures. . . . It
now becomes clear how the habit pattern [of consumption] can be
broken without a change in income or prices. For any particular
family the frequency of contact with superior goods will increase
primarily as the consumption expenditures of others increase. When
that occurs, impulses to increase expenditure will increase in frequency, and strength and resistance to them will be inadequate." [5]

In these consumer comparisons it is one's *standard of living* as a
whole which is important, which is compared with that enjoyed
by others. The traditional emphasis on the price of goods as being
the chief concern of consumers is somewhat muted. Price remains
important, but only in relation to one's standard of living. There is
nothing important in price considered by itself. The price of Lin-
colns and Cadillacs tells us nothing about the consumption patterns
of workers. It is only the price of such expensive automobiles taken

[5] Duesenberry, *op. cit.*, p. 27.

in conjunction with the standard of living culturally imposed on workers that tells us we need not expect workers to buy such cars: for them to do so would make impossible the maintenance of their standard of living as a whole. To put the matter another way, the housewife's query, "Can we afford it?" does not usually mean, "Have we got the money?", but rather, "Will this expenditure make it impossible for us to maintain the general standard of living which is expected of us and which we have come to expect?"

The price of a good, then, is important in that it potentially affects one's standard of living as a whole. Small price changes or price differentials that have a negligible impact on one's apportionment of income can be and often are frequently ignored—even the workman on a small income may buy a pack of cigarettes in one store for a penny or two more than it would cost him across the street, simply to avoid making an extra trip, since the saving would be too small to affect his way of life. But the individual who repeatedly ignores price changes and price differentials, who gives little regard to price, will find greater difficulty in maintaining a standard of living comparable to that of his associates. His carelessness will result in a pattern erratically combining luxury with poverty, perhaps a fine set of golf clubs but an overly worn pair of shoes, a magnificent contribution to the Community Chest but a threadbare coat for his wife, trading in a two-year-old car on a new one while the house is badly in need of paint, and so on. Such consumption behavior is generally viewed as irrational.

We might then paraphrase Adam Smith's comment concerning the profit interest of shopkeepers by saying that the significance of price is not that one expects an individual always to buy cheapest in every specific instance, even where identical goods are involved, since this would tend to suggest a penuriousness not commonly found. What one does expect to find, however, is a *general* regard to prices, a *general* consideration of price ranges and differentials, because such consideration is necessary if a particular standard of living is to be maintained.

PRODUCER COMPARISONS

In the category of producers we include all those who hold a job or follow a career, all those whose time is consumed at an occupation which carries remuneration. As we observed in the preceding chapter, the aspirations of such individuals include both income (command over consumption goods) and satisfactions arising out of the work process to which they necessarily commit their persons and personalities. The achievement comparisons relate to these two types of aspiration.

Most people appear to judge the acceptability of their remuneration by comparisons with what others are receiving.[6] Bill Jones's wage of $100 a week is satisfactory as long as Bob Smith is receiving the same amount, but if Smith's pay should be increased to $125 while Jones's salary is not adjusted, Jones may consider himself inequitably treated.

A person tends to regard certain other individuals or groups as the basis for justifiable comparison. The comparison may be made with a fellow worker, a relative who holds down a similar job in another plant, with workers of similar skills wherever found, or with workers of different qualifications who are rated as of equal, lesser or greater "worth." Thus a truck driver may feel himself underpaid relative to the clerk who checks in his shipment; a railroad engineer may be dissatisfied because a customary wage differential between his own job classification and that of brakeman has been eliminated; schoolteachers may complain that they earn less and work harder than a waiter in a night club, and so on. For most individuals and groups, then, there are certain other individuals and groups with whom wage comparisons are made to determine the equity of the going wage or the wage increase or decrease. We may refer to this process as one of equitable comparison.

The importance of certain of these comparisons is greater than

---

[6] This analysis has been most fully developed by Arthur Ross, in *Trade Union Wage Policy* (Berkeley: University of California Press, 1948).

others. Each individual or group not only believes there are others with whom wage comparisons may rightfully be made, to determine the justice of one's own rates; for each individual or group there are certain others with whom he compulsively compares himself. The comparison acquires greater emotional significance, carrying an impact that distinguishes it from other comparisons. The lathe operator may believe that, equitably, he should receive at least as much as his next-door neighbor, a maintenance electrician in another company, but unequal changes in their wage receipts may give rise to nothing more than bitter comment to his wife. On the other hand, should the same lathe operator find that a junior employee working alongside him was being paid more, or that less skilled workmen in the same shop were being paid as much, such comparisons would probably impress themselves on him in such a manner that they could not be ignored. They would acquire an emotional force possibly giving rise to a heated argument with his foreman, possibly stimulating him to look elsewhere for a job, possibly leading him to join the union in his shop or file a grievance with the union steward; relations might cool between the worker and those with respect to whom the comparison rankled; the aggrieved employee may become less coöperative. That is to say, certain equitable comparisons force themselves on the minds of individuals and groups so decisively that they move to action, they elicit behavioral responses. We may refer to these as coercive comparisons.

It is equitable comparisons, then, and in particular the coercive comparisons which chiefly determine whether an individual is satisfied with the remunerative rate attaching to his job. "The worker's interest in wage rates . . . is not simply an interest in consumption. It arises partly from the fact that wage rates are an important element in fairness of treatment. From this standpoint, the important thing is not the absolute level of the wage, but its level *relative* to the wage rates of others with whom the worker thinks he should be compared. Depending on the circumstances, the comparison may be with other workers on the same job, in other departments of the plant, in other plants in the area, or even in plants some distance away." [7]

At the same time, one's satisfaction with the *income* from his employment is not wholly determined by his attitude toward the *rate*. An hourly rate which the employee considers equitable, by all the comparisons he normally makes, may nevertheless yield an annual income which is quite unsatisfactory compared with the earnings of others, due to recurring unemployment. The greater emphasis on wage comparisons probably reflects only the absence of a clear relation between wage rates and employment. The latter depends on so many elements other than any wage rates which might be won that discernment of a functional relationship would require prophetic vision. If annual flows exhibited sufficient constancy, it seems clear that they, rather than hourly rates, would become the basis of comparison. We may feel sure that producers at all levels, from common laborer to corporate president, are mindful of remuneration over a period of time longer than an hour. Indeed, higher hourly rates have sometimes been justified, in collective bargaining negotiations, in certain trades such as construction, on the ground that fewer hours can be worked over the year. Nevertheless, in the absence of employment stability, rates are perhaps as good an indication of flows as anything else, and modifications are easily ascertainable. Whether hourly rates or annual income, however, it is the equitable and coercive comparisons which determine satisfaction with one's present income achievement and which dictate the proximate objective.

In addition to income goals there are other values sought from the work process. We may summarize these nonincome objectives, outlined in the preceding chapter, as consisting of satisfactions from job occupancy (the enjoyment of the social contacts and social prestige associated with the job itself) and satisfactions with personal performance (the psychic satisfactions of the work and the opportunities of distinguishing oneself from others). In the former

[7] Lloyd Reynolds and Joseph Shister, *Job Horizons* (New York: Harper & Brothers, 1949), p. 85.

category the relevant comparisons are how "human" is one's superior, how congenial his colleagues, the extent to which the workflow facilitates social intercourse, and the extent to which the job is respected by one's neighbors. In the latter category the relevant comparisons are the degree of enjoyment (the degree of the play or sport element) which one experiences in the tasks for which he is held responsible, the degree of discretion which he enjoys in performing his tasks, the degree of recognition accorded performance.

These matters are all relative—relative to jobs previously held or about which one has heard or which one imagines are to be found. The autocratic boss is autocratic in contrast to his predecessor, or to a boss known in a different company, or to a brother-in-law's boss, or to the union representative's conception of what a boss should be like. A new employee coming into the plant fresh out of the Navy may not perceive the boss as autocratic until after he has been on the job long enough to absorb the attitudes of his associates.

Such comparative estimates of satisfaction from job occupancy are made at all levels of employment, but there is no reason to believe that the satisfactions which are sought or expected, and therefore the comparisons which are made in evaluating achievement, are the same for all individuals. There is reason to believe, however, that the satisfactions which are sought through the job are not simply the product of individual idiosyncrasy but of institutional conditioning, so that generalizations with respect to job aspirations are possible. For example, satisfaction from one's personal performance is something which is more accessible to higher levels of the work hierarchy than to the rank and file. Pride in personal performance relative to what others are doing requires personal responsibility for the result and satisfactory recognition by others of the achievement. Neither of these conditions is adequately met in most shops—at least in the shops of the large corporations which collectively account for more than half of total employment. As the production process has become specialized and fractionalized, personal responsibility for the final result has been lessened, and (with the earlier unsophisticated application of time-and-motion study) recognition of high productivity came in the form of cuts in incentive wage rates with sufficient frequency to introduce into shop language a new term for the high producer—"rate buster." Workers often are thus unable to gain much satisfaction from high levels of personal productivity, and for many this aspiration may cease to apply to the job but seek its satisfaction outside the job.[8]

As one goes up the job ladder, however, the opportunity for developing pride in one's personal performance increases; the section head, the departmental supervisor, the plant manager, the company president, each can distinguish himself from others by the quality of his achievement. The quality of his performance becomes, indeed, not only a matter of prestige but a condition of holding his job. Poor performance can create nervous tensions, an unhappy home life, and stomach ulcers, while outstanding performance carries with it community respect, professional reputation, and a sense of achievement. The corporation president points with pride to a high earnings figure for his company, from which he himself may not directly profit, in contrast to the shop worker who normally (and understandably) takes little pride in the level of his productivity, from which he may even profit under an incentive plan. The latter may feel little satisfaction in a result which comes out of a mechanized and fractional operation over which he has little discretionary control, while the former experiences a sense

---

[8] Managements who complain of worker disinterest in productivity may thus be complaining of results for which they themselves are responsible. And at least with respect to the specialization of production, the result may have been a *necessary* accompaniment of the productive efficiency on which our higher consumption levels depend. Loss of job satisfaction may have been the *necessary* price of an increase in consumption. In this connection Professor David Riesman suggests, in *The Lonely Crowd* (New Haven: Yale University Press, 1950), that we would do well to forget about making production jobs interesting—they are inherently uninteresting in our specialized processes, he maintains—and concentrate on a more satisfactory use of our increasing leisure time.

of achievement in a total result in which he believes his judgment played a decisive part. These may be regarded as the extremes in a continuum measuring the possibility of satisfaction in personal performance (involving responsibility and recognition) on which all participants in the production process might be spotted.

To the extent that the rank and file of workers cease to aspire to psychic satisfaction from the work process, adjusting aspiration to reality, this is likely to carry as consequences: (1) a greater (compensating) emphasis on the income and social satisfactions deriving from the job, and (2) less interest in promotion to higher levels, the attraction of which stems partly from the possibility of distinguishing oneself from others in his work performance, an attraction which, however, has lost importance in the worker's system of aspirations.

CAPITAL-SUPPLIER COMPARISONS

In the previous chapter it was argued that the aspirations of capital suppliers, like those of other individuals, run to consumption and work satisfactions. The comparisons which are important to such suppliers are therefore the comparisons which are relevant to consumers and producers.

Where capital is supplied to obtain an income, whose use is ultimately for consumption, it is the profit return which is significant. The comparison that identifies the relative achievement is with the rate and steadiness of return earned by capital elsewhere. As in the case of the influence of prices on consumer demand, however, so here we may expect that capital suppliers will not insist on maximizing their return at every moment of time but only on securing a return which stands up well alongside other performances, over time. It is a *general* regard for the profit flow which characterizes the individual capital supplier, a general consideration of relative profit rates which determines his satisfaction or dissatisfaction with his achievement. There is no need to assume a constant and unremitting consideration of whether a further gain could be had by diverting capital into whatever line happens momentarily to offer the highest reward.

Where capital is supplied partly to obtain work satisfaction, as through the establishment of one's own business, the relevant comparisons are those to which all producers are subject: a regard both for the rate of return, some comparison with rates earned elsewhere, since this determines one's consumption standard and cannot be ignored, but also an evaluation of the satisfaction of the job relative to satisfactions which could be gained elsewhere.

What are the effects on aspirations, in summary, of living in a perpetual context of comparisons? Our culture encourages us to match or exceed the consumption planes of our regular associates, since consumption is so intimately related to accomplishment. Rising incomes are wanted to increase the quality of one's consumption, and an increase in income for one or more within a social group, when translated into a higher plane of consumption, creates pressures on others within the group to match or exceed that performance. Incomes are thus significant because of their connection with the consumption process, and higher incomes are sought to support consumption goals.

Incomes are derived from the production process, either through the contribution of personal services or the supply of capital. What constitutes a satisfactory return to those who supply these services is determined by comparisons with the returns of others relative to the services performed by them. Those who supply capital for use by others judge the satisfactoriness of their income achievement by comparisons with the capital earnings of others, and those who supply their labor and entrepreneurship likewise rely on comparisons with the wages and salaries of others.

Suppliers of personal services differ from suppliers of capital, however, in the major respect that they themselves go with their services. Living their lives on their jobs, they develop other desires than for the consumption of goods. These aspirations relate principally to the satisfactions that come with a particular job, such as camaraderie and prestige, and the satisfactions that come from one's personal performance. The possibility of achieving such satisfactions differs among jobs, and jobs are compared on the basis of these qualities just as on the basis of the incomes attached to them.

Dissatisfaction occurs when the gap between one's achievements and the achievements of those with whom one compares himself (whether on the basis of a consumption plane, rate or flow of income, or job satisfaction) is too great to be acceptable. The proximate aspirations are indicated by the lack of satisfaction. Satisfaction occurs when the relationship with others' achievements is accepted, whether gaps exist or not, and reveals no immediate aspiration except possibly one of continuity.[9]

The comparative achievements thus determine the proximate aspirations. They represent the satisfactoriness or unsatisfactoriness of one's present position in a continuing process of attainment. They are significant because they are one of the principal means by which we can break out of the wilderness of individual idiosyncrasy and establish uniformities and similarities—classes of cases. By setting up standards based on social *patterns* of achievement we acquire a logical basis for norms, by which to judge and predict behavior on a probability basis. We turn now to consider in further detail the element of continuity—of time—in the process of aspiration and achievement.

[9] Where consumption comparisons and income comparisons run between the same individuals, there is likely to be less occasion for dissatisfaction: a common plane of consumption is likely to be related to common income levels. Where individuals move in a social group which differs from their work group, however, consumption aspirations and income aspirations have less relationship—the satisfaction of one does not necessarily lead to the satisfaction of the other. In the United States, where there has been substantial social mobility, social ties do not follow occupational ties with any regularity. The culturally implanted ambition to improve one's social position requires, for its satisfaction, the purchase of goods of a quality level which may be disproportionate to one's income. The resulting pressure of expenditures on income may help to account for the primary concern of American workers with wage rates.

CHAPTER 4

The Time Stream of Aspirations

ASPIRATIONS are projections from the present. They embody hopes of future states—of intellectual, moral, familial, social, economic, political states—in which the individual would like someday to find himself and toward the achievement of which he therefore commits himself to strive. Such projections cover an individual's life span (and, vicariously, may extend beyond his own life by projections into the lives of his children). At the moment we are concerned only with "economic" aspirations—those which involve the consumption or production of goods.

Because aspirations cover the time span between now and the grave, they include hopes the fulfillment of which is sought at various stages of the time stream. The youth entering high school has perhaps fifty years ahead of him. His aspirations embrace states toward which he would strive (with varying degrees of intensity of application) at various intervals along the fifty-year span. He has immediate aspirations of what he would like to accomplish in high school—a place on the football team, a chance to work on the school newspaper, perhaps development of a special interest in chemistry and a vague notion that it would be a good thing for him to do well in all his studies. At the same time he holds aspirations for the years beyond high school. These are sometimes conflicting and ill conceived and generally shifting. There may be some rough idea of a college degree, beyond that of a job in business which promises a chance to get ahead, an acceptance without much actual contemplation of the prospect that perhaps in his mid-twenties he will marry and raise a family. Later, he hopes, he will achieve a comfortable income and a place in the community, or perhaps he pictures himself as becoming a captain of industry or a crusading newspaper editor. His youthful aspirations for his old age are probably buried in his consciousness but might include at least the hope that he would never be dependent on others, and beyond that may run to thoughts of indolence at Miami Beach or a chance to travel after retirement.

Every individual at every stage in life has some such stream of aspirations. The separate hopes and objectives are obviously of different levels of significance and immediacy. The wish to become a successful businessman is of a different order than the wish to get a good grade on tomorrow's examination; the consequences flowing from the former aspiration or from its achievement will be much more affecting of the individual's behavior over his life span, but the latter aspiration is more likely to affect his behavior today. At every stage in his life, however, and increasingly as the years go by, the individual is subjected to the necessity—imposed both by self and society—to relate meaningfully the aspirations which he holds for various future periods in his life span. This system of related aspirations is really a person's conception of himself, in which he unites his past, present, and future. Aspirations which cannot be fitted into this conception, fuzzy and imprecise though it is, we call daydreams—desires which are recognized as "impractical" or unlikely of fulfillment in view of the direction our lives have taken and are taking. Ultimate ends, proximate goals, and all the intermediate objectives are thus linked in a continuous stream of projected behavior, interacting with each other. The selection of any end or goal or objectives—whether ultimate, intermediate, or proximate—influences the selection of all other ends or goals or objectives, since these are meaningfully related.[1]

[1] Paul Weiss, in *Man's Freedom* (New Haven: Yale University Press, 1951), has systematically developed this idea; I have here abridged what he elaborates with penetration of thought and beauty of language.

As an individual moves through time, his more or less integrated bundle of aspirations undergoes change. At age 5 his conception of what he is becoming is different from his conception at age 20, and that in turn differs from what it will be at age 50. As he matures, the picture which he holds of his future adjusts to the realities of which he is increasingly a better judge. He is a better judge not because his intellectual powers are improving but because there is more of his past on which to base projections to an increasingly shorter future. Consumer and producer aspirations are affected by this passage of time;[2] they are a function of the position in his life span which the individual occupies at the moment.

Present behavior is doubly related to this time stream of aspirations: it both dictates aspirations and is dictated by them.

Every act, whether deliberate or not, affects our achievement, and as we observed in the preceding chapter achievement affects proximate goals. Proximate goals in turn are systematically related to intermediate objectives and ultimate ends, as the individual builds a meaningful conception of himself in terms of what he has been, is, and is becoming. Every present action taken (and every alternative course of action which is therefore foregone) is related to the future, whether intentionally or not. Every present action or inaction makes certain future actions less possible and others more possible. Under the necessity of meaningfully relating our aspirations over our remaining life span, we necessarily adjust our aspirations to our experience, relating the hoped for to that which experience makes possible. Consumption standards futilely pursued will ultimately be scaled down and a new standard of comparison adopted which is more possible of fulfillment. The worker whose wage rate fails to move comparably with that of some other occupational group with which he has been comparing himself will—if he can do nothing about it—adjust his sights downward, finding new comparisons by which to gauge satisfaction with present achievements. The man who started out to be president of the

[2] Eli Ginzberg has written of this process in *Occupational Choice* (New York: Columbia University Press, 1951).

company over time finds that the rate of his progress (that is, the course of his experience) requires a downward readjustment of goals, first perhaps to being general manager, later perhaps to being a division manager. What we have been influences what we hope to become, what we have achieved affects our present choice of goals.

While present behavior is thus a determinant of aspirations, it is equally true that aspirations are a determinant of present behavior. As long as we maintain that all actions are not predetermined (nor undetermined either), then past actions do not wholly dictate present behavior. The notion of complete determinism is foreign to modern scientific trends, which picture relationships as only probable. Past experience is, then, not wholly determinative of either aspirations or behavior, and aspirations may guide present behavior. In this sense it is possible for the projected future as well as the actual past to control an individual's conduct.[3]

It is only because we can attribute to individuals some degree of control over their actions, some element of nondetermined behavior, that choice becomes a meaningful consideration. If all actions inescapably flowed out of the past, choice would denominate only the mechanical process by which action unfolds. Every event would be determined by a prior event. In such a system rationality would have no meaning, since *all* actions would be rationalized by their antecedents. Commonly, however, by rational behavior we mean actions which are consistent with a person's aspirations, and by rational choice we mean a deliberative decision which imple-

---

[3] It is clear now why the notion of infinite and insatiable wants, taken at face value, is unacceptable as a conception of human nature, suggesting as it does a disorganized mind and a person lacking a sense of direction. A literally boundless appetite provides no links between past, present, and future. It is possible to conceive of an infinite capacity for increasing one's aspirations following successive achievements, but at every stage in the time stream for the normal individual there are real proximate goals, which have value (capacity to satisfy) only because they are meaningfully related to a projected future, a feat which is impossible if an individual's wants cannot be contained even in his imagination. Moreover, since for normal individuals aspirations help to determine present behavior, literally insatiable wants are too formless to provide present direction, except in the daydreaming wish sense rather than in the economic want sense.

ments a person's conception of what he is becoming and intends to become.

RATIONAL BEHAVIOR

Price economists from Bentham on have considered rational choice to be a characteristic of human nature. They have argued that a consumer's choice of goods or a producer's choice of employment is governed by a conscious consideration of such relevant factors as relative prices. In more recent years this assumption has been questioned. It has been shown by empirical investigations that both consumption and job choices are governed frequently by habit, chance, proximity, and other nonrational elements.[4] Nevertheless, we must be cautious in our interpretation of the data. Such studies reveal the existence of nonrational economic choices only by a narrow construction of that term.

It is unquestionably true that choice among a number of alternatives all satisfying some given objective frequently proceeds according to chance or habit. Such *isolated* choices, because nondeliberative, must be viewed as nonrational. If we think of the individual as attempting to effectuate a set of systematically related aspirations through time, however, we discover that rational choice may apply to the category even if not to the specific item. The fact that an individual impulsively buys a Plymouth does not mean that he impulsively bought a car; he may have deliberated long before concluding that purchase of a car at this point in time was, under all the circumstances, appropriate to the realization of his ongoing stream of aspirations. He may also have calculated that in view of the total standard of living to which he aspires a low-priced car is called for. Having thus narrowed the alternatives by rational thought, he may leave final choice to impulse. We cannot there-

[4] Studies of this sort are numerous. Two examples will suffice. On nonrational consumer behavior, Karl W. Kapp, "Rational Human Conduct and Modern Industrial Society," *Southern Economic Journal*, vol. 10 (1943–1944), pp. 136–150. On nonrational worker behavior, Lloyd G. Reynolds and Joseph Shister, *Job Horizons* (New York: Harper & Brothers, 1949).

fore describe his behavior as nonrational, even though the final act of choice was. Similarly, an individual may have narrowed his job choice to some occupational category such as machinist by due regard to his aptitudes, inclinations, and skill. Having made such a conscious decision, he may then accept the first such opening that comes to his attention. His particular job choice, while perhaps nonrational by itself, is, however, consistent with his rationally conceived objective.

Any single action, isolated from the individual's stream of aspirations and related behavior, may appear to be nonrational. Choices may be made at random or on impulse from among a number of alternatives. But if these alternatives belong to a category any member of which satisfies some consciously identified want in a person's system of aspirations, then so-called nonrational behavior can be traced back to rational choice. We are faced with a problem of the degree of specificity of objective which rationality requires. Let us agree to distinguish actions which while seemingly nonrational in themselves nevertheless fulfill some rationally specified objective as reasonable behavior.

One conclusion which follows from this analysis is that the marginal calculations do not apply to the whole range of behavior to which they were assumed to apply, since some consumption and job decisions are relegated to the category of reasonable rather than rational choice, with habit or impulse accepted as a reasonable guide within the range of alternatives meeting rationally determined standards of specificity.

Most economic actions, then, are intended (at some level of specificity) to realize some objective which has meaning because of its relation to the stream of aspirations. No matter how rational the choice, however, rationality is no guarantee of a *good* choice. The alternative selected may prove to have been unsuited to the objective, or the objective may prove to have been inconsistent with other aspirations. Such results are not necessarily indicative of poor judgment. They are not even necessarily indicative of a lack of knowledge which theoretically could be remedied by collection of data or the development of scientific understanding. Uncertainty is inescapable once we admit the element of indeterminacy, that at best a given result is probable but not certain. Because of uncertainty, choice—however rational—must be based on expectations, never on complete knowledge. Our decisions can never rest on anything more substantial than informed judgments.

ECONOMIC DECISIONS

The business of living requires a continuing stream of economic decisions based on expectations. We are constantly either making expenditures or not making expenditures—the latter requiring a decision as much as the former; we are forever reëvaluating our jobs in a manner that affects our determination to remain where we are or not to remain—the former involving a decision, just as the latter. Some choice is always in the process of being made; some choice—to do or not to do—is thrust on us and cannot be escaped. And since inaction is always an alternative to action, choice among alternatives is not only always possible but always necessary.

Risks

The alternatives from among which any choice is made must be assessed for the gains and risks which accompany them. The gains of an action are the progress which it promises toward achievement of one's aspirations and the protection or security which it affords to one's present position, that is, his past achievements. (Progress toward more or less defined aspirations and security of past achievements are inextricably related. As we have seen, they are both aspects of a single time stream in which aspiration and achievement leapfrog each other.) The risks of an action, in contrast, are its possible adverse effects on present position and future achievement.

These gains and risks of alternative actions must be weighed to determine their relative consequences for one's stream of aspirations. By weighing the gains and risks of an action is meant a calculation of (1) the significance of the gain to the maintenance of one's position or the achievement of his aspirations relative to (2) the significance of the risk—assuming it to materialize—to the maintenance of one's position or the achievement of his aspirations.

This kind of balancing of values is not reducible to mathematical terms, since it involves incommensurable items. The gains of a decision to accept a job offer may be an increase in one's wage rate, but the risks may include a probability of less satisfaction from the job. Despite our present inability to reduce these terms to a meaningful common denominator (the same problem which Bentham faced), the fact is that such balancing is done by individuals and is made the basis of choice. The following ratio may be viewed as representative of the judgment process, and any numerical ratios used in subsequent examples may be considered as symbolic of the judgments reached, even though we have no unit of measurement.

$$\frac{\text{gain}}{\text{risk}} = \frac{\text{significance for the improvement of one's position}}{\text{significance for the deterioration of one's position}} = \frac{3}{1}$$

This ratio we shall call the consequence ratio. In the above example, the effect of the action on achieving one's goals would be three times greater than its adverse effects on one's position, should both beneficial and adverse effects actually be realized. Or to put it another way, if one's judgment about the possible unfavorable effects accompanying the contemplated action were borne out, their impact would be relatively slight compared with the expected favorable effects of the action (in the ratio of 1 to 3). If the action under consideration were movement to a new job, for example, the above ratio would indicate that if the favorable consequences materialized as expected, say a wage increase, the result would be three steps forward, whereas if the unfavorable possibilities materialized, say some loss in job satisfaction, the result would be one step backward. Again it should be emphasized that there is no intimation that people actually place numerical values on their expectations; we use the consequence ratio only to suggest the kind of evaluations which lead to economic choices.

As we have seen, choice must always be made from among alternatives, and for each alternative a consequence ratio is estimated. If the consequence ratio of moving to a new job is three to one, then the consequence ratio of remaining on the present job may be two to one, indicating that the gain in staying, say transfer to a more interesting assignment at a slightly higher remuneration, would be greater than the likely risk, say the prospect recently rumored of an unwelcome change in supervisors.

The consequence ratios are only expressions of likely or expected outcomes. Prediction based on certain knowledge is not possible, as we know. In addition to the consequence ratios, then, we need some estimate of the probability that the consequences will occur. It may be that some loss of job satisfaction is likely if Jones moves to a new company, but *how* likely is it that this will happen? It may be certain that income on the new job will be higher at the time of transfer, but how probable is it that over time it will remain higher, so that the estimate of significance to one's time stream of aspirations will be justified?

For the same reason that possible consequences of an action cannot be wholly foreseen, the probability that those consequences which *are* envisaged *will be* realized can be only a judgment. Like the potential consequences to which they apply, the probability ratios are only expectations. If the individual believes that there is a 3-to-1 likelihood of a new job's providing higher income, over time, than one's present job, this expresses his rough estimate of the probability of the outcome. Three chances out of four the favorable result will materialize. We can express this as a probability of 0.75. On the other hand, if he believes that the loss in job satisfaction which he fears as a consequence of the move has only a 50 percent chance of developing, that the chances are even that he will like the new job as well as he does his present one, he expresses a probability of 0.50 with respect to the risk of the action. These probabilities must then be applied to the consequence ratio to obtain a measure of all the expectations which are relevant to the decision. If we take the consequence ratio of our first example, three to one, and apply to it the probabilities mentioned in the preceding sentences, we would have:

$$\text{Action X } \frac{\text{gain}}{\text{risk}} = \frac{3}{1} \times \frac{0.75}{0.50} = \frac{2.25}{0.50} \text{ or } 4.5$$

We shall call the final result the inducement to act. It has no significance by itself and obtains meaning only when laid alongside other inducements to act. If, to continue the example we have been using, the alternative to moving to the new job was remaining on one's present job, an action which had a consequence ratio of two to one, then if the probability of the gain eventuating was nine chances out of 10 (0.90) and of the risk materializing was one out of two (0.50), we would have:

$$\text{Action Y } \frac{\text{gain}}{\text{risk}} = \frac{2}{1} \times \frac{0.90}{0.50} = \frac{1.80}{0.50} \text{ or } 3.6$$

The inducement to act is here 3.6. The inducement to remain on the present job is thus less than the inducement to move to the new job. We may therefore expect the individual to move. In general, we can say that an individual will choose that action, from among the alternatives presented, which offers the greatest inducement to act. Once more it should be stressed that the mathematical formulations used here are illustrative only of the general process of analysis by which an individual, in the making of a rational choice, determines which of the alternative courses of action presented he will pursue.

For many choices the gains and risks attending the action are so slight that rational choice of this nature is not called for. The choices are reasonable but not rational, following rule of thumb, custom, or impulse. Such reasonable choices are answerable to a rational choice made at a higher level of specificity. The daily decision whether to buy the *New York Herald Tribune* or *The New York Times* is made on the basis of habit, the buying of a bouquet of flowers for one's wife is made on the basis of impulse. These are reasonable choices, as long as they do not threaten the budget which protects the standard of living, a budget which has been arrived at with as much rationality as most individuals bring to economic decisions and which makes calculated and appropriate allowances for something like "education and advancement" and "miscellaneous" expenditures.

With respect to the rational choices, a person's estimates of the relative inducements to act are the primary basis for decision. As we have seen, he is likely to choose that course of action which offers the greatest inducement to act. Nevertheless, at times he may be faced with alternatives offering equal inducements to act. Unless some greater specificity of objective is introduced as a basis for distinguishing between them, the choice among such equal alternatives will then be nonrational, following personal inclination. If the equality of inducements to act is due not to the similarity of consequences and the similarity of probabilities, but to the off-setting of dissimilar consequences by dissimilar probabilities, then the gambler nature of the individual is necessarily revealed. He must choose between a high probability of low returns and a low probability of high returns. Suppose the inducements to act of two alternatives were as follows:

$$\text{Action A } \frac{\text{gain}}{\text{risk}} = \frac{20}{1} \times \frac{0.10}{0.50} = \frac{2.00}{0.50} \text{ or } 4.0$$

$$\text{Action B } \frac{\text{gain}}{\text{risk}} = \frac{4}{1} \times \frac{0.50}{0.50} = \frac{2.00}{0.50} \text{ or } 4.0$$

Then the gambling instincts of the individual would stand exposed by his choice between Action A, the long shot, and Action B, the fifty-fifty bet.

The two principal streams of "economic" aspiration, as we have seen, deal with consumption and production activities. With respect to each of these the individual faces a variety of alternative course of action between which he must choose. His choice, at the level of specificity necessary for rational pursuit of an objective, will tend to fall upon that line of conduct which offers the greatest inducement to act. We may be sure, however, that the inducement of a particular action will depend importantly upon the point of time in his life span at which a person stands, from which he projects his aspirations. His proximate objectives are the consequence of comparing his own achievements with the achievements of others whose streams of aspirations have driven them along similar channels, but the relevant comparisons depend upon where a person stands in his own time stream.

The Budget Decision

With respect to consumption behavior, the major decision is one's budget, how one's income shall be apportioned. As we have seen, this involves a choice (partly determined by social grouping, partly by income) as to one's place on the consumer-goods quality spectrum and at the same time a rough determination of the amounts required for shelter, food, clothing, transportation, and other goods and services, as well as for savings. This is a decision which is commonly made by rational consideration of how well the possible alternatives will allow one to achieve his consumer objectives. Rational consideration here does not require a precise formula reduced to writing. The rational decision is more often made "on the run," in the process of disbursing income. Most individuals follow a pattern of expenditures, over short spans of time, which shows a substantial degree of consistency, evidencing a choice of budget which through experience (trial and error) has been found to hold out the greatest inducements, in the sense of promising a most favorable balance between achievement of aspirations and the assumption of risks threatening such achievement.

Budget A, for example, which calls for a higher level of expenditures relative to saving than does Budget B, gives greater promise of achieving one's comparative aspirations, but at the same time holds greater threat that one's achievements will be washed out by an emergency such as accident or serious illness which subjects the individual to expenses for which he is financially unprepared. The consequence ratios and probabilities of various alternative budgets must be weighed before the person settles down to some choice. The weighing process does not often involve careful or concentrated consideration. It is likely to be something which occurs in the process of deciding on particular purchases or in the form of thoughts that come to an individual as he reads a novel or talks with friends or is subjected to the arguments of advertisements. That it is made piecemeal over time does not deprive it of its rationality; it is not simply an impulsive acceptance of spending habits which can be expected to change from week to week. A pattern of expenditures is developed which accords with a person's conception of himself and what he is becoming, and which has been deliberatively chosen, even though more on the basis of a "stream of consciousness" than of a process of ratiocination.

This deliberative choice varies with a person's age. Younger people have more unsatisfied material needs and experience relatively less concern about their ability to maintain past achievements in the face of emergencies or old age.

To a husband and wife under 30 old age seems far away. Earnings are likely to advance—not decline, as they are almost certain to do at the other age extreme of life. Why save now when so many wants and needs compete for every dollar? Why not wait—at least until a car and a mechanical refrigerator have been bought? Some such balancing of present versus future probably explains why families [in] which the wife was under 30 spent more of their income and saved less than those in which the wife was 60 or more in a group of 46 villages in the Middle Atlantic and North Central region. With incomes in the range $1000–$1499 (average about $1200) the younger families just about broke even; that is, the amounts saved by some just about balanced the deficits of the others. In contrast, the older families kept outlays for living far enough below income that savings averaged $125.[5]

[5] *Family Spending and Saving as Related to Age of Wife and Age and Number of Children* (U.S. Dept. of Agriculture: Miscellaneous Publication 489, 1942), p. 1. Data relate to 1935–1936. On p. 4 it is reported:
"Both the young and the elderly families (those in which the wife was under 30 and those in which she was 60 or more) at the income level $500–$999 had a deficit for the group as a whole, that is, aggregate living expenditures were [larger] than aggregate income. But the average deficit for the older group was less than one-third as great as for the younger—$12 compared with $40. About

With advancing years and increasing family responsibilities, income security (that is, the security of one's consumption position) [6] seems to be weighted more heavily. Emergencies are more carefully guarded against in the form of accident, sickness, and life insurance. Liquid savings increase. The realization that future income—and the maintenance of one's social position—depends on present savings becomes sharper; annuities may be provided for through retirement insurance. As the strength of these considerations increases over the years, the consequence ratios and probabilities can be expected to change, altering the inducements which accompany one budget in contrast to another and influencing choice among the alternatives.

Finally, we should recognize that the individual's investment decisions—what use shall be made of his savings—is also part of the stream of consumer choices, since the purpose of investment is usually return which has significance because of an ultimate relation to consumption. It seems probable that a great deal if not most of personal saving takes place without respect to the interest rate, since it is designed to serve a purpose which is not much influenced by the interest rate. Some saving is in anticipation of a definite purchase—a house, an automobile, a refrigerator, an education, on which a payment must be made which cannot be financed out of current income. Other saving serves a security purpose, as we have seen. For at least these two categories of savings, the interest rate is not likely to be controlling of whether savings occur or not. The decision is part of the budget problem. Once saving occurs, however, the individual is faced with a choice of the forms in which

---

one-third of the older families 'went in the red': a larger proportion, more than one-half, of the younger.

"The point on the income scale at which the families, as a group, broke even (i.e., changed from a deficit to a surplus status) was about $775 for the childless families 60 or older; $1350 for those under 30. In other words, the younger families had to reach an income point $575 higher than the older before the aggregate surplus of the group with savings reached or exceeded the aggregate deficit of those that 'went in the red.'"

[6] Since "consumption" aspirations include vicarious consumption, the security of one's consumption position includes the continuity of vicarious consumption, as notably through bequeathal.

savings can be held—as bank account, as insurance payments, as corporate stocks, as government bonds, as land or property. The form in which savings are to be held involves a consideration of the relative inducements to accept one alternative over the others. Here the interest or profit rate plays its part. Investment A seems likely to pay off at a rate of 10 percent, a gain of substantial importance in the achievement of one's aspirations. On the other hand, it ties up funds in a manner that would make it difficult to draw on them in the event of an emergency, an emergency the probability of which depends on one's health, age, hazard of occupation, and so on. The consequence ratios and probabilities are calculated for this and other alternatives before commitment. The calculation, as we know, may take place over time and is likely to lack precision, and the final choice may well reflect a gambling instinct that turns to the long shot or the sure bet. Nevertheless, we would be justified in considering it a rational decision—that is, reflective, deliberative, considered in the light of more-or-less-specified objectives.

Negative saving—the incurring of debt which must be financed out of current income—reflects similar considerations. Debt is assumed either to maintain or to improve present consumption (as in the case of home mortgages or installment buying) or to secure a future return that gives greater promise of achieving one's stream of aspirations than would current use of the debt-repayment installments (as in the case of investment in some business enterprise).

THE REVENUE DECISION

If these are the considerations affecting the budget decision, the same balancing of gains and risks in weighing one action against alternatives governs the stream of decisions relating to a person's job aspirations, and again the point in one's life span at which he finds himself influences his estimates. Here the principal decision relates to the use of one's time. Time has many possible alternative employments, just as does money income. A part of it can be sold to others—so many hours which carry with them a person's peculiar productive skills and abilities; a part of it is devoted to sleep, part to family life, part to recreation and amusement, part to self-improvement.

At every moment of time some choice as to its use must be made or remade. Some balance of satisfactions among alternative uses must be sought over time. It would be possible, for example, for an individual to hold down two or more jobs simultaneously (as some people do), an arrangement which increases money income and hence command over goods and services but which also reduces one's command over time in which to enjoy not only such goods as the added income makes possible but also all other phases of living. Personal command over one's own time, in contrast to someone else's purchased command over one's time, can be viewed as self-employment in distinction to market employment, and a person can be viewed as rationally budgeting not only his money but his time in an effort to achieve his aspirations.

The use of time which is of greatest interest to economists is the individual's market employment—that portion of his time (necessarily carrying with it his skills, abilities, and personal traits) which is sold to others, as part of a production process. We shall call this allocation of one's time to some remunerated production process the revenue decision. In the case of most individuals it is closely equivalent to job choice.

In the revenue decision as in the budget decision the weighting of risk relative to gain appears to increase with a person's age. There are several explanations for this. First, as one grows older he develops family and financial responsibilities which increase the consequences of any unfavorable outcome. Second, at some point in his career he may reconcile himself to the fact that he has bumped the ceiling of job progress. With whatever company he is connected, he has gone about as far as he is likely ever to go. At that point his estimate of the gain likely to come from any job movement will reflect by its pessimism his resignation to or acceptance of the situation. His stream of aspirations has been so substantially run that his principal remaining objective is to make sure of his present position (past achievements). Finally, the longer one stays on a job or with a company—either for the reasons above or because of satisfaction with job progress—the greater security does he feel in his employment and consequently the more does he risk by moving to another job.

The point in his life span at which an individual tends to become increasingly security-minded varies from person to person. Where he is in the job hierarchy at that time has a special significance, for it largely determines the manner in which he can seek the security which he more and more prizes. Let us consider the two extremes of the job hierarchy—the rank and file of employees and top management—to observe the difference.

The career stages of the manual worker have been analyzed in an investigation by Professors Reynolds and Shister.[7] There is little initial planning on an occupational career. "Careful calculation of the relative advantages of different careers, and a long-range planning for the child's training and induction into a particular kind of work, appears to be a middle-class luxury not found to any extent in working-class families." The young person makes his entry into the working world by casual contact. "He goes through a 'fumbling-around period' of several years, during which he tries out two, three, or perhaps many more jobs. . . ." Such conduct may not be nonrational, though there are, to be sure, degrees of rationality. Rational decision does not require long-range planning but only reflection and deliberation. Here—as in the case of the budget decision—reflection may occur "on the run," in the course of experience.

In this period the young jobholder is likely to be moving in a

---

[7] Lloyd G. Reynolds and Joseph Shister, *op. cit.* This study was conducted in 1947 and is based upon two groups of workers, one a cross-sectional sample of 450 manual workers in a manufacturing center of about 350,000 population, a sample which showed a bias toward older-age workers, and another consisting of 350 workers who had changed jobs within the last year, which was found to be skewed in the direction of the younger-age group. The study admittedly understates the amount of upward job progression, since interviews were conducted only with those who were currently manual workers. Others who had started as manual workers but who had moved into other career lines were thus not included in any of the tabulations.

generally upward direction in the occupational progression. He expects advancement and is inclined to move to another job if it comes slowly. This period of restless interest in something better ends, for a great many men, soon after marriage. They are likely to settle down in a given company, where occupational progress for perhaps half of them comes to an end. While some will continue to move from company to company in answer to brighter prospects, and others will rise within the company where they have settled down, a substantial number remain on the same occupational level for the greatest part of their working lives. Of this latter group perhaps half appear to be content with their position and some have even refused advancement.[8]

For substantial numbers of manual workers, then, from some point—sometimes occurring rather early in their occupational life—onward, any advancement comes not in moving to higher job levels but in the form of "a change from the second shift to the first shift, from hourly rated work to incentive work, from a job in labor grade 9 . . . to another job in the same labor grade which is more desirable for one reason or another. Beyond this most workers have little expectation of going." Similarly, from this point on any improvement in remuneration comes not as a reward for personal progress but as a sharing in greater productivity in the firm, the industry, or the nation. One may continue to expect rising wage income, but as a consequence of general wage increases while on a given job rather than as a result of movement to higher-level jobs.

Why is it that so many workers tend to bump their ceiling of advancement relatively early in their careers? There appear to be two principal explanations. (1) The limitation on further upward movement is a result of conditioning factors over which individuals

[8] This picture of an upwardly mobile younger group of workers and an older group characterized to a greater extent by job stability has been confirmed by every labor market study of which I know which has touched on this matter. Further evidence on the basis of census data is supplied by Seymour L. Wolfbein in "Job Tenure of American Workers," *Monthly Labor Review*, vol. 75 (September, 1952), pp. 257–262.

have no control. Among the most important appear to be the size of the plant in which they are located (small plants are less conducive to continued progress than large plants), personal ability (whether due to innate deficiencies or lack of training), and luck. (2) Advancement ends largely through choice. Only 2 percent of those interviewed in the Reynolds and Shister study expressed any desire to advance to a foreman's job, and a number had refused to accept a foremanship when it was offered. "Too much responsibility" is the reaction to such an offer, a responsibility that endangers one's future by requiring a gamble on success. Many will put up with a smaller return rather than expose themselves to the risk of gambling with the security of present income and employment. "Most workers who have more than five years' seniority or who are more than forty years old are unresponsive to alternative opportunities."

"Those who said they were too old to learn a new job did not usually mean that they would be physically incapable of doing so. They meant rather that they were not willing to face the risks and perhaps the temporary loss of income involved in trying out on a new job." "The worker with years of service in one plant has more protection against layoffs than he would have if he started in at a new plant with no seniority. This is an important consideration with many workers. Most of them seemed to regard the present high employment as abnormal and temporary, to be followed in all likelihood by a period of depression. Many of the workers interviewed said that one of their main concerns was to 'get set before the bust comes.' One way to prepare for 'the bust' is to pile up as many years of seniority as possible on your present job."

When security-mindedness comes to rank-and-file workers in the production process, then, it expresses itself in the form of piling up years of experience on a given job, with the expectation of establishing a claim to that job. Holding on to one's present job becomes a course of action offering special inducement. Seniority offers security.

The probability of continued employment for any individual depends equally on two considerations: his personal performance and his company's performance. The individual who satisfies his company's needs can expect job continuity as long as his company needs him. The individual can himself seek job security, then, only through actions which are designed to control the impact of personal and corporate performance. At the level of the individual manualist, corporate performance is beyond his power to affect significantly. While his productivity has its impact on overall performance, it is too small a component to control the whole. At the same time, for many a rank-and-file worker production operations have become enough standardized to rob him of an opportunity to distinguish himself from his fellows. Moreover, even where distinction is possible any personal performance which shows up fellow workers—perhaps endangering their security—is likely to cost him a place in the society of the shop, threatening that job satisfaction which occupies an important place in his stream of aspirations, particularly if attaching to a job on which he hopes to remain for the indefinite future. Where personal performance cannot be significantly distinguished from the performance of others (except grossly, as satisfactory or unsatisfactory when compared with the average), where corporate performance lies beyond one's control, the job claim has come to depend largely on seniority—the years of service. This seniority claim is generally supported in our culture. Most people tend to believe that as long as a senior employee can perform his work with reasonable efficiency his years of service to the company should be rewarded by giving him greater claim to employment than is given to a junior man.[9]

[9] One investigator has described how little questioned among workers themselves is the policy of basing preferment on length of service. "During several years of railroad experience the author shared the feelings of the typical railroad employee toward seniority," he writes. "This attitude, as probably is the case with most employees, was gained more by a process of absorption of the general opinion of fellow workers than by independent thinking. And it is extremely important to note that, although employees more or less continually express their opinions concerning specific instances of application and interpretation of seniority, they rarely discuss its validity as a method of job allocation." Dan H. Mater, "Effects of Seniority Upon the Welfare of the Employee, the Employer and Society," *Journal of Business of the University of Chicago*, vol. 14 (1941), p. 384.

If we turn to the other end of the job hierarchy, however, to top management, we find a situation quite in contrast. Here are those individuals who have either been so fortunate as to start at a higher rung on the occupational ladder (by reason of family, training, or luck) so that even a short progression carries them close to the top, or those who have continued to progress (by reason of greater aspiration, greater ability, or luck) beyond the stage at which their fellows sought security. Such individuals are nonetheless concerned with security—necessarily concerned with it in rationally choosing among alternatives on the basis of relative inducements to act, since risk to present position (past achievements) is risk to aspirations. Moreover, even for individuals at this level of advancement we may assume that some point in their life span is reached where security considerations carry increasing weight: the risk of loss of position becomes more compelling than hope of additional gain. For persons in this top-level category, security must be sought in other forms than seniority, however.

If security in employment depends on personal and corporate performance, these are *both* matters which are significantly within the control of top management. Corporate performance is attributable to the action of all those who compose the enterprise, to be sure, but the contribution of an individual in the upper echelon has a vastly greater marginal value than the contribution from an individual in the ranks. The difference corresponds to the part played by the President and individual legislators in the conduct of the United States in contrast to the part played by the individual voter. Because of the greater degree of individual control over and responsibility for the outcome, the personal performance of top management is identified with corporate performance.

Under this circumstance the security of top management would appear to stand or fall on how well corporate performance matches the expectations of those to whom management owes its job, the owners. The basis for owner satisfaction, as we observed in the preceding chapter, is a profit showing comparing favorably with profit performance elsewhere. Top management, for its own security, must thus match the returns of competitive enterprises. And if among these competitors there are some which are run by managements still bent on further achievement, an achievement which itself is measured in terms of comparative profit rates, then security for any management can be gained only by keeping up with the performances of its more aspiring competitors! For top management, under the circumstances, there is no security of past achievement except through further achievement.

This is, indeed, the situation from which workers in the shop have largely freed themselves. Competitive performances in the production process have been recognized by them as threatening the security of those who fail to match the records of the better performers. Through their shop society, by the sanction of ostracism, they have a means of restraining this interpersonal competition. It is partially through this means that they have been able to effect a job security which depends not on competitive performance but on seniority. No such means of achieving job security is available to top management, however. There is no managerial society comparable to the shop society, in which overambitious managers can be ostracized. Quasi agreements may provide some surcease from competitive rigors in the case of oligopolists, but where there is lack of opportunity for interpersonal contact and control there is an understandable unwillingness to entrust the future of one's company to an agreement reached through conjecture and subject to violation by some management bound on further achievement.

This continuing pressure on top management cannot be much relieved by weakening the control of owners (stockholders). Typically in the large American corporation stockholder control is nominal rather than real, and management is to this extent freed of an effective needling by its capital suppliers, whose recourse in the event of dissatisfaction with the way the business is run is not to change the management but to sell their stock. But even in these instances there is no security for management except through further achievement. Since its job security is identified with corporate security (irrespective of the degree of ownership control) it must continue to compete effectively with all in its field, including the aggressive managements which are "on the make," in order to assure its own survival.

For top management, then, the possibility of substituting security for achievement, of foregoing further achievement in order to avoid gambling with past achievement (present position), depends less on its own inclinations than on the behavior of its competitors. The same competitive threats to position which top management faces face too the rank and file of production workers, to be sure; jobs of the latter as well as of the former depend on corporate survival. But the rank and file possess neither the power nor the personal responsibility for meeting the threat; relieved of such responsibility, they can individually seek such job security as the corporate performance permits, through seniority. Top management possesses both authority and responsibility; unable to evade that responsibility, it cannot protect what it has by refusing to accept risk; it must continue to risk in order to protect what it has. It must meet and match the performances of its competitors. Only through cartel action— the restraint of competition—can it find relief from this competitive pressure. And cartel action is unlawful in the United States.

We have here contrasted the position of the rank and file production worker with top management. Between these extremes of the industrial hierarchy are numerous layers of lesser management personnel. It appears a reasonable conjecture that the farther one progresses up the career ladder, the less possible of attainment is job security—the freedom from risking what one has already gained. *Degrees* of risk to one's present position, attending alternative courses of action, always exist, of course, for those at all levels of the hierarchy. But as one goes up the ladder he has less chance of avoiding actions which necessarily threaten his position; despite personal inclination his occupational position will less and less allow him to forego the action which, while it may bring further achievement, requires gambling with what he has achieved. Small wonder, then, that American businessmen, living in a competitive economy, are known for the bulging brief cases which they take home at night! Their degree of success demands the price of eternal competitive vigilance. Small wonder, too, that numbers of American workers voluntarily drop out of the competitive race, satisfied to remain on a lower rung of the ladder where risk of position is less and the pace is not so exacting.

In the stream of job decisions which face the individual over his lifetime, then, the nature of gain and risk and the relative weight attaching to them vary depending upon a person's age and the position he occupies in the job hierarchy. The younger person, at any level, is likely to be more ambitious, counting the gain as relatively more significant than the risk. The older person is more security-minded—first, because he has more to protect and, second, because in most instances his stream of aspirations has been shortened by experience, dimming earlier optimisms, so that the next step diminishes in value because it may lead no higher (the division superintendency must be valued only for its own sake and not additionally because it is a stage on the way to a vice-presidency—there is not enough time remaining in his life span for that). But how the older person seeks security depends on his position in the hierarchy. At lower levels, with limited personal responsibility for corporate performance, seniority is the trustiest device. At higher and higher levels, with increasing personal responsibility for corporate performance, less and less is job security possible except through continuing achievement: relaxation does not avoid but carries risk.

Every person has his stream of aspirations, his conception of himself and his place in society as influenced by his past and his becoming. Every person makes rational choices, at some level of specificity of objective, which are designed to achieve his ongoing aspirations. The rational choice consists in a calculation of the consequences of the probable gain from an action for one's future achievements relative to the consequences of the probable risk to one's present position (past achievements), coupled with an estimate of the relevant probabilities of the consequences occurring.

The result is something we can call the inducement to act. Such estimates can never be made on the basis of certain knowledge; both consequences and probabilities necessarily embody only judgments and expectations.

At any time a person is faced with alternative courses of action, since not doing is always an alternative to doing. An expenditure may be made or not made; a job may be thrown up or retained. Decisions are thus always in the process of being made, though much of the time the alternatives may be unworthy of conscious consideration or the consequences of choosing between the alternatives may be of such limited significance for the achievement of aspirations as to permit choice to be governed by habit, impulse, or chance. When conscious, rational choice is called for, however, it is made on the basis of the relative inducements which alternative actions carry. The course of action offering the greatest inducement will be selected.

The two principal streams of economic decisions for all individuals are those affecting the uses of income (the budget decision) and the sources of income (the revenue decision). These decisions—based on the calculation of the inducements of alternative actions—will be affected by the position which the individual occupies in his time stream of aspirations, by where he is, how he got there, and where he expects to go.

The theoretical significance of this is that it removes economic decisions from being comparisons of relative prices at an isolated moment of time and converts them into comparisons of alternative actions which have consequences over time. Price (including the profit, interest, and wage rate) enters as a determining variable only when it affects the budget and revenue decisions at a level of specificity of objectives that calls for rational choice, with the specification of objectives depending on the individual's position in his time stream of aspirations.

CHAPTER 5

The Concomitance of Aspirations

THE English economist Wicksteed spoke of a person's wants as mirroring his personality. To know a person's preferences—his choices among the goods and services representing the many sides of life, such as food and drink, home furnishings and home location, sports, aesthetic pursuits, his clothing, vacation tastes, and so on—to know these preferences is to know the individual. If this is only a partial truth it is nevertheless an important one. It helps to remind us that when we speak of "consumption" aspirations we are using the term loosely, intending it to embrace all those aspects of a person's life which involve the consumption of goods. The aspiration is not actually for goods but for the things which goods make possible—creature comforts, religious development, intellectual attainments, play and amusement, political participation, protection of person and property, and so on. It is these and not the goods themselves which constitute our bundle of wants. It is our choices among these objectives which are reflected in the budget decision.

The satisfaction of these aspirations, depending on goods, is in an exchange economy first dependent on income, which is derived from current or previous work. But work—thus made necessary—has its own satisfactions which are not dependent on goods but which are sought for themselves and to which consumption aspirations may at some level be sacrificed. We have therefore spoken of "job" or "producer" aspirations, which include not only a desire for income, making possible the satisfaction of consumption aspirations, but also job satisfactions, such as the enjoyment of social contacts on the job, a degree of pleasure in the work itself, prestige deriving from one's occupation or his personal performance. By the definition of "work," these psychological satisfactions would not have been sought in this manner unless income attached to the effort, but whenever energy is expended to obtain income these satisfactions will also be sought from the job. In the revenue decision the individual decides what kind of work he shall pursue in the light of his income needs balanced against the nonincome satisfactions of alternative employment and his desire for personal command over his own limited time (self-employment).

The choice of a job, through the income attaching to it, affects a person's choice of a standard of living. But the level of income is in turn partially determined by one's valuation of the satisfactions attaching to alternative jobs, so that consumption standards and job satisfactions must be weighed against each other. It is thus equally correct to say that choice of a standard of living affects one's choice of a job. Work satisfaction becomes an objective alongside consumer satisfaction, and choices are required which in some degree sacrifice one to the other.

For the individual, then, the economic problem is one of balance —a balance achieved through the revenue and budget decisions, a balance affected by the social role in which the individual is cast and by his position in his time stream of aspirations (both conditions influencing the standards by which he compares his own achievements).[1]

In psychological terms this effort to achieve balance can be viewed as the attempt of the individual to achieve personality integration, to relate all his activities in a meaningful and satisfying pat-

---

[1] This conception of a balance of satisfactions over time does away with the old value hierarchy of production as means and consumption as end, since as soon as we are in the time stream, production and consumption follow each other, depending on each other, each valued for its contribution to a single process, neither absolute, both a means and both an end in the individual's realization of his stream of aspirations.

tern. This effort is as compulsive as the effort to maintain good health and has in fact been conceived as an aspect of health. Individuals vary in the extent to which they achieve this personal integration, but they cannot escape the compulsion itself since failure provides its own physical and mental sanctions.[2]

Individual acts of choice are meaningless in themselves. They take on meaning only as part of a pattern. That a person will prefer one good over another, because of what it is or what it sells for, is a chance bit of information until it is related to many other choices which collectively describe behavior. Even the occasional spree or binge to which most of us succumb drops its aberrant connotation and acquires its reasonable explanation when placed in context, achieving recognition as a means of escape from normal routine and rational conduct which at times becomes oppressive. (As Bertrand Russell has observed, "A quiet life may well be a boring life.") At some level of specificity room may be made, by rational choice, for such infrequent, irrational (but reasonable) outbursts.

The notion of balance, of the need of the individual to integrate his economic activities in a meaningful pattern, replaces the conception of the individual as a rational maximizer. Maximization as a description of economic behavior shows weaknesses in at least two major respects: (1) What constitutes the maximum gain resulting from some action ceases to be clear when concomitant aspirations are introduced. One objective—the acquisition of consumer goods, let us say—can be maximized, and we can objectively describe the behavior of an individual who seeks to maximize that one thing. But if an individual has more than one objective and

---

[2] The compulsion of personal integration implies no necessary ethical norm nor does it assume that a person's drives are necessarily in the direction of utilizing his full range of capacities. It simply posits the compelling need facing all individuals to organize their lives in some fashion which is meaningful and satisfying to them.

There is, however, a relationship between capacities and personal integration. If an individual adopts ultimate ends or intermediate objectives or proximate goals which are impossible of attainment because of a lack of ability, unless he rescales his aspirations he will lead a life of frustration and fail in some measure to accomplish that personal integration which he is driven to seek.

these are to some extent competitive with each other (in the expenditure of time and effort, if nothing else) we cannot argue that he seeks to maximize them all.

A businessman, for example, like any other individual, is involved in a network of relationships—with his employees, with his customers, with other businessmen, with the public generally. There is no reason for believing that one motive—the pursuit of profit—is so dominant that it dictates the character of all his relationships, governing all his responses, directing him to make certain marginal adjustments irrespective of the resulting impact on the complex of relationships of which he is the focus. There is substantial and convincing evidence that businessmen in their relations with employees are concerned not only with marginal value products (though they cannot ignore that consideration) but also with ethical, moral, and social aspects of those relationships. Wages are sometimes maintained when market considerations alone would warrant their being reduced. Superannuated employees have been kept on the payroll out of a sense of responsibility. Contributions have sometimes been made to tide employees over emergency periods, out of a sense of sympathy. Similarly with respect to customers, a firm does not always charge "what the traffic will bear"—not simply from fear of the effects of customer retaliation on the firm's future but because the management may, as members of a community, be sensitive to the effect on their social relationships. Again, wage and price policies are sometimes adopted in the light of how business colleagues will react—not simply due to the conjectural interdependence of oligopolistic relationships, since some colleagues operate in different product or labor markets, but out of a desire to maintain a compatibility of relationships with individuals with whom there is an occupational or social-class bond.

These aspects of business behavior involve the satisfactions of vicarious consumption or of prestige from one's personal performance or the enjoyment of one's work society. The balancing of these satisfactions with the drive for income and personal consumption reveals an integrated pattern of behavior explaining economic conduct more satisfactorily than does the maximizing approach. There is no need to water down the fact that the businessman is necessarily spurred by profit considerations, the desire for pecuniary gain. Our culture indeed requires of him that he earn a profit as the condition of surviving as an independent entrepreneur. It does not require, however, that he pursue maximum profit. When the desire for pecuniary gain is tempered by consideration of other goals which the individual would achieve we leave behind us the concept of rational maximizing and necessarily move toward the idea of balancing satisfactions according to a culturally influenced behavior pattern.

(2) Maximizing ceases to be an adequate description of behavior as soon as the time element is introduced. And this for two reasons.

(a) Actions affect the future, but the future is uncertain; the consequences of present behavior must be expressed as expectations, with respect both to progress toward aspirations and security of past achievements. Large gains and large risks must be weighed against small gains and small risks, and low probabilities of favorable consequences against high probabilities of less favorable consequences. The result of such rational calculation is preferred courses of action but nothing which could be described, objectively, as maximization. It was the worker's uncertainty about future employment prospects, especially in the light of the insecurities of the 'thirties, that explains why he and so many of his fellows during World War II refused to give up the seniority they had accumulated with current employers to transfer to other companies engaged in more pressing war work and paying higher wage rates.[3] What was it here that was being maximized?

(b) There are some who would argue that in the above case what

[3] Accounts of this attitude in two industries are to be found in "Seniority in the Automobile Industry" and "Seniority in the Rubber Industry," *Monthly Labor Review*, vol 59 (1944), pp. 463 and 789, respectively. We may expect that except for younger workers seniority generally acts as a direct counter to wage rates in inducing employee movement. Higher rates in other companies lose some of their attraction because they are necessarily coupled with low seniority. Low rates on long-held jobs lose some of their repelling power because they are coupled with high seniority.

was being maximized was income *over time*. Aside from the fact that there is evidence to suggest that this was not the case (since workers appear not to consider that a brief spell of high-paying work is to be preferred to a steadier duration of lower-paying work, even though the former may result in a greater total income), there is a further difficulty with this formula. Maximization over time is possible only when some finite span of time is assumed. When time is a continuing stream it becomes literally impossible to calculate within what period of time income will be maximized. Maximization is logically defensible in a static system, with each moment of time isolated from the time stream. It is logically indefensible in a system in which time runs on without providing any discrete intervals within which there is some reason for maximization.

This time element provides the answer to those who may wonder how a balance of satisfactions differs from maximizing satisfaction. Even admitting that work satisfactions must be considered along with consumption satisfactions, one may ask why we cannot phrase the problem as one of maximizing *all* satisfactions.

The problem may indeed be formally so stated, but it is then robbed of any meaning sufficient to permit investigation. Maximization in such a formulation has only the loose sense of subjective decisions with respect to what total course of conduct is most preferred at a moment of time. To speak of "satisfactions" as that which is to be maximized in any more precise sense is to set up a purported common denominator, as Bentham sought to do. But it is a common denominator which—as yet, in any event—we do not know how to use and with which we can only make empty generalizations about behavior. By leaving behind the meaningless common denominator and concentrating upon the identifiable aspirations of people in various circumstances, we can—statistically—learn something about the probable behavior of people in their economic relationships. We can find out more about the revenue decisions— about the job choices of younger workers, and about the circumstances under which seniority becomes important, and about the characteristics of those who seek promotion, and how the production process itself affects worker aspirations. We can explore the circumstances conditioning budget decisions—under what conditions saving will take place, the influence of price on purchases, how the age factor affects buying habits, what contributes to the consumer acceptance of innovations. By such investigations we can, over time, build a picture of patterns of economic conduct which will be genuinely explanatory of budget and revenue decisions; with the further question of whether such patterns of behavior as are discerned maximize something called "satisfactions" over an indefinite time stream we can afford to be unconcerned.

It is thus the pattern of behavior as related to the time stream of aspirations, it is a person's conception of himself and what he is becoming, his changing integration of concomitant objectives in a meaningful and satisfying perspective that explain economic behavior, and not his effort to maximize some single quantity at a moment of time. But does this conception of a balance of satisfactions which is influenced by an individual's position in his time span leave us with something vague and imprecise and therefore analytically less useful than the more precise concept of maximizing?

There is no need for such pessimism. Rather, it appears that content must be supplied to the concept of balance on a different plane of analysis. We are seeking not logical certainties, such as the maximizing approach seeks to provide, but statistical probabilities, such as can be secured only by an examination of the behavior of numerous individuals in parallel circumstances. The interplay of the individual and his culture creates the expectancy that individuals in common cultural settings will reveal certain behavior traits in common. Subjected to reasonably similar conditioning, they are likely to respond to types of situations with sufficient consistency to make statistical analysis meaningful. The budget and revenue decisions of people in various subcultural groupings requires examination to elucidate the kind of balancing of concomitant goals, and the kind of balancing of gains and risks, which goes on at different periods in their life streams. Here we encounter the concrete data of the economic process which have as yet been insufficiently exploited, which have to some extent been obscured by our preoccupation with price data, but on which our theoretical understanding depends.

In all this, however, the economist need not surrender his primary concern with the use of scarce resources. His interest lies in the flow of goods and services and in the related flows of receipts and expenditures. The revenue and budget decisions are of economic significance only because they determine the inflows and outflows of income.

The element of time precludes us from saying that the revenue decision governs the inflow of income and the budget decision the outflow. Saving out of current income occurs only because of a time horizon and then gives rise to assets which become available in the form of income at a future time—income which is not determined by the revenue decision at that future date. A past budget decision (itself influenced by a past revenue decision) may thus give rise to current income, affecting both revenue and budget decisions in the present. (If current job income is supplemented by income from past savings, more weight may be accorded to job satisfaction in the revenue decision, and in the budget decision expenditures can be larger than otherwise they would have been.)

Current revenue and budget decisions are thus affected by past revenue and budget decisions (even by past decisions on the part of others, in the case of such vicarious satisfactions as lead to bequeathal or setting up a favored individual in business). But current decisions may also be affected by expectations of future income and expenditures. Present expenditures may be reduced or income emphasized where there is expectation of greater future need or smaller future income; savings may be negative (expenditures in excess of current income) where there is expectation of a rising income.

Thus past revenue and budget decisions interact, giving rise to assets and liabilities.

Future (expected) revenue and budget decisions interact, giving rise to expected income flows.

Present revenue and budget decisions interact, determining the balance of inflows and outflows, but the level and manner of their balance is influenced by the past (through assets and liabilities) and by the future (through expectations).

These relationships suggest the analytical treatment which we shall adopt. Although the interaction of revenue and budget decisions prevents us from saying that the revenue decision—*over time*—governs the inflow of income and the budget decision—*over time*—the outflow, we can nevertheless say that any revenue decision *in the present* (influenced by past decisions in the form of assets, and future decisions in the form of expectations) governs inflows, and that the budget decision *in the present* (likewise influenced by assets and expectations), governs outflows. We shall explore this relationship between present decisions and assets and expectations more fully in a later chapter.

There is, however, no escape from the proposition that, even in the present, revenue and budget decisions are mutually influencing. Income decisions are partially determined by outlay decisions, and expenditures are partially governed by the job choice. But neither wholly controls the other: income is adjusted, within limits, to satisfy consumption aspirations, and outflows are controlled, within limits, to satisfy producer's aspirations for work satisfaction.

When we speak of the concomitance of aspirations, then, we refer not only to the fact that a balance of producer and consumer satisfactions is sought (and that each of these categories itself represents balanced choices), but also to the fact that past and expected (future) aspirations are merged with the present. But the significance of this concomitance lies, for economists, only in its determination of the inflows and outflows of income.

CHAPTER 6

Bargaining Power

IN seeking to further the achievement of their aspirations at the particular points where they stand in their time streams, individuals are necessarily drawn into relationships with each other. These relationships may be competitive or coöperative. The ability of individuals to achieve their aspirations through these relationships depends upon their bargaining power and how they exercise it. The concept of bargaining power emerges from an examination of these economic relationships and the bargaining process.

COMPETITION AND COÖPERATION

A competitive relationship exists when the attempted achievements of two or more individuals are incompatible with each other. It is this relationship which has preoccupied the attention of economists.

The basis of competition is scarcity—that more for some must mean less for others, affecting relative positions. Even when objectives other than the satisfaction of consumption wants are admitted, competition is bound to persist, since it is an inevitable product of the urge to compare oneself with others. As long as prizes and distinctions are sought, if only pieces of ribbon or buttons or the favor of others, there is competition. There is an absolute scarcity when there is only one first prize, one foreman's job to be won, one union steward to be elected. There is scarcity whenever groups of workers seek to top each other in the wage gains which each makes or when businessmen seek to better each other's rate of profit. There is scarcity whenever occupational prestige is at stake or personal performances are compared, wherever relative ranking is significant. Scarcity and competition are of concern to the economist, however, only when they affect the use of scarce resources.

Competition is not the only type of relationship which is evoked by an individual's pursuit of his economic objectives. Specialization of function, division of labor, and exchange are characteristic of any organized society. The resulting functional dependence of an individual on others establishes as necessary a basis for coöperative relationships as scarcity does for competitive relationships.[1] A coöperative relationship is necessitated whenever an individual's objectives are unobtainable through his own unaided efforts, requiring the collaboration of others. Despite the common connotation attaching to the word, coöperation does not imply willingness but only the joint pursuit of a given objective. Coöperation may be forced, when the common objective is imposed by some on others, as in a military organization or a master-slave relationship.

In the system of economic relationships through which aspiration is linked to achievement, then, competition arises because of scarcity, and coöperation arises because of interdependence. Coöperation, based on interdependence, is no less fundamental a rela-

[1] What appear to be exceptions to this proposition do not involve societal relations. (1) An individual may overcome the scarcity imposed by nature, in the Robinson Crusoe sense. With free land, seed as the gift of nature, self-improvised tools, and his own efforts he may wrest his own living from the soil. But this is not a society. (2) As soon as others are introduced who seek the use of resources which are not plentiful enough for all, three possibilities emerge: (a) a situation of *conjectural* interdependence arises, with one individual's actions dependent on the reactions of others and vice versa, so that a quasi agreement results, but with all individuals *functionally* independent; this too is nonsocietal; (b) the individual resorts to piracy, thievery, marauding, which it is true may satisfy his material objectives without benefit of coöperation, but which at the same time denies the societal relationship; (c) the individual coöperates with others, satisfying his objectives by sharing the scarce resources on some agreed basis. Functional interdependence arises. It is this last resort which we take here as the general rule.

tionship than is competition, based on scarcity. Except in a Robinson Crusoe economy (a situation with less interest to the *social* scientist than a community of ants or a swarm of bees), interdependence is as pervasive and unavoidable an influence as is scarcity. Both are inescapable and together they give rise to the network of economic relationships characterizing society.[2]

The same individuals may be competitive in some respects and coöperative in other respects, since their relations involve both scarcity and interdependence. In a master and slave relationship, for example, joint production objectives are compulsorily imposed by the former on the latter, establishing a forced coöperation in which the achievements of one (the master) depend on the achievements of another (the slave). In the division of the product, however, even though the master is privileged to take whatever he likes without any possibility of protest by the slave there is still a competitive relationship between them—more for one means less for the other. Between the two there may also arise at times instances of voluntary coöperation, as for example in the erection of a church for the worship of a common god.

In order to establish more explicitly the nature of the connection between competition and coöperation, let us adopt certain terminology. If we identify any individual with some economic function as we do when we refer to him as a worker, an employer, a lender, a seller, and so on, there are always other individuals who are similar to him in the respect identified—other similarly skilled or similarly situated workers, employers, lenders, sellers. All individuals who are alike in the given respect, so that one might be substituted for the other (with similar but not necessarily identical results, as one machinist might substitute for another even though he cannot do the job so expertly) we denominate *commensals*.

---

[2] Neither competition nor coöperation requires a face-to-face relationship, nor do they indeed necessitate a consciousness of the existence of the relationship. In an ecological sense they may be induced by simple environmental or spatial relationships of which the individuals are not in fact aware. In treating, as economists, of the use of limited resources, however, we shall find it necessary to deal only with conscious relationships.

In contrast, there are others who stand in a complementary relationship to these same individuals: the employer is a complement of the worker, the worker of the employer; borrowers complement lenders, and buyers complement sellers. Such complementary pairs are linked together in a coöperative relationship in which each makes some unique contribution. The relationship is sought *because* the functional contribution of one is different from that of the other. These functionally interdependent relationships we denominate *symbiotic*, and the complementary types we call symbionts.[3] All exchange relationships are instances of symbiotic coöperation since they involve two parties in the common objective of a trade of goods (or titles to goods, such as money), where each is able to supply something that the other needs or wants. All situations where production specialization occurs are instances of symbiotic coöperation, since each specialist's services carry meaning only when joined with the efforts of other specialists.

We are now in a position to arrive at certain interesting conclusions. Because functional interdependence is unavoidable and in a modern exchange economy is completely pervasive, the objectives of competition can be won only through symbiotic coöperation. A number of workers compete for a job opening, but the prize can be won by any of them only through an ultimate coöperative relationship with the employer. One firm competes with other firms to dominate some market, but the objective can be gained only through coöperative relationships with a number of customers. A consumer wishes to obtain some product which is also desired by others (or which embodies resources which others desire in different commodities), but his wish is fulfilled only when he establishes a coöperative relationship with some seller.

It is difficult to conceive of a situation in an organized exchange economy, with its division of labor, where objectives calling for the use of limited resources can be achieved independently of others. Even so simple a project as the growing of vegetables on one's own

[3] The terms commensal and symbiotic have been adopted in preference to others because of their current use in the allied fields of sociology and social ecology.

land requires implements (which even if self-made are seldom made without nails or use of a knife), water (which even if obtained from a stream or spring is seldom conveyed by means not involving some good manufactured by others), and customarily the payment of a property tax (for one's share in the benefits of government).

If competition depends, for the achievement of its objectives, on some symbiotic relationship, it is no less true that the symbiotic relationship depends on competiton. Since a symbiotic relationship is one of coöperation, it can exist only by decision of all those who are party to it. That decision depends on the *terms* of coöperation, terms which must be reached through agreement, whether implicit or explicit. A union and management enter into a collective bargaining agreement, establishing symbiotic coöperation, only after a contest over terms, a contest which may include strike or lockout. A symbiotic relationship between housewife and grocer in the form of purchase and sale takes place only when each is satisfied with the terms of the sale.

An agreement between symbionts on the conditions of coöperation involves a competitive relationship since the element of scarcity is present. In arriving at terms, more for one necessarily means less for the other. The resolution of this competitive relationship is a precondition of coöperation—inescapable regardless of the good will of the coöperants. *Wherever* a scarcity relationship exists competition is unavoidable.

This dependence of coöperation on the competitive resolution of the scarcity problem is fundamental to all economic theory. Its prevalence can be emphasized by examples which involve economic relations usually judged insufficiently important to incorporate into systematic analysis. A coöperative relationship between church and devotee—economic if involving the use of scarce resources to foster the work of the church—depends first on the settlement of the competitive relationship between the church and its follower: the making of a contribution by the latter to the former invokes a competitive relationship in the economic sense that more for the church means less for the giver, even though the latter may feel adequately recompensed in terms of spiritual satisfaction. Similarly, a coöperative relationship between parent and child to further the child's development, perhaps through piano lessons—again economic if requiring the use of scarce resources—can be undertaken only after a prior determination of the terms of coöperation, involving a competitive relationship between parent and child because a greater use of family resources on behalf of the child necessarily means less of the family's resources which can be spent on the behalf of the parent, however great the joy of the parent in the child's advancement.

Thus symbiotic coöperation is sought as a means of achieving one's objectives, but coöperation depends on agreement as to the conditions of coöperation. This competitive relationship between symbionts over the terms of their coöperation is resolved (necessarily so, as will become evident) by a bargaining process, in which each party seeks a working agreement which is advantageous to its own interests.

With two primary exceptions—withdrawal of one's productive power (time) from the market in the case of the revenue decision (that is, self-employment) and withdrawal of one's purchasing power (money) from the market in the case of the budget decision (that is, saving), with these two exceptions economic actions run in terms of coöperation by agreement. Previously we spoke of the inducement to act as though it constituted an array of alternative courses of conduct, each carrying its own gains and risks to the achievement of aspirations, based on terms that were given to the individual. We spoke of the inducement to act as though it involved a unilateral decision only: the individual's choice was determinative of the course he pursued. We now wish to emphasize that since actions depend on agreements with others, two (or more) parties must be induced to act before any action can be taken, so that an individual's course of conduct is dependent on another's decision as well as his own. And the terms of the alternative courses confronting the individual are not fixed but are subject to his influence, an influence which depends on how important his coöperation is to the opposing party. The influence which a person has over another, in the setting of the terms of their coöperation, is his power to withhold the gains that his coöperation would make possible, thus imposing on the other a cost of disagreeing on his terms. But the amount of the gain (as well as the amount of the risk) attaching to his coöperation is itself dependent on the terms which he sets. A bargainer who sets a high price on his coöperation thereby lessens the gains and increases the risk attaching to coöperation with him. By modifying the terms which he asks he modifies the gains and risks which the other faces in agreeing on his terms.

BARGAINING

To emphasize the dependence of economic action on agreement, let us convert our expression for the inducement to act into an expression for the inducement to agree. The inducement to agree may be defined as

$$\frac{\text{the cost of disagreeing on X's terms}}{\text{the cost of agreeing on X's terms}} \quad \begin{array}{l}(= \text{ the gains from coöperating with} \\ \quad \text{X that must be given up}) \\ (= \text{ the risks presented by agreeing} \\ \quad \text{with X that cannot be avoided})\end{array}$$

In the case of either agreeing or disagreeing with X, the gains and risks are relative to other possible bargains or to no bargain. We are interested in the achievement of aspirations made possible by coöperating with X, in contrast to the achievements made possible by coöperating with Y or Z. We are interested in the risks to one's aspirations accompanying agreement with X in contrast to the risks accompanying agreement with Y or Z.

Each bargainer will seek to propose terms of coöperation which are as favorable as possible to himself and yet sufficiently favorable to the opposing bargainer to win his affirmative response. Each will seek the advancement of his own aspirations, and hence will propose terms on which he himself is willing to coöperate with another; but each seeks agreement, and hence will propose terms which offer an inducement to the other, which do not drive him to disagreement. In this relationship two different sets of proposals are likely to be advanced, one by each of the bargainers, since each may be expected to favor his own interests over the other's. Such initial differences do not necessarily preclude ultimate agreement, however; since each seeks coöperation with the other he may make concessions to secure it. The effort to win the consent of the other constitutes what we call bargaining, and a successful outcome of the bargaining process involves a movement of one or the other or both parties toward the terms offered by the bargaining opponent until there is finally agreement on some common set of terms.

The outcome of the bargaining process—whether agreement is reached, and if it is on what terms—depends on how much one or the other or both can be led to move from some preferred position which favors itself toward a less preferred position which is more favorable to the other party. The degree of influence which one possesses over the other, to force such concessions, is what we refer to as bargaining power. Bargaining power can be defined as the capacity to effect an agreement on one's own terms; operationally, one's bargaining power *is* another's inducement to agree. If X and Y are in a contest over the terms of their coöperation, X's bargaining power is represented by Y's inducement to agree (the cost to Y of agreeing on X's terms relative to the cost of disagreeing on those terms), while Y's bargaining power is X's inducement to agree (the cost to X of agreeing on Y's terms relative to the cost of disagreeing on those terms). The terms proposed are sometimes understood rather than made explicit, but the principle is not thereby vitiated. And the costs, both of agreement and disagreement, must be regarded as the subjective estimates of the parties, the *expected* probabilities of the consequences which are *expected* to affect the realization of their aspirations.

If for both parties the cost of agreement is greater than the cost of disagreement on the other's initial terms, then no agreement between them will be forthcoming unless concessions are made. In order for a bargaining agreement to be concluded at least one of the parties must find that agreement on the other's terms is less costly than disagreement on those terms. As a condition for any agreement, then, we can say that the ratio of the inducement to agree must be 1 or greater for at least one of the parties.[4]

There is no reason to conclude, however, that whenever a party finds its inducement to agree equal to 1, it will thereupon consent to the other's terms. Depending upon the nature of the relationship, it is also possible that that party will simply offer more favorable terms to its bargaining opponent, perhaps making repeated concessions, in a continuing effort to find some terms short of those to which it is prepared to agree where the inducement to agree of its bargaining opponent is also equal to 1. As the party with the weaker bargaining power (greater inducement to agree to the other's terms) gradually moves toward the other's position, it will thereby strengthen its own bargaining power by increasing the other's inducement to agree on its terms. The union which demands a 20-cent wage increase may be ready to agree to the 10-cent offer of the employer, sooner than strike; its cost of agreeing on management's terms may be less than its cost of disagreeing. But sooner than settle at once for 10 cents, it will lower its own demands, first to 15 cents, then to 12 cents, in the hope or expectation that at some point above the employer's 10-cent offer the employer will also be placed in a position where it will be cheaper to agree on the union's terms than to disagree on those terms. By its progressive lowering of its terms, the union will have increased its bargaining power.

When for both of the parties the inducement to agree is equal to

---

[4] Although we have expressed the inducement to agree as a ratio, and given it the appearance of an arithmetic calculation, in practice this is seldom feasible. For the costs of agreement and disagreement are often not reducible to a common denominator, but involve a comparison of incommensurable items, a balance of satisfactions, as we have already noted with respect to the gains and risks in the inducement to act.

1, an area of indeterminacy is created. At any point within this range each would prefer to settle on the other's terms rather than not settle at all, but the terms of the two parties still differ. Resolution of the difference which separates them involves a continuation of the same bargaining process in which they have been involved all along, each trying to win the advantage. In this game of bluff and persuasion relative bargaining power is important. Whichever party has the lesser inducement to agree will be relatively the stronger in bargaining power. It may therefore be inclined to carry its bluff a little farther than the other, conveying the threat of a disagreement which it itself wants to avoid, in an effort to compromise the difference to its advantage. If the other party believes that *only* bluff is involved, however, its refusal to agree involves no actual cost of disagreement, since it can expect that its continued disagreement will only cause the other party to reduce its demands further.

It is here that the uncertainty of the bargaining process becomes most apparent. Neither party can ever be sure of its own bargaining power, since this depends on the subjective estimates which the other has made, the nature of which can only be surmised. X's estimate of the relative bargaining powers, for example, depends on his calculation of the costs of agreement and disagreement on Y's terms, laid alongside his estimate of Y's estimate of the costs of agreement and disagreement on his own (X's) terms. Because of the high degree of uncertainty involved here, as each party tries to gain the advantage in the final terms of settlement, it is possible that if one's bluff is called a disagreement may be precipitated which neither wishes, involving both in expected costs greater than if they had conceded the whole difference between their respective demands to the other.

In many cases an individual faces not simply one bargaining opponent but a number, each of whom stands as a possible alternative to the others. An employer interviews half a dozen applicants for a single job opening, with each of whom some bargain might be made. Each of the applicants likewise is negotiating with other possible employers, with any one of whom an agreement may be reached. Whether an agreement is arrived at between A and B, rather than between A and C and between B and D, depends on the relative inducement to A to agree on B's terms or on C's terms, and the relative inducement to B to agree on A's terms or on D's terms. Only if the terms offered by A are more favorable than those offered by D will B be induced to agree with A. Only if the terms offered by B are more favorable than those offered by C will A be induced to agree with B. B faces A and D, offering its coöperation on stated terms and considering their offers of coöperation on their stated terms. A similarly faces B and C. B may move only a short way toward the position of A, because D is willing to move much farther toward its (B's) own demands. If A then seeks agreement with B it must make even greater concessions than D, perhaps wholly accepting B's last terms. It will be unwilling to make such concessions, however, if in the meantime C has moved closer to its position than has B. When more than two sets of bargainers are involved the relationships are even more complex. Nor are they made any simpler by the fact that bargainers standing as alternatives to each other are sometimes unaware of the terms which their commensal competitors are offering or that they are sometimes played off one against the other—whipsawed—by the bargaining opponent.

Coöperation between two parties thus depends on whether the terms on which agreement can be reached between them offer each the greatest inducement to agree of all the alternative bargains which each faces. (This is equivalent to our earlier proposition that an individual will pursue that course of action which offers the greatest inducement to act.) [5] If, however, the cost of agreement is greater

---

[5] The question might be raised as to whether this choice among possible bargains on the basis of the one offering the greatest inducement to agree does not imply maximizing. This question was raised and answered in the preceding chapter. If some meaningful common denominator for all satisfactions existed, within a defined time span, then maximizing would apply. As it is, we can say that choices may be taken as revealing maximum satisfaction only in the sense that each choice is evidently preferred over all other competing choices. But the basis of such preference is not thereby revealed, and in the absence of a common denominator of

than the cost of disagreement for all bargains faced, no agreement will be forthcoming. The consequence is withdrawal from the production process, in the case of the revenue decision, and liquid saving, in the case of the budget decision. As we have already seen, the budget and revenue decisions are *continuing* decisions, *continually* demanding choices which cannot be avoided, choices which we now see require (1) agreements or self-employment [6] and (2) agreements or liquid saving.

THE BARGAINING RELATIONSHIP

Since relationships of symbiotic coöperation are essential to the achievement of competitive objectives, and since bargaining relationships are essential to the establishment of symbiotic coöperation, it follows that the bargaining relationship must be viewed as in some sense fundamental. It is the relationship which joins the scarcity and interdependence conditions, owing its existence to both. In contrast to this view of the basic importance of the bargaining relationship, however, there are many who contend that bargaining is not economically significant, since it rests on a power by the bargainer to exclude suitable alternatives, a power which is not commonly possessed in an exchange economy, where alternatives are normally available (other employers, other workers, other buyers, other sellers) to stop anyone from seeking to exact a greater price

---

satisfactions the conception of a person's balancing a variety of aspirations is less misleading than a conception of maximizing. In this sense choices represent best balances of statistically ascertainable aspirations rather than the maximum of some unknown quantity called "satisfaction," "good," or "happiness" which might be seized in some moment as though the actors could order, "Time, stand thou still."

A related question is what determines the alternatives which are compared. From among the almost unlimited number of bargains possible, how are some few selected to be compared with each other? The answer would appear to be that one's aspirations themselves are selective of the alternatives considered. As will be repeatedly stressed, individual bargains are understandable only in the light of an integrated pattern of behavior.

[6] It is because of this continuing necessity to decide the use of one's time—to divide it between self-employment and agreements for market employment—that *all* activity can be said to have an economic component, namely, the use of the scarce factor time (or energy). Self-employment, it will be recalled, here refers to all uses of time except those for which a wage or salary is received.

for his symbiotic coöperation than his commensals are willing to take.

This argument is not without merit, but it has one great defect. Reliance on numbers of alternatives available to anyone who seeks a symbiotic relation may explain many exchange transactions more or less satisfactorily. But if, as economists, we are concerned with the allocation of all the limited resources available to a society, there are many types of transactions which do not fall into the same pattern and cannot be so well explained by the principle of large numbers of alternatives. Most taxes paid to governments (city, state, and federal), contributions to churches, the allocation of resources within the family unit, the expenditure of funds upon military establishments, the provision of economic assistance to develop foreign countries, and so on, in an impressive list which includes all nonmarket transactions, can hardly be explained so readily in terms of exchanges where numbers of equally satisfactory alternatives are available.

Before we accept the conclusion that the bargaining relationship is essential to all symbiotic relationships (where the use of limited resources is involved), however, we shall want to examine six special cases which raise questions concerning that conclusion, the answers to which should help us in passing judgment on the significance of bargaining as an economic relationship. These are: (1) the case of perfect competition; (2) the case of perfect coöperation; (3) the case of unilateral imposition of terms; (4) the case of terms imposed by outside authority; (5) the case of commensal agreement for individual bargaining; and (6) the case of commensal agreement for collective bargaining.

1. The case of perfect competition. As we have seen, because of interdependence one's aspirations can be achieved only through relationships of symbiotic coöperation. The perfectly competitive price analysis recognizes this condition: although its explicit emphasis is on competition, underlying the whole theoretical fabric is a conviction of the need for economic coöperation. Adam Smith opens the first chapter of his *Wealth of Nations* with a discussion

of division of labor that leaves no doubt as to the importance of coöperation in his system.

Perfect competition is the condition of large numbers of homogeneous economic agents—homogeneous not in the sense of being similar in all respects but only in that respect which is significant to the symbionts with whom coöperation is sought. Workers may be short or tall, young or old, colored or white, blonde or brunette, of Irish or German descent, and so on, but if the employer is interested only in their skills as machinists or lathe operators or bench hands or salesmen or in some other functional capacity, these personal differences have no bearing on their homogeneity or nonhomogeneity. Among such homogeneous agents (commensals) there occurs competition to become party to some desired symbiotic relation, a relationship desired because it is the key to achievement of their economic aspirations.

This competition takes the form of a bidding process, with the best bids winning the desired relationship. No individual can hope to win the desired relationship with any bid less favorable than that made by one of his fellow commensals, since all stand as perfect substitutes for each other.

Bidding is a species of competition—not between symbionts but among the commensals seeking to be party to some symbiotic relationship, not between workers and employers, but among workers and among employers. Its significance lies only in its effect on the terms of symbiotic coöperation, however. That effect is to reduce to zero the bargaining power of any commensal who seeks to win the desired relationship with an offer less than the most favorable bid of his fellows. Under such circumstances the cost to the other party of disagreeing with the bidder's terms is zero—alternatives are available at better terms; no gains that would come from coöperating with that bidder are sacrificed by coöperating with another bidder.

Perfect competition actually involves a double bidding process, in which each would-be party to some type of symbiotic relation bids against its own commensals—employers bidding against employers (the high bid winning) and workers against workers (the low bid winning) to become parties to the employer-worker relationship. Identical bids by employer and worker (a coincidence of high employer bid and low worker bid) represents agreement between the two parties on the terms of their symbiotic coöperation. This double bidding process puts a limit on the bidding: there is no need for workers to bid lower than employers bid, or for employers to bid higher then workers bid, since when identical bids are entered by workers and employers—by the symbionts—there is agreement between them.

This double bidding process, no less than the customary auction bidding, is significant only because related to symbiotic bargaining. The bargaining power of *both* parties is reduced to zero, since if any commensal—on either side of the relation—seeks to exact terms more favorable than his fellows are offering, the cost to the other party, the symbiont, of disagreeing on those terms becomes zero.

We conclude, then, that bidding, like bargaining, is a competitive process. There is a general scarcity condition present, a scarcity of the symbiotic relationships which represent access to limited resources, a limitation on the number of workers, of employers, of sellers, of buyers whose coöperation will aid in the achievement of economic objectives. Bidding becomes an element in the determination of the terms on which coöperation takes place, by affecting the costs of agreement and disagreement, that is, by affecting bargaining power.

Bidding does not occur only in cases of homogeneity. Competitive offers may come from some who stand not as precise substitutes for each other but who are nevertheless interchangeable. The real estate pages of any metropolitan newspaper carry columns of advertisements of houses for sale at a variety of asking prices; none of the houses is precisely the same, but each competes with the other and affects the terms of the bargain which is ultimately struck between the buyer and one of the many sellers. There is no doubt that in such a case the bidding process is supplementary to the bargaining process, an element affecting the bargained outcome. The situation is changed when the rival bids come from perfect substitutes for each other only by the fact that bargaining power is affected in a particular manner.

Competitive bidding by perfect alternatives to each other is most uncommon. It is least to be expected when the performance of some service is called for, as typically in the production process. Because individuals are unique the services of one are seldom quite the same as those of another, and personal characteristics unrelated to functional performance become important in the social contact. All the elements of personal discrimination, some of which we approve and others which we tend to disapprove, become relevant considerations.[7] Homogeneity is most likely to be found in the product transaction, though even here the prevalence of product differentiation drastically reduces its incidence. The best examples are perhaps provided by the organized stock and commodity exchanges.

Perfect competition is thus a relatively uncommon form of competitive bidding (commensal competition) which has significance in the economic system only because it is related to another form of competition, symbiotic bargaining. It is a case where bargaining power is at its minimum limit, becoming zero because the cost of disagreement on the other's terms is zero.

2. The case of perfect coöperation. Let us consider now the situation where not only would symbionts effect a coöperative relationship but each desires the same apportionment of costs and benefits resulting from the relationship. We may refer to this as the case of perfect coöperation. But in what sense is such coöperation a bargained relationship?

In instances of this sort the terms of coöperation are usually implicit. They are, however, the same for each party. Since the terms

---

[7] A comprehensive survey of the preferences of employers in the hiring process is contained in E. William Noland and E. Wight Bakke, *Workers Wanted* (New York: Harper & Brothers, 1949); and of the preferences of workers in the employment process in Lloyd G. Reynolds and Joseph Shister, *Job Horizons* (New York: Harper & Brothers, 1949).

which one seeks are precisely those which the other offers, there is a cost of disagreeing on the other's terms, but no cost of agreeing on the other's terms instead of one's own terms. We have here, then, a situation complementary to that of perfect competition, with bargaining power for each of the symbionts at the opposite limit, being infinite.

This is not the same thing as saying there is no cost of agreement at all. Any economic relationship implies a cost, since it is the necessity of choice between alternatives—imposed by the scarcity condition—which creates the economic problem, and as soon as choice is necessary there is a cost—the cost of that which must be sacrificed by choosing this. In the case of perfect coöperation, however, the cost of agreement is at its absolute minimum—there are no other terms of coöperation which either party would prefer.

Two examples of this type of coöperation have already been provided, one involving a contribution by a religious devotee to the church of his persuasion, the other an expenditure by a parent for the training of his child. That these two instances are not commonly considered in economic analysis does not deprive them of their economic nature, since both involve an allocation of scarce resources, though with consequences that are usually of more interest to the sociologist than the economist. We are not here interested in them for their significance or insignificance to economic theory, however, but only for their illustration of the case of perfect coöperation. In both instances a competitive relationship is present, as we have seen: the general scarcity condition applies, in that more for the use of one means less for the use of the other. In the case of the religious association, we may assume the implicit terms of coöperation to be the member financing, to an amount of his own discretion, of the propagation of a common creed. In the case of the family association, the implicit terms of coöperation are the child's adherence to a parent-financed program of study.

That the bargaining relationship is actually present, with an exercise of infinite bargaining power by each of the symbionts under the given circumstances, is demonstrable. Suppose that the religious follower offered to make a contribution only on the condition that the church modify its program in some respect. Perhaps the minister had been active in his efforts to inject Christian principles into industrial relations, offending either an employer or a union official who was affiliated with the church and who offered to maintain his contribution to the church's work only on condition that the minister confine the application of his religious beliefs to nonindustrial affairs. The bargaining relationship would immediately become apparent. For the minister there would now emerge a cost of agreement on the other's terms—a denial of his ethical convictions and perhaps the loss of the support of others—against which must be weighed, as cost of disagreement the loss of the member's contribution and perhaps the contributions of those whom the member might influence. Or suppose that in the family situation the child desires to pursue a course of musical study but only on condition that he be allowed to take lessons from a more expensive teacher who is also patronized by his friends. The parent would now face a cost of agreement on the child's terms where previously there had been none, involving a greater expenditure than he wishes to make, against which must be laid a cost of disagreement in the form of giving up the musical training which he desires his child to have. In neither of these two cases would the bargain now be assured, since what had previously been an infinite bargaining power on both sides has now been converted into a situation in which the desires of each are in conflict and must be resolved by a contest of necessarily limited bargaining powers.

3. The case of unilateral imposition of terms.[8] We distinguish two types of situations here: (1) unilateral imposition of terms but discretion as to acceptance of the coöperative relationship, and (2) unilateral imposition of the relationship on dictated terms. These two situations which appear distinct on first encounter will be found, on reflection, to blend imperceptibly into each other.

[8] In *Collective Bargaining* (New York: McGraw-Hill Book Co., Inc., 1951) I distinguished unilateral imposition of terms from bargaining. I now appreciate that the distinction which I sought to make was between unilaterally imposed terms and negotiation, since each in fact constitutes a species of bargaining.

Both raise the question of whether terms which are coerced by one of the parties can be construed as bargained.

Symbiotic relationships which are optional to us but which can be elected only on conditions fixed by the other party are common. Most retail stores in the United States operate with posted prices which the customer is free to accept or reject but not to modify. Employers sometimes complain that union agents confront them with demands which are already written into a collective bargaining agreement, ready for signature, and a statement that "That's all we'll listen to—take it or leave it." Can such "take it or leave it" demands be called bargaining?

Bargaining does not require negotiation. A bargaining relationship exists whenever symbiotic coöperation is contemplated (as when any purchase or sale is considered) in the furtherance of one's aspirations, provided only that satisfactory terms are obtainable. Satisfactory terms are not necessarily terms which are regarded as "fair," in any sense; they are satisfactory only in the sense that the cost of disagreement on those terms is greater (or no less) than the cost of agreement. For the manager who is confronted by a union ultimatum, backed by threat of strike, the cost of accepting the union's terms, however strong his dislike of them, may be less than the cost of the alternative of not accepting the terms. For the shopper who compares the offerings of a number of merchants, the cost of paying the price demanded by one store may be less than the cost of refusing to meet those terms, costs which consist of going without the desired object or paying a higher price elsewhere or being subjected to inconveniences in marketing. In both cases a bargaining relation is present, even though negotiation may be absent.

Moreover, the party to whom the demand is made is not always without the bargaining power to force some modification in the terms demanded. The manager may have means at his disposal of convincing the union leader that the latter's disagreement on his terms is more costly than agreement, opening an area for compromise settlement. If a customer threatens to buy elsewhere, the merchant may deviate from his posted-price policy and make a "special offer"; in any event, if enough customers turn away he may be induced to lower his price.

We are not accustomed to thinking of coöperation as a relation forced by some private individuals upon others, but less than a hundred years ago the master-slave relationship still existed in the United States. In that instance the symbiotic relationship itself was forced upon one of the partners to it, on terms which were dictated by the other. Perhaps the most common existing area of such economic coöperation compelled by one of the parties on his terms is in family life. Children are frequently subjected to parental authority, at times involving physical coercion, to compel coöperation on dictated terms, in the performance of household tasks.

These situations still embody the bargaining relationship, however, since in a literal sense coöperation can never be compelled. The party subjected to coercion can always accept the penalties of refusal to coöperate, however drastic these may be. Such penalties enter into his calculation of the costs of disagreement, and must be laid alongside the costs of agreement before it can be determined whether the coercing party possesses sufficient bargaining power to attain his objective. These situations are fundamentally no different from the case of "take-it-or-leave-it" terms, except in the harshness of the penalties associated with disagreement. The history of union-management relations in the United States, for example, contains numerous instances where one or the other of the parties sought to compel agreement on its terms by resort to violence in a ruthless effort to make the alternative to agreement excessively costly.

4. The case of terms imposed by outside authority. The same two types of situations may be distinguished here as in the case of unilateral imposition of terms: (a) The relationship is discretionary but if entered into the terms are fixed: compulsory arbitration, minimum wage determination, public utility and railroad rate fixing are examples. (b) The relationship itself is compelled on terms laid down; examples here are tax payments and military service. Again it may be asked, Where terms are so fixed by force or authority,

how does bargaining enter as a necessary preliminary to the relationship?

Again, these two types of situations, apparently dissimilar, represent only a range of similar situations. Where authoritative terms of coöperation are imposed, the terms may or may not include penalties for noncoöperation. Where it is intended to compel coöperation, penalties for noncoöperation are provided and become part of the cost of disagreement on the terms imposed. Military service may be avoided if one is willing to pay the price for disagreeing on the terms of symbiotic coöperation laid down by his government. Bargaining, as we have noted, does not imply negotiation but only a calculation of the cost of agreement and disagreement on the terms proposed—terms which, it is true, are in this instance not proposed by the other party to the relationship but by an outside authority.

5. The case of commensal agreement for individual symbiotic bargaining. Here agreement is sought not between the symbionts themselves but among a relatively small number of commensals who are competing with each other to become party to some symbiotic relationship. The agreement may be overt, effected by negotiation (though in the United States this is usually illegal); an example would be industry collusion in the submission of bids, or any price agreement among competitors. The agreement may simply be understood, developing out of the learning process (quasi agreement), as in the case of oligopolists, as Professor Fellner has so lucidly demonstrated. In either case the agreement relates to the terms which any one of the group is free to offer in bargaining for the desired symbiotic relationship without evoking retaliation from his commensal rivals.

The agreement is thus a form of coöperation designed to strengthen the position of each member of the commensal group in his bargaining with symbionts. To the extent that rivalry among themselves is reduced, the bargaining power of all of them is increased. In the case of price collusion, for example, the cost to any firm of disagreeing on the customer's terms is reduced when that cost does not include the certain loss of a sale to some competitor offering more favorable terms. By thus reducing the cost of disagreement on the customer's terms, each firm increases its bargaining power.

Such commensal agreement depends on commensal bargaining (quasi agreement on quasi bargaining). It can be assumed that the terms which the commensals agree among themselves that each of their number can offer to those for whose symbiotic coöperation they are all competing do not equally favor them all. One (a high-cost producer, for example) would be benefited if the common terms were set higher, another (who hopes to expand its markets) if they were fixed lower. These disagreements among themselves can be resolved only by bargaining. The terms which are finally accepted depend on the interplay of their bargaining powers, the determination by each of the costs of agreement and disagreement on the terms proposed by each of the commensal group.

Commensal coöperation of this sort thus depends on bargaining, just as does symbiotic coöperation. But commensal coöperation has significance only in so far as it aids the coöperants in their bargaining for symbiotic relationships. Each of the small number of commensals stands as an alternative to the others in the symbiotic relationships which all desire, a condition which, if allowed to stimulate competitive bidding among them, would weaken the bargaining power of all. Agreement among themselves as to the limits to which any of their number will push his bid, without evoking retaliation from his fellows, is a means of strengthening the position of all in their symbiotic bargaining. Such agreement can normally be effected when only small numbers are involved, however.

6. The case of commensal agreement for collective symbiotic bargaining. This is similar to the case above, except that here the agreement is not on the terms which each individually will offer, with each continuing to stand as an alternative to the other in symbiotic relationships which all desire but which only one can have; here the agreement is on the terms which all will collectively offer, for a symbiotic relationship which includes them all. The

purpose of agreement is less to prevent competitive bidding by commensals within the group than to forestall competitive bidding by commensals *outside* the group for the positions of each one *in* the group. When the group acts collectively, the only alternatives facing its opponent are a symbiotic relationship with another similar group, or noncoöperation. Because whole groups can be replaced only with more difficulty than individuals, the cost to the other party of disagreeing on the terms proposed by the group increases, strengthening the latter's bargaining power.

Agreement on the terms which will be collectively offered to the other party requires bargaining among the commensals themselves. The terms which appear most advantageous to some may not satisfy others. In labor unions, for example, skilled members may wish to hold out for a higher wage increase than unskilled members are willing to settle for, and before agreement on common proposals can be reached concessions will have to be made, based on relative bargaining power. If it should happen that there is unanimity of opinion on the terms to be supported, this is simply the limiting case of infinite bargaining power, since the cost of agreement to all, on the others' terms, is zero. In the course of negotiation, however, differences are likely to emerge within the group over the concessions to be offered to secure agreement. In any event, such commensal coöperation has significance only in being an instrument of bargaining power in the effort to effect a symbiotic relationship with others.

We have now examined six special cases, in each instance finding that the bargaining relationship is fundamental to the symbiotic relationship, the bridge between the two inescapable conditions of scarcity and interdependence. We should remind ourselves, however, that all agreements do not involve rational choice any more than do all actions. Agreements may be effected from routine or chance or sudden inclination. As we know, such decisions (agreements) are commonly referable to some higher level of specificity of objective, however, which gives them their reasonableness if not their rationality. The cost of agreement may simply be too negligible to be significant to the continuing revenue and budget decisions, so that the terms of one party are willingly accepted by the other, with a result approaching perfect coöperation.

Figure 1 suggests the connections between the various types of relationships which we have investigated. Because of general scarcity and interdependence, particular symbiotic relationships are

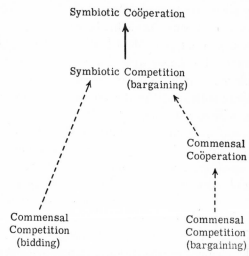

FIGURE 1. Dotted lines indicate that symbiotic competition may—but need not—be influenced by commensal competition.

sought which will satisfy the demands of both conditions. These coöperative relationships can be attained only through bargaining. In addition, in most (but not all) instances such competition among symbionts is influenced by competition in the form of rival bids by commensals, which sometimes leads to commensal coöperation (a bargained relationship).

We thus have the picture of a society whose scarce resources are distributed in accordance with the relative bargaining powers of its constituent members. Each individual is the manager of his own scarcity and interdependence position, a management which takes the form of making day-to-day bargains, through the exercise of his bargaining power, which are both a reflection and a determinant of his continuing revenue and budget decisions. The results of his bargains appear in the form of an inflow of resources to him and an outflow of resources from him, whether those resources are actually embodied in goods and services or constitute a command over goods and services in the form of money.

Each individual stands as the focus of a large number of symbiotic relationships, arising out of his bargained transactions. Each of those with whom one individual has a symbiotic relationship in turn is the center of a similar web of relationships, and so on, with every individual's web interconnected through some chain with every other individual's web in the economy, a connection which may be immediate or very remote.

The changes which an individual makes in his system of bargained relationships are influenced by his aspirations. The nature of his drives—their direction and intensity—helps to determine how he administers his position of scarcity and interdependence, whether he initiates changes to which others respond or whether he responds to actions initiated by others, how he reacts to modifications in the general conditions of scarcity and interdependence such as are brought on by changes in population and resources. Whatever the nature of one's aspirations (in so far as they require scarce resources for their fulfillment), they can be sought *only* by bargaining for terms on which the facilitating symbiotic relationships can be erected. In a world of interdependence, the effort to achieve one's objectives can *only* be met by effective management of one's bargaining power.

SUMMARY

Let us now summarize the principal findings of this chapter.

1. Because of a scarcity of the resources available to all aspirants for their use, for whatever purpose, all individuals in a society are

competitive with each other. More for some means less for others. This is the general scarcity condition.

2. Because of functional interdependence, the objectives of com- petition—the aspirations of the individual—can be achieved only by symbiotic coöperation. This is the general interdependence condition.

3. The general interdependence condition can be resolved only through particular interdependence (symbiotic) relationships. Establishment of such particular symbiotic relationships requires agreement between the symbionts on the terms of their coöperation.

4. Agreement on the terms of coöperation must be reached through a competitive process, since the costs of coöperation (which must be met from limited resources) and the fruits of coöperation (which are necessarily limited) must be apportioned among those competing. More for one means less for the other. We call this competitive process bargaining, and any agreement eventuating depends on relative bargaining power (the other's inducement to agree on terms proposed). A bargained agreement is the particular scarcity relationship which resolves the general scarcity condition.

5. The achievement of aspirations involves one's management of his position of scarcity and interdependence through bargains which simultaneously effectuate and mold the fundamental revenue and budget decisions on which inflows and outflows of income depend.

CHAPTER 7

The Determinants of Bargaining Power

A PERSON'S bargaining power consists in his ability to effect agreements on his own terms. Its measure is another's inducement to agree on his terms. Whatever affects another's costs of disagreement and agreement on one's own terms thus determines one's own bargaining power. In this chapter we shall consider, first, methods of measuring bargaining power and, second, its determinants.

THE MEASUREMENT OF BARGAINING POWER

There are two approaches to the calculation of the costs of disagreement and agreement, either of which is satisfactory and both of which arrive at the same result. Clarity will be served if we understand the differences and similarities in these approaches. Let us begin with one which differs slightly from the formulation with which we are already familiar, and end with that which we previously encountered. In this first approach the calculation of the costs of disagreement and agreement on the terms of any possible bargain *incorporates* the costs of disagreement and agreement on the terms of all other possible bargains.

The cost of disagreement is the sacrifice of those special advantages for the achievement of one's stream of aspirations which flow from the prospective relationship. Although as economists our touchstone remains the use and allocation of scarce resources, we cannot fail to be concerned with the impact of the transfer of resources on a person's whole goal structure. The benefits accompanying the relation may be "noneconomic" (job satisfaction, for example) and yet be as determinative of the special advantages of this bargain, which would have to be given up if some other bargain were made, as the scarce resources which accompany it (as represented by a wage rate, for example).

The special advantages which are given up by not agreeing on another's terms include advantages both of the quality of what is offered and the terms on which it is offered. If two identical products are offered on different terms, the cost of disagreeing in one case involves only a price advantage. If two products of differing quality are offered on the same terms, the cost of disagreeing in one case involves only a quality advantage. If two products of differing quality are offered on different terms the cost of disagreeing in one case may involve a quality advantage, a price advantage, or both a quality and price advantage. The cost of disgreeing on another's terms is whatever gains in the achievement of one's aspirations are foregone by giving up this symbiotic relationship.

The cost of agreement on the other's terms is the adverse consequences to the achievement of one's aspirations accompanying this bargain which could be avoided if some other decision were made. These are the disadvantages associated with this agreement—what other objectives must be sacrificed to this one, what risks to present or future achievement are incurred. The disadvantages which are accepted in agreeing on another's terms are disadvantages both of the quality of what is offered and the terms on which it is offered.

Advantages and disadvantages are, however, only relative. A quality advantage possessed by one product in comparison with another may be considered a quality disadvantage in comparison with a third, and the same is true of price comparisons. Or one product may be superior in one respect and inferior in another.

Since the cost of disagreement consists in the special advantages offered by a particular bargain, the cost of agreeing on some *other* bargain must be equivalent to the sacrifice of the special advantage offered by the first. Since something can be considered of special advantage only with respect to the achievement of one's aspirations, then the foregoing of this aspirational achievement involves not only a cost of disagreeing on *this* bargain but a cost of agreeing (a consequence adverse to the achievement of aspirations) on some *other* bargain. Let us suppose that a young man is considering the choice of a college. He is faced with the possibility of going to ABC College, which has a reputation for scholarship which would be highly advantageous to the achievement of his career ambitions but which has little social life, or of going to XYZ College, whose scholastic standing is good but not superior, but which is noted for sponsoring an extraordinarily full extracurricular program. The cost of agreeing with the authorities at ABC on the terms of his admittance thus carries, as one ingredient, the giving up of good times outside class hours, while the cost of agreeing with the authorities at XYZ carries as one cost of agreement the foregoing of a superior training. The special advantage which characterizes one choice thus becomes something which must be given up by making another choice, a cost of agreeing on the alternative.

This relationship between the costs of disagreement and agreement approximates the notion of opportunity cost which we encounter in the price analysis—the cost of a good or service is what must be given up in order to obtain it, the opportunities which one necessarily foregoes by making one decision rather than another. There has been some tendency, however, to regard opportunity costs as involving only scarce resources—the cost of a course of action is the goods and services which could have been obtained through alternative courses of action. No such connotation applies in the present analysis. The special advantages which are given up if this bargain is *not* made (the cost of disagreement) and the special advantages which are given up if this given bargain *is* struck (the cost of agreement) relate to a person's total stream of aspirations.

Some flow of resources must be involved, but it is not only the resources acquired or given up which determine whether this bargain or that bargain will be made, but the total effects on one's goal structure. It is not only agreement on a product or service which is involved, but agreement on a personal relationship, and the advantages and disadvantages which are relevant are those pertaining to the relationship, not just to the good.

This relationship between the cost of disagreement on one bargain and the cost of agreement on another follows inescapably from three conditions which we have already established: (1) the number of alternatives is limited; this is the scarcity condition; (2) some alternative must always be chosen, some decision must always be made, in consequence of the ongoing nature of a person's activity (his time stream of aspirations) and the condition imposed by interdependence; (3) individuals in the pursuit of their aspirations make rational (or reasonable) choices among the alternatives presented; this is the condition imposed by the compulsiveness of personality integration. In necessarily choosing among the limited alternatives which are presented at any moment, the rational individual must inescapably weigh the relative advantages and then sacrifice what is less important to that which is more important, as measured alongside his aspirations.

The relationship between the cost of disagreement on one bargaining proposal and the cost of agreement on another bargaining proposal can be made clearer by illustration. Suppose we are comparing two products or jobs. In the first instance, we have:

	Product/Job A	Product/Job B
	Superior good at higher price	Inferior good at lower price
	Superior job at lower wage	Inferior job at higher wage
Cost of disagreement	Quality advantage	Price/wage advantage
Cost of agreement	Price/wage disadvantage	Quality disadvantage

In this instance it is clear that the advantage of one offering (its cost of disagreement) constitutes that which has to be sacrificed when the individual chooses the other (its cost of agreement). Consider a second instance:

	Product/Job A	Product/Job B
	Superior good at lower price	Inferior good at higher price
	Superior job at higher wage	Inferior job at lower wage
Cost of disagreement	Quality and price advantage	Zero
Cost of agreement	Zero	Quality and price advantage

Here A has advantages both of quality and price which would have to be given up by choosing B. But B has no special advantages, hence offers nothing which has to be sacrificed by choosing A. (This zero cost of agreeing with A is *only* in comparison with B; because scarcity of resources prevents the satisfaction of all aspirations, there must always be a cost of agreeing on *any* bargain, in the light of the whole range of available alternatives.)

This method of calculating the costs of disagreement and agreement involves a consideration of the special (unique) advantages and disadvantages attaching to each possible course of action. The calculation is made with direct reference to the alternatives. Because the cost of disagreement is the special advantage offered by this bargain, any improvement in the alternatives which incorporates the advantages of this one reduces the cost of disagreement. Because the cost of agreement is the special advantages of other bargains, any unique improvement in the alternatives raises the cost of agreement. The *relative* costs of disagreement and agreement of the several alternatives are thus incorporated in the calculations, and from the calculations there can emerge only one bargain where the cost of agreement is less than the cost of disagreement (that is, where the inducement to agree is 1 or greater).

There is another method of estimating the costs of disagreement and agreement which arrives at the same result but by a different

procedure. The estimates are made independently of the alternatives, with reference only to the structure of aspirations. The cost
of disagreement is the measure of the aspirations whose achievement must be sacrificed if this bargain is rejected, and the cost of
agreement is the measure of those aspirations which must be
risked or sacrificed if this bargain is made. It is not the special or
unique advantages and disadvantages of each bargain which enter
into the calculations but the *total* advantages and disadvantages.
The *relative* costs of disagreement and agreement are thus not incorporated in the calculations but are ascertainable only by laying
the ratios of all bargains alongside each other. A change in the
character of the *alternatives* to any given bargain does not affect
its costs of disagreement or agreement. Any number of bargains
(rather than just one) may have costs of agreement which are
lower than their costs of disagreement, but if choice is rational only
one bargain will be chosen—that which offers the greatest inducement to agree.

This second method of calculating the costs of disagreement and
agreement has certain advantages. It carries no connotation that the
rational individual will in fact consider all possible alternatives, only
that from among the alternatives which he does consider he will
choose that which is most compatible with his aspirational structure. Moreover, it avoids the unwarranted inference that there are
always alternative *bargains* which may be made: in some instances
the alternative is not another bargain but only no bargain (as in
the tax relationship), with whatever penalties disagreement entails.
The cost of agreement may not be only the special advantages of
other bargains which must be foregone; in some instances the cost
of agreement may be the advantages of disagreement on this one
bargain, which must be laid alongside the advantages of agreement
(the costs of disagreement) in order to determine whether the advantage lies with acceptance or rejection of the other's terms. (Such
considerations must have motivated at least some of the American
colonialists in their resistance to certain royal taxes, for example,

where the cost of disagreeing with the King's collectors involved threat to family security but the cost of agreement involved loss of principle.)

It is this second method of calculation which we employed in deriving the inducement to act, in an earlier chapter. Nevertheless, either method of estimating the costs of disagreement and agreement is satisfactory in terms of the results derived. Both have been set forth here because confusion is possible if one moves back and forth between these two approaches without an explicit awareness of their differences.

We should remind ourselves that the costs involved, by any method of calculation, include *anything* which is relevant to the person's stream of aspirations. For the economist, however, the only significance of costs lies in their influence on the flow of scarce resources, or income.

ASPIRATIONS AND ALTERNATIVES

It is now time to pin down the determinants of the costs of agreement and disagreement, changes in which lead to changes in bargaining power. Costs of agreement and disagreement depend on the interaction between the aspirations and alternatives of all those in the society. Changes in others' aspirations or in the nature of the alternative which an individual constitutes to them (an alternative worker, an alternative employer, an alternative seller of groceries, an alternative lender, and so on) make him a more or less desirable symbiont, affecting the cost to others of agreeing or disagreeing on his terms. Similarly, changes in the alternatives which others constitute to him and in his own aspirations make others more or less desirable symbionts, affecting his cost of agreeing or disagreeing on their terms. It is this interaction between an individual's aspirations and alternatives and the aspirations and alternatives of others which determines for him his position of scarcity and interdependence, which both establishes his bargaining power at the moment and which he must manage through the exercise of his bargaining power.

As we shall see, the effects of changes in aspirations and alternatives differ as between buyers and sellers. But because the analysis presented here is designed to apply to a broader category of transactions than is normally encompassed in economic theory, it is necessary to establish what is meant by buying and selling. If all transactions consisted simply of an exchange of goods or services, the terms buying and selling would not distinguish the transactors. Each would be both buyer and seller, each selling some good or service in order to buy some good or service. We would more commonly designate such a transaction as "trading." Where exchanges consist of money given for goods or services, however, we can distinguish the transactors in terms of who gives money and who gives goods or services. The former we designate the buyer and the latter the seller. It is in this basic sense that these terms are used here. In this sense, buying and selling extends to the tax relationship or the charitable relationship or the church relationship, for example, the buyer being the taxpayer or the donor or the tither, all givers of money, the seller being the government or the beneficiary or the church, all givers of some service or satisfaction. It is as between buyers and sellers, in this more comprehensive sense, that the effects of changes in aspirations and alternatives differ.

Changes in aspirations may be of four general types.

1. We have already encountered one influence of the movement of time in a previous chapter, when we noted how the ongoing nature of a person's life stream affects the integrated bundle of aspirations which he holds. We now note a different effect of time on aspirations, with something that we might label the cultural time stream rather than a personal time stream, influencing not a person's position in his life span but the society's position in its evolutionary stream. Cultural change influences the aspirations which can be said to characterize a society, in the sense that there is a statistical probability of their occurring in any of its members.

Changes in culturally encouraged aspirations occur unevenly among individuals, however, so that there are always those who refuse to accept the objectives which are commonly pursued within the society. We can describe the culturally induced aspirations as the modes, and individuals' aspirations may change by being more or less identical with the modes.

At present we have little more than an impressionistic basis for establishing the cultural patterns which affect the use of economic resources, for identifying the changes in family life (as exampled by apartment living), the conception of the role of the state (as in relationship to individuals, groups, and other nations), the differing place of religion in life (as exampled by a decreasing concern with Sabbath observance), and so on. The economist is concerned with cultural changes of this nature only in so far as they affect the flow of resources, but he should be unconcerned with them only to the extent they do *not* affect the flow of resources.

2. In addition, people's aspirations may be modified by a movement along the comparative-achievement scale. Such a change is likely to be a reflection either of a shift in personal income flows or of identification with a different social group. Under either of these influences, a family may shift its sights upward, aspiring to higher-quality goods and services, or alternatively, it may be reconciled or satisfied to adopt lower material standards.

3. A shift in the time element of the stream of aspirations is also possible. Material goals may be advanced or delayed.

4. Finally, there may be a shift in personal taste or inclination, the idiosyncratic element of style and preference, in which color and model and shape and size (not related to levels of quality on the quality spectrum) govern choice at a level of specificity of objective halfway between rational and reasonable.

Changes in aspirations can come by any of these four routes. Wherever any change in aspirations occurs, it has a potential effect on the distribution of bargaining power within the system as a whole, since it potentially increases or decreases the number of individuals seeking certain scarce goods or the intensity with which they seek them.

Changes in alternatives likewise fall into four major categories.

1. Innovation involves the creation or introduction of something categorically new. The invention of new products for the direct satisfaction of wants or of tools for making existing products more efficiently or more satisfactorily are examples. So too is the development of new forms of social organization, such as the modern corporation. So too is the introduction into one society of the products or practices of another—cross-cultural fertilization.

2. Imitation consists in the proliferation by others of the fruits of the innovator. The imitations need not be identical but may consist of differing species of some genus of product or service in the form which we commonly associate with product differentiation.

3. Alternatives may change through discovery, which differs from innovation in that it does not involve the creation or introduction of any new product or process but the uncovering of more of something which is already familiar to us. Natural resources are the principal subject of discovery—new lands, fresh mineral deposits, additional water resources, virgin forests, better transportation routes.

4. Changes in the population composition involve changes in numbers, age distribution, functional skills, intelligence, sex, and location. Such changes carry a differential impact on various groups within the society, some of which are now subjected to relatively more or relatively less bidding competition from their commensal rivals in effecting symbiotic relationships either for the satisfaction of aspirations or for the provision of their own services.

Let us consider for a moment this last type of change in alternatives—changes in the composition of the population. Wherever the number of commensals increases, the relative bargaining power of each one within the group declines. This is because: (1) there is an absolute increase in the number of those whose aspirations are competitive with his own; (2) there is no increase in the number of those who offer alternative means of satisfying his aspirations; (3) there is an absolute increase in the number of those offering services (alternatives) similar to his own; (4) there is no increase in the number of those whose aspirations his services satisfy. In either buying or selling the cost to the other party of disagreement on his terms declines. To the extent, then, that individuals are commensal competitors—either in their aspirations or in the alternatives which they constitute to others—on the basis of age, skill, function, intelligence, sex, or location, a change in the numbers or quality of these characteristics in the population affects their relative bargaining power in the particular symbiotic relationships which are relevant.

An increase in the number of lawyers and a decrease in the number of engineers, for example (a change in the skill composition of the population), in the absence of other change decreases the bargaining power of the former and increases the bargaining power of the latter. Alternatively we might say that such changes increase the relative bargaining power of those on whom lawyers depend and who depend on lawyers (their symbionts), as, for example, the suppliers of office space in law buildings, law books, legal secretaries, and the users of legal services. Similarly, the relative bargaining power of those in symbiont relationship to engineers declines in those relationships. Such a straightforward case of "supply and demand" is readily enough incorporated within the price analysis. But other types of population changes have their similar repercussions which we are sometimes more inclined to disregard.

An increase in the age group 50–59, relative to other age groups, for example, increases the commensal competition for those jobs which (because requiring less exertion or adaptability) are more suited to older workers, and thus reduces the bargaining power of all in the group. A relative decline in the number of younger workers available for the more exacting employments may raise the bargaining power of this group relative to their employers. Initially the change in age composition may also increase the commensal competition for certain types of goods or services which are sought by older people, decreasing the demand for the goods or services more suited to younger persons. The bargaining power of those supplying the former services (let us say geriatricians) rises, while the bargaining power of those supplying the latter type (let us say tennis instructors) declines.

Moreover, if we recall the time stream of aspirations which appears to characterize major groups within our society, we will remember that with increasing age the revenue and budget decisions are otherwise affected. The proportion of income saved increases as retirement becomes more imminent, and job security takes on added importance. The bargaining power of this older-age group relative to all sellers of goods and services thus rises, with heightened awareness of the risk of present expenditures to the postretirement future (cost of agreement), while bargaining power relative to the buyers of their services declines because of the higher cost of disagreement.

If the increase in the older-age group represents a relative decline in the group of, say, 20–29, then further consequences are likely to follow, since it is this age group which is most risk-minded, most willing to migrate to new areas, to try out new jobs, to adjust to technological innovations. This shift in the aspiration structure of the population will affect the alternatives available to others and hence the relative bargaining powers of certain groups within the society.

These population changes which have just been discussed illustrate how changes in alternatives (by any of the four routes enumerated above—innovation, imitation, discovery, population changes) have the immediate effect of modifying the number and quality of the alternatives available for the satisfaction of aspirations. More specifically, if the number and quality of the alternatives to some particular symbiotic relationship increase, the cost of disagreement on the terms of coöperation laid down by that symbiont declines to the extent that the special advantages which previously characterized it have been incorporated in the modified alternatives, and the cost of agreement with that symbiont rises to the extent that the modified alternatives offer further advantages not characterizing that particular relationship. Suppose, for another example, that Company X offers better working conditions but lower wages than any other firm in town. As between other firms and X, the worker's inducement to agree on X's terms (that is, X's bargaining power) is given by

$$\frac{\text{cost of disagreement}}{\text{cost of agreement}} = \frac{\text{the greater job satisfaction at X}}{\text{the higher wages at other plants}}$$

Now Company Y moves into town, offering working conditions which, while poorer than those at X, are superior to those at all other firms, and wages which are higher than are offered by any other firm. The worker's inducement to agree on X's terms (X's bargaining power) now declines:

$$\frac{\text{cost of disagreement}}{\text{cost of agreement}} = \frac{\text{the greater job satisfaction at X, but not greater by so much as formerly}}{\text{the higher wages at other plants, now even higher at Y}}$$

There are, then, the possibilities of change in aspirations (in the four forms which we have considered), coupled with the possibilities of change in alternatives (also in four forms, which we have considered). It is the interaction between the changes of a person's aspirations and the alternatives which he offers to others, on the one hand, and the changes in the aspirations of others and the alternatives which they provide for him, on the other hand, which defines his bargaining power in the society, and which (considering all individuals) distributes bargaining power among all those in the system.

Our personal aspirations (conditioned as they are by the culture) define the existing alternatives which others offer to us, at the same time that the particular kind of service which we supply to others (the alternative which we constitute to them) is defined by their aspirations. It is equally true that the existing alternatives define our personal aspirations, and that the kind of alternatives we offer to others defines in part their aspirations. These are the conditions of personal interdependence and scarcity. (What goods or services provided by others in limited quantities will satisfy our special wants, what goods or services which we provide will satisfy the objectives of others, what jobs provide the conditions we consider important to our well-being, what kind of personal attraction we have for others that promotes an exchange relationship—these are all aspects of scarcity and interdependence as we encounter them at the personal level.)

But the distribution of aspirations among all members of the society defines the *extent* to which others seek the same relationships which satisfy our personal aspirations, as well as the *extent* to which is wanted by others the kind of services (alternatives) which we offer. The distribution of alternatives likewise defines the degree to which others offer services which are similar to ours, as well as the degree to which others can satisfy aspirations similar to those we hold. These are conditions of general interdependence and scarcity. (How many others want and how many others supply the same goods or services or satisfactions which we offer—these are aspects of scarcity and interdependence at the social level.)

It is the interplay between these personal and socially distributed aspirations and alternatives which determines bargaining power. It is the degree of coincidence between one's wants and offerings (the individual component), on the one hand, and the extent to which these same wants and offerings are wanted and offered by others (the social component), on the other hand, which measures the relative inducements to agree.

If a person's aspirations can be satisfied by numerous alternative relationships which the culture encourages, his bargaining power improves through this interdependence condition, except as this effect is offset by a competitive coincidence between his aspirations and the aspirations of others (a scarcity condition). Similarly, if the services or advantages which a person offers to others in his relationships satisfy aspirations which are widely shared in the society, his relative bargaining power improves through this interdependence condition, except as this is offset by a competitive coincidence between the services he supplies and the alternatives offered by others (a scarcity condition). We can generalize these relationships as follows:

	Bargaining power varies directly	Bargaining power varies inversely
As buyer	with the degree to which personal aspirations can be satisfied with the alternatives offered by others	with the degree to which personal aspirations coincide with the aspirations which are competitively sought by others
As seller	with the degree to which a person's services (the alternatives which he constitutes to others) satisfy the aspirations of others	with the degree to which a person's services coincide with the alternative services competitively offered by others

A person's bargaining power is, then, strongest as buyer when he is seeking from others some service or advantage which is in general supply but which no others want, and as seller when he is offering some unique advantage (of quality, of price) satisfying some general aspiration.

As yet there has been no systematic exploitation of the statistical data already available, let alone collection of data obtainable but not gathered, sufficient to permit a description of the aspirations and alternatives confronting the major commensal groups within our society, on which over time depend the definition and distribution of our society's scarce resources. It is the characteristics of the interrelated budget and revenue decisions of people in common circumstances which we need to know in order to define the symbiotic relationships which are relevant to their integrated bundle of aspirations. It is the alternatives which they face (as defined by their aspirations) and which they oppose to others (as defined by the aspirations of others) which we need to know to establish the relative bargaining powers which determine the terms on which those symbiotic relationships are effected. It is the interplay of changing aspirations and changing alternatives, over time, which we need to know in order to give concreteness to the process by which bargaining power is redistributed within a society.

INCOME AS A DERIVED DETERMINANT

Changes in alternatives and aspirations affect an individual's bargaining power in particular bargains. An increase in the number and quality of bargains affects an individual's bargaining power in those particular bargains to which the number and quality of alternatives have improved. A shift in a person's aspirations affects those particular bargains which are now valued more or less than formerly. As we have already seen and as we shall see again later, the effects of such changes in particular bargains may be generalized through the interrelationship of the revenue and budget decisions. But this is to say that the generalized effects work themselves out through the medium of changes in income flows. We shall find it useful to examine changes in income as a determinant of bargaining power, one which is a derivative of changes in aspirations and alternatives, and one which operates less particularly and more generally in the sense of affecting whole classes of bargains.

Income obviously does not change autonomously. Income movements can themselves be traced back to changes in a person's aspirations or alternatives or in those of others with whom he is in a commensal or symbiotic relationship. Consider, for example, the revenue decision. If one's job alternatives improve, and his aspirations incline him to take the benefit in terms of wages rather than job satisfactions, then his income will rise. A similar result may follow from a change in aspirations which prompts him to work longer hours or to prepare himself for a better job. A rise in the aspiration level of those for whom he constitutes an alternative may likewise lead to a change in income, either greater or lesser, depending on whether he constitutes a more or less desirable alternative than formerly. Or consider the budget decision. A change in a person's aspirations (as perhaps through contraction of a malignant disease) may reduce his estimate of the special advantages attaching to saving and reduce his efforts to earn an income out of which he formerly had regularly set aside some sum. An increase in the demand by others for the goods which satisfy his objectives may turn the terms of bargains adversely to him and lead to efforts to augment income so that he may retain the level of his past achievement. The provision of new alternatives by others, satisfying his aspirations more fully but at a greater outlay, may have a similar effect. Income may also come from past investments, but such investments are themselves attributable to the person's stream of aspirations at positions in the past (inducing saving) and the alternatives then available both in his revenue and budget decisions, including alternative investments. Thus changes in income are ultimately derivatives of either past aspirations and alternatives or present changes in aspirations and alternatives.

An increase in income, so attributable to past aspirations and alternatives or to changes in present aspirations and alternatives, exercises a general effect on a person's bargaining power. In all buying transactions the cost of agreement and hence relative bargaining power tends to decline, since the risk to one's income position attributable to *any* particular purchase diminishes with the increase in either money or real income. In all selling transactions (except that responsible for the increase in income) the cost of disagreement will fall, thus tending to increase relative bargaining power, since there is less risk to a person's income position in rejecting the terms offered by *any* buyer of his goods or services.[1] Let us examine these general effects more closely.

Let us assume that in a relationship where X has been buying

[1] The degree to which costs of agreement in other buying transactions is reduced may be quite minuscule where the effect is attributable to an increase in real income, since the amount of any price reduction—except in major purchases such as a house or automobile—is not likely to be significant. Similarly the degree to which the cost of disagreement in other selling transactions is reduced may be slight. If through an improvement in his alternatives an individual managed to secure better terms in the sale of vegetables which he grew in his spare time, for example, the increase in income might have an insignificant impact on his cost of disagreeing on the terms offered by his regular employer. On the other hand, an increase in income on his regular job might lead to lower costs of disagreeing on the terms

some good from Y, Y lowers the price he is asking. This suggests that Y's bargaining power on his original terms, relative to X, had been shown to be weak. His lowering of his terms strengthens his bargaining power by reducing the cost of agreement to X. The effect of this reduced cost of agreement is to increase X's real income. This increases in real income then causes a reduction in the cost of agreement on other bargains, since the terms demanded in other bargains now constitute less of a threat to the achievement of one's bundle of aspirations than formerly, raising the inducement to agree and thus improving the bargaining power of those with whom X contemplates buying relationships. This is not true, however, with respect to buying transactions which would replace Y, since the cost of agreement on their terms would now include additionally the sacrifice of the real-income advantage accruing from agreement with Y.

Now assume a relationship in which X is selling some good or service to Y. Y raises the terms of his offer, implying that his bargaining power relative to X had been shown to be weak; by improving his offer he strengthens his bargaining power relative to X. X, with his improved income position, now need rely to a lesser extent on income from other sources, so his cost of disagreement in other selling transactions declines. This is not true of selling relationships which would replace that with Y, however, since in their case the cost of agreement must include additionally the sacrifice of the income advantage resulting from the improved terms with Y. Whether cost of disagreement is reduced or cost of

---

offered by his vegetable customers, even to the point where he willingly sacrificed the income which he had previously derived from that source.

The income effects on bargaining power may of course be modified by concomitant changes in aspirations and alternatives. If, for example, a consumer's position in the quality spectrum of goods tends to vary directly with income, so that with higher income he buys higher-quality goods, and vice versa, then such a change in aspirations may offset the change in income. In such a case the cost of disagreement on inferior goods declines, increasing bargaining power, and it would be only with respect to the newly wanted superior goods that cost of agreement—and bargaining power—would fall.

agreement raised, however, the effect is to increase relative bargaining power.[2]

Similarly, a drop in one's income raises his cost of disagreement in selling bargains (since disagreement constitutes a greater threat to his level of achievement) and raises his cost of agreement in buying bargains (since agreement has a like effect). We can then generalize that in selling transactions bargaining power tends to move directly and in buying transactions inversely with changes in income.[3]

THE INFLUENCE OF THE PERSONAL TIME STREAM ON BARGAINING POWER

The individual, in his economic activities, may be regarded as managing his inflow and outflow of income. He does this through his revenue and budget decisions, which take the form of agree-

[2] Another way of phrasing these conclusions would be as follows. In both buying and selling transactions the effect of an increase in income (real or money) is to increase the cost of agreement on any transactions which would substitute for those on which the newly acquired income advantage depends, their cost of disagreement remaining unchanged. In the case of buying relationships, however, *supplements* to real income (the additional things which can be purchased with the increased income) are no less important than they formerly were, hence the cost of disagreeing is unchanged, but the means of acquiring them has increased, hence cost of agreement is lower. In selling relationships, supplements to income are less important than formerly in view of the increase in income, so that cost of disagreement falls, while the cost of agreement remains unchanged. Thus, following an increase in real income, an individual's bargaining power falls with respect to purchases supplementing that on which the rise in real income depends and rises with respect to purchases substituting for it. In the case of an increase in money income, an individual's bargaining power rises with respect to all sales except that on which the rise in money income depends.

[3] If the decline in income is attributable to a decrease in money inflows, then we should have to amend the statement of the text to read that the cost of disagreement in selling bargains would rise except in that bargain whose poorer terms are responsible for the decline, if alternatives remain as formerly. If the decline in (real) income is attributable to a rise in price, the exceptions to the general increase in the cost of agreement would be those goods whose prices had not risen (or risen as much) and which could be substituted for those whose prices had increased. These exceptions would apply, then, to the generalizations concerning the effects of a decline in income on bargaining power, but as exceptions they are less important than the general effect stated.

ments with others reached on the basis of relative bargaining powers. His income flows through time, and the element of time is present in all decisions which he makes. The past makes its presence felt through the specific medium of assets, the fruits of past bargains which are available now to supplement current income. The future makes its influence felt through expectations, the judgments about future bargaining power on the basis of which present choices are made. The yesterdays and the projected tomorrows are thus represented in decisions which are reached today. The inflows and outflows of the past and the expected inflows and outflows of the future thus govern the current stream of inflows and outflows. All this is ground which we have covered before. We wish now to explore how assets and expectations influence bargaining power.

Assets are held in various forms, ranging from goods which are stocked for consumption in the imminent short run (such as food on the shelf) through goods which are used for current consumption but which have longer life expectancies (such as household appliances, automobiles, homes, and office buildings), from savings which are held for specific, assigned purposes (such as payment of the month's bills) through liquid funds or investments set aside for less specific but nonetheless assigned purposes (retirement, sickness contingency, a safety reserve), and finally the unassigned funds and investments which can be drawn on as opportunity dictates.

As far as their effect on bargaining power is concerned, all these forms of assets have one characteristic in common: they act as a potential supplement to current income. Assets which are held in the form of goods for future use can have their usefulness extended, thus in a sense adding to income. Though provision is made out of current income for their ultimate replacement, the fact that the life of the washing machine or the adding machine has been extended by two years means that replacement costs are spread over a longer period, freeing some portion of current income for other uses. Assets which are held in the form of savings assigned for future specific uses can be reassigned for present use, and un-assigned funds can of course be tapped.

The existence of this potential supplement to a person's income modifies his cost of agreement on the terms proposed by those with whom he is doing business. How it modifies these costs depends on whether he is a buyer or seller in the prospective relationship and on whether his assets include goods of the type which are the subject of the bargain.

As a buyer, his inducement to agree on another's terms increases with the amount of his assets, since the cost of agreement declines. (The risk to his standard of living that is associated with any given purchase is less than it would have been in the absence of assets.) Such an increase in his inducement to agree on another's terms is equivalent to an increase in the other's bargaining power, which in turn is equivalent to a relative decline in his own bargaining power. Hence we can say that a buyer's bargaining power tends to fall as his assets increase and to rise as his assets diminish.

There is a significant exception to this functional relationship, however. To the extent the buyer's assets consist of goods of the type which is the subject of bargaining, then the functional relationship is reversed. The more of such assets he holds the stronger is his bargaining power, and the fewer of such assets the weaker it is. The householder whose assets include two automobiles will be less inclined to purchase a third, even though the carryover from the past of assets in the form of automobiles actually reduces the risk of purchasing a third. (The risk is less since current income could be supplemented, if need be, by selling one of the cars already held or by not replacing it as quickly as had been contemplated.) Similarly, the businessman whose assets include inventories of his product has a lesser inducement to agree to the terms of his employees and suppliers than if he held no stocks of their output. The cost of disagreeing on the terms of buying some good is thus reduced when one already possesses goods of the type. The principle underlying this functional relationship is the familiar one of diminishing marginal utility or rate of substitution of one good for another.

We can generalize, then, that a buyer's bargaining power tends to move inversely with the size of his assets, except as these assets include goods of the type which are the subject of the bargain. Both aspects—the size and the composition of assets—have their effect. If a buyer has inventories of a good which someone seeks to sell to him, his bargaining power will be raised over what it would have been in the absence of such inventories, *except* as reduced by the existence of other assets which make the purchase less of a risk to his income position than it otherwise would be.

The circumstances of the seller are the reverse of those of the buyer. For him the existence of assets lowers the cost of disagreeing on a buyer's terms, lessening his inducement to agree, increasing his relative bargaining power. (The danger to his standard of living that comes from foregoing any given sale—any given addition to his income—is reduced by the cushion of assets on which he can fall back.) Here again, however, we encounter an important exception when the seller's assets include goods of the type which he is trying to sell. The more of such goods which he holds, the lower is his cost of agreement, since the less likely that he will be giving up something which might be of greater value to him later. (Thus the larger a businessman's inventories the weaker is his bargaining power, that is, the more likely that he will make concessions to his buyers.)

We may generalize that a seller's bargaining power tends to move directly with the amount of his assets, except as these assets include goods of the type which he is trying to sell. Again both the size and the composition of assets affect the result. If a seller has large inventories of his product, for example, his bargaining power will be depressed over what it would have been in the absence of such inventories, *except* as it is increased over what it otherwise would have been by the existence of other assets which can serve as a supplement to income, offsetting the need for income through sales.

Let us now turn to the effect of expectations on bargaining power. Expectations can relate to any of a number of variables—the price of goods, their quality, their rate of obsolescence, the level of economic activity, costs of production, and so on. The theoretical significance of such variables is their effect on the achievement of one's aspirations in the future. For the economist, this significance can be further limited to their effect on the flow of goods and services (income) on which the achievement of aspirations in part depends. It is, then, income flows (as related to aspirations) that we are really concerned with when we speak of expectations.

By expectations we will mean an individual's judgment as to how his present decisions are related to the future achievement of those aspirations which depend on income. Such a judgment involves either or both of two considerations: whether future bargains are likely to make this present bargain more or less compatible with the time stream of aspirations; whether this present bargain is likely to make future bargains more or less compatible with the time stream of aspirations. The first involves the influence of the expected future on the present, the second the influence of the present on the expected future.

The relevant expectations are those which affect one's cost of agreeing or disagreeing on the terms of contemplated relationships, that is to say, those which affect his bargaining power. From our prior analysis of the determinants of bargaining power, the relevant expectations can be identified as those which relate to aspirations, alternatives, and income. The effect of expectation of change in these variables is similar to the effect of present change in these variables.

Thus an *expected* increase in the number and quality of the alternatives which satisfy a person's aspirations operates to raise a person's bargaining power by lowering his cost of disagreement, just as does a *present* increase in the number and quality of alternatives. The expectation held by some individuals in 1953 that color television was imminent increased for them the number and quality of the alternatives available (though available only in the future), lowering their cost of disagreement with merchants then offering only black-and-white television sets. A belief that prices will decline in the future similarly increases the alternatives facing an individual, who will under the circumstances consider that present purchases of postponable items carry a higher cost of agreement, raising his bargaining power. Likewise any expected changes in the alternatives to the services one provides which better satisfy the aspirations of others increases his cost of disagreement and diminishes his bargaining power. Thus the makers of silk goods could foresee the continuing deterioration of their selling position due to the advent of the cheaper rayon, just as in the 'forties manufacturers of rayon, cotton, and woolen products suffered a loss of bargaining power in selling transactions due to the increasing availability of nylon. In essence, the future constitutes a more or less desirable alternative to the present, depending upon the nature of one's expectations as to the likely changes in the relevant variables.

Present and future aspirations are also substitutable against each other. Any expected change in aspirations which lessens the value of those alternatives satisfying the aspirations being shed decreases one's cost of disagreement and raises his bargaining power, while an expected change in aspiration raising the value of alternatives satisfying the new aspiration lowers the cost of agreement (or raises the cost of disagreement), thereby reducing one's bargaining power. Any expected changes in the aspirations of others which lessens the demand for the services (alternatives) which one offers, increases his cost of disagreement and lowers his bargaining power. (The passing fad lessens the faddist's interest in the services which satisfy the diminishing want, at the same time stimulating those who provide such services to reach whatever bargains they can in their declining market.)

Expected (future) income and present assets are likewise substitutable against each other. An expectation of rising income diminishes the risk from using current income and assets, lowering bargaining power (young couples spend all and incur liabilities), while an expected fall in income encourages frugality in present expenditures, increasing the cost of agreement and raising bargaining power (the worker approaching retirement foresees a greater future than present need for income).

The influence of changes in assets and expectations on one's bargaining power is, however, only a *tendency*. Whether the tendency materializes depends upon the changes simultaneously influencing these with whom one is seeking agreement. For purposes of exposition we have been speaking as though the assets and expectations of all others remain fixed, so that we might determine the effect on a person's bargaining power of changes in his assets and expectations alone. In reality all bargainers are subject to such change, and the change in their relative bargaining power depends on the *relative* changes in assets and expectations. That the savings of one individual are increasing tells us nothing about his bargaining power until we investigate the savings pattern of those with whom he is trying to effect agreements. That the income expectations of one person are unfavorable reveals nothing about the consequence for his bargaining position until we discover the expectations of those with whom he is doing business. Even more, that the assets of one have increased tells us little about changes in his bargaining power until we know, too, whether his expectations have been subject to change, and whether the asset *and* expectation positions of his symbionts have been modified. It is not the absolute changes in the bargainers' assets, considered by themselves, or the absolute changes in bargainers' expectations, considered apart, of which we must take account, but the effect on relative bargaining powers of changes in assets and expectations concomitantly of those who are contemplating coöperative relations.

An individual's management of his position of scarcity and interdependence necessarily involves the calculation of his asset position and the estimation of his expectations as effectively as possible, in order to maintain or improve his bargaining power relative to others, as the only means by which his stream of aspirations can be achieved. For the same reason that any single choice has significance only in relation to a pattern of behavior, any individual bargain has economic significance only in relation to the inflows and outflows of personal income. The influence of assets and expectations on bargains is analytically important only because of the relationship of bargains to the income stream.

SUMMARY

Let us summarize what has been said about the determinants of bargaining power.

1. A person's bargaining power can be changed in particular bargains by a change in aspirations, with alternatives remaining constant, or by a change in alternatives, with aspirations remaining constant, or by some disproportional change in both aspirations and alternatives.

2. In general, a person's bargaining power as a buyer tends to move directly with the number and quality of the alternatives satisfying his aspirations and inversely with the degree to which others seek to satisfy the same aspirations as his. An individual's bargaining power as a seller tends to move directly with the prevalence of the aspirations which he can satisfy through the services which he offers and inversely with the degree to which others offer the same services that he offers.

3. A change in alternatives or aspirations, through its effect in particular bargains, may change income, affecting one's bargaining power generally. Income flows may also be affected by the present impact of past aspirations and alternatives. In general, a person's bargaining power as a buyer tends to move inversely with present changes in income, and his bargaining power as a seller tends to move directly with present changes in income (the principal exceptions occurring in selling bargains responsible for a change in money income).

4. In addition to the effects of present changes in income, the influence of time makes itself felt through assets and expectations, as embodiments of past and future aspirations and alternatives. In general, a person's bargaining power as a buyer tends to move inversely with the amount of his assets (except for assets of the type

which are the subject of bargaining). As a seller his bargaining power tends to move directly with the amount of assets (except for assets of the type which are the subject of bargaining). Expectations relate to changes in aspirations, alternatives, and income. Expected changes in these variables have the same direction of influence on bargaining power as present changes.

5. A person's bargaining power as a buyer thus tends to move:

(a) Directly with the present and expected number and quality of the alternatives satisfying his aspirations.

(b) Inversely with the present and expected degree to which others seek to satisfy the same aspirations.

(c) Inversely with present and expected changes in income.

(d) Inversely with the amount of present and expected assets (except for assets of the type which are the subject of bargaining).

6. A person's bargaining power as a seller tends to move:

(a) Inversely with the present and expected degree to which others offer the same service which he offers.

(b) Directly with the present and expected prevalence of the aspirations which he can satisfy through the services he offers.

(c) Directly with present and expected changes in income (except in selling bargains responsible for the change in money income).

(d) Directly with the amount of present and expected assets (except for assets of the type which are the subject of bargaining).

Again we should remind ourselves that such a summary statement of the determinants of bargaining power omits one dominating consideration, however—that bargaining power must always be expressed relative to another's bargaining power, that it has no meaning as applied to an individual. We can say that an increase in the number and quality of the alternatives open to an individual *tends* to increase his bargaining power in the relevant transactions. Whether his bargaining power has actually improved, however, depends on whether there have been simultaneous changes in the alternatives or aspirations or the income position both for himself and for those with whom he seeks symbiotic relationships, changes which may have so altered their inducement to agree as to have improved their relative position. Changes in bargaining power cannot be ascertained until one knows the total impact of changing aspirations, alternatives, and income flows on the costs of disagreement and agreement of all the parties to a possible bargaining transaction.

CHAPTER 8

The Manipulation of Bargaining Power

THE achievement of an individual's stream of aspirations depends on the management of his position of scarcity and interdependence, through his revenue and budget decisions, on the strength of his relative bargaining power. Relative bargaining power, as we have seen, is determined by the interaction between the aspirations and alternative means of satisfying those aspirations of all those in the society, or to phrase it another way, by the degree of coincidence between an individual's aspirations and alternatives and those which the culture (in all its aspects) encourages. This interaction is partly but not wholly outside the individual's control. To some extent he is capable of manipulating his relative bargaining power to his advantage. The manipulations with which the economist is concerned are only those which affect the use of scarce resources, which have their impact on income flows.

Because it takes many separate bargains to make up the inflows and outflows of income there are many points at which bargaining power can be manipulated. In not all such instances, however, does an individual attempt to modify the relative bargaining positions to his advantage. In many of them the consequence of the separate bargain on one's stream of aspirations is too slight to warrant an effort to alter the bargaining relationships. In numerous situations the decision is simply to accept or reject the relationship on the basis of the bargaining powers as they are given, without consideration of the possibilities of altering the terms of relationship through a manipulation of bargaining power. But in matters which touch more significantly the achievement of one's aspirations, bargaining power is often not taken as given but attempts are made by one or the other or both of the parties to alter the relative costs of disagreement and agreement to secure greater advantage.

The bargains which are most likely to be the focus of attempts at manipulation of power are those which most directly involve coercive comparisons—proximate objectives which are compulsive on the individual because they constitute the immediate measure of achievement or the lack of it, such as the comparison of wage and profit rates of flow and standards of living. These comparisons provide the most irresistible targets at which the management of the income stream is aimed. They set up states of tension which may lead to actions which otherwise would not be taken.

The coercive comparison, to be significant to the economist, must carry with it some impact on the person's income flows. Whatever the aspiration, to be "economic" it must have some intended or actual effect on a person's inflow or outflow of scarce resources. A worker may be stimulated to seek a wage increase simply to maintain a relative standing with some other worker who has won an increase, but he does so only in the expectation, perhaps implicit, that his income will not thereby suffer (endangering his relative consumer position) and that it will probably be augmented. This expectation may not prove justified, to be sure, but the increase is not sought without regard to the effect on income. Similarly, the worker may seek satisfaction on the job, but this has no economic significance unless it is somehow related to his income flows, as through the fact that he is willing or unwilling to sacrifice income to achieve or maintain job satisfaction.

The decision as to the amount of one's savings (and thus his asset position), the influence of expectations on one's decisions, the choice of consumer goods, the balance between job satisfactions and income—these are all largely based on the nature of the compulsions implicit in the relevant comparisons. Job satisfaction may be sacrificed for a higher wage if one's rates begin to lag behind those with which they have traditionally been compared. Savings may be reduced if one's standard of living fails to keep pace with one's customary associates. But before such drastic readjustments are undertaken, necessarily involving new risks or disadvantages to one's whole structure of aspirations, the effort may be made to manipulate one's bargaining power to regain or improve position without incurring (or at least minimizing) further risk or disadvantage.[1]

By the manipulation of bargaining power is meant any action which is designed to effect a desired relationship which another party is reluctant to undertake or to effect such a relationship on more preferable terms. An individual who seeks to manipulate his bargaining power must necessarily operate through another's inducement to agree. His actions must therefore be directed to increasing another's cost of disagreement or decreasing his cost of agreement. The costs of disagreement and agreement, the advantages of a given bargain, have been identified as relating to both price and quality. The determinants of the costs of disagreement and agreement are a person's aspirations and alternatives, as these inter-

---

[1] The comparisons which are compulsive at any time are themselves the resultants of past bargaining power. That a machinist compares his wage rate with, let us say, a lathe operator (in terms of some customary differential) is reflective of the fact that the relative bargaining powers of machinists and employers, on the one hand, and lathe operators and employers, on the other hand, in previous years were such as to establish this comparison as "reasonable" and expected. If their relative bargaining powers had been different, machinists might now be comparing their rates not with lathe operators but with some other occupation either more or less highly remunerated. If the two rates should now diverge or converge in consequence of a shift in the relative bargaining powers of these two occupational groups, we might expect either that over the years a new form of wage comparison would emerge (a different conception of the wage relationship between machinists and lathe operators, or a new comparison between machinists and some other group) or that machinists would seek to manipulate their bargaining power to take the sting out of the comparison with lathe operators if that comparison was now to their disadvantage. It is thus that past exercise of bargaining powers is a determinant of what comparisons are coercive today, and the latter in turn affect one's exercise of present bargaining power.

act with the aspirations and alternatives which are encouraged in the culture. The manipulation of bargaining power can thus be said to be any action designed to affect the relative advantage of the relationship which one offers (whether an advantage of price or quality), by modifying the existing structure of aspirations and alternatives.

Although, as we have seen, an individual's "economic" aspirations can be fulfilled only through symbiotic relationships, those aspirations can sometimes be more fully achieved by bargaining with one's commensals as a preliminary to symbiotic bargaining, to limit or prevent commensal competition which weakens one position vis-a-vis the potential symbiont. The manipulation of bargaining power can thus be with respect to either symbiotic or commensal bargaining.

THE MANIPULATION OF BARGAINING POWER IN SYMBIOTIC RELATIONSHIPS

Although the methods of manipulating bargaining power are basically the same whether one is buying or selling, let us separate these two situations to simplify the discussion.

A seller's bargaining power can be increased relative to that of a potential buyer to the extent that the latter's aspirations cannot be so readily satisfied by alternative relationships. This result can be attained if the seller can distinguish his offering by incorporating in it some advantage previously offered only by competitors (imitation), while retaining its own special advantages, or by endowing his offering with some additional quality not offered by competitors (initiation). By either of these means he raises the buyer's cost of disagreeing on his terms. A seller may also enhance his bargaining power by lowering his price, thereby reducing the cost of agreeing on his terms.[2]

[2] If one uses the alternative method of calculating costs of disagreement and agreement, as set out in the preceding chapter, he would have to rephrase the above propositions. In the alternative method, the relative advantages and disadvantages of competing bargains are incorporated directly into the computations.

With respect to price changes, the seller may make downward adjustments not only by overt price cuts but by such covert means as secret rebates, special discounts or deals, increased trade-in allowances, time-payment plans at no extra cost, or tie-in sales. By any of these means the seller can lower the buyer's cost of agreement.

The matter of quality changes is more complex. The possibilities for a seller's manipulating the buyer's inducement to agree are several. Three will be noted.

First, the seller can initiate a new product or service, or differentiate his product or service to endow it with some unique advantage, or he can incorporate into his own distinctive service some additional advantage previously offered only by his commensal competitors. By any of these methods he increases the cost of disagreement on his terms—at least for some buyers.

By endowing his offering with some unique quality a seller can expect to increase its attractive power to some unknown number of individuals. At the same time, however, he runs the danger that the special quality may repel others. Product differentiation thus creates special markets, with each seller more firmly attaching some buyers to his orbit and more certainly repelling others, thereby opening opportunities for other sellers to come forward with offerings designed to attract those whom the others have repelled. The manipulation of one's bargaining power through product differentiation is thus a two-edged sword: it increases the cost of disagreement for some and lowers it for others, and the problem which faces the seller is to discover the form of differentiation which can be expected to induce a more rather than less favorable symbiotic response.[3]

We would then have to say that any adjustment of either quality or price which created or increased a seller's advantage would raise the buyer's cost of disagreement on his terms, since the buyer gives up more by not agreeing, while any adjustment of either quality or price which met or more nearly approached a competitor's advantages would reduce the buyer's cost of agreeing on his terms, since the buyer gives up less by agreeing.

[3] As Wroe Alderson has suggested, good strategy sometimes dictates that a new firm or a small firm or a struggling firm adopt product policies which run counter to those of the leaders in the field, since it will then meet a demand which is not as well met by its stronger competitors, carving out a group of buyers vis-a-vis

As a second form of quality change, the seller can provide certain guarantees that the buyer will not be disappointed in the special advantages which he presumes to be purchasing. Examples of such guarantees are "satisfaction-or-money-back" terms, agreements to service or maintain the good for a specified period, and assurance of a resale value. As another form of such guarantees we would have to include "good will" or "reputation," whether based on a buyer's belief that he will secure some certain quality advantage by concluding an agreement with this seller rather than another, or that he will secure a favorable adjustment in the event that his expectations of advantage are disappointed through no fault of his own. Such guarantees increase the probability that the advantage expected will in fact be realized or diminish the probability of a risk attaching to the bargain, thereby raising the cost of disagreement or lowering the cost of agreement, in either case increasing the buyer's inducement to agree.

As a third form of nonprice change, in some situations the seller can impose penalties on the potential buyer for refusing to agree on the terms asked. The penalty threatened may be lawsuit, slander, violence, fine, strike, refusal of future sales, or other harmful action which raises the cost of disagreement. Such sanctions may impinge harshly on the buyer's stream of aspirations, constituting adverse effects to be avoided and conferring on the selller's offering the special advantage of avoiding these adverse effects. Refusal to effect the coöperative relationship on the terms offered may subject the symbiont to injuries which carry greater risk to his objectives than do the costs of agreement. To the businessman, under certain circumstances, a strike may be more costly than the wage increase which his employees demand. To the distributor of XYZ Company's washing machines and refrigerators, refusal to handle their newly added home air-conditioning unit (in place of that which the dis-

---

whom it is likely to be in a superior bargaining position because its offerings carry a unique advantage. "Survival and Adjustment in Behavior Systems," in Reavis Cox and Wroe Alderson (eds.), *Theory in Marketing* (Chicago: Richard D. Irwin, Inc., 1950), p. 82.

tributor has handled to his satisfaction in the past) may mean the loss of his XYZ franchise.

Aside from these manipulations of price and quality, by which the seller seeks to raise the buyer's cost of disagreement or lower his cost of agreement, there is one other way in which he can affect relative bargaining powers to his advantage. His relative position can be improved to the extent that consumer aspirations requiring the use of his product or service spread to others, who thus offer alternative relationships to the seller. If additional buyers appear, ready to conclude agreements on his terms, the seller can afford to be less concerned with the reluctance to concede his asking price of those with whom he originally sought to bargain.

The obvious mechanics for raising up alternative buyers is advertising. The effect of advertising is to make people want what they previously ignored or to want something more than they had before, in either case raising their cost of disagreement on the seller's terms. To the extent their cost of disagreement rises, the seller's own cost of disagreement on the terms of some original prospective buyer falls—he now has others with whom he can effect symbiotic relationships if the latter remains adamant. If a seller has but one potential customer (a monopsonist), his cost of disagreement on the other's terms is greater than if he has other customers ready to bargain with him. Advertising creates these other customers and confers on the seller the power to say no to this buyer because another will come along to accept the terms which he refuses.[4]

There are, then, these basic ways in which a seller can manipulate bargaining power to his advantage: By downward price adjustments or other price concessions he can reduce the cost to others of agreeing on his terms. By imitation or initiation in the matter of quality, he can attempt to distinguish his offerings from those of his commensal competitors, to assure that buyers' aspirations can be better satisfied by a relationship with him rather than with those

---

[4] We rule out any attempt by the seller to raise his own cost of agreement on the other's terms as improbable or irrational, thus disregarding this fourth possible means of affecting relative bargaining powers.

who stand as an alternative to him, thus increasing buyers' cost of disagreement on his terms. He can secure the same effect by guaranteeing performance or by threatening penalties for refusal to agree. By advertising, he can attempt to induce in others the kind of aspirations which he stands ready to satisfy, thereby lowering his own cost of disagreement with any one buyer.

Turning to the other side of the symbiotic relationship, we observe methods by which the buyer can manipulate bargaining power to his advantage which are similar to those available to the seller. A seller's cost of disagreement on the buyer's terms is, as we know, the satisfactions which are made possible because of the relationship. Any increase in a buyer's offer thus raises the seller's cost of disagreement. A seller's cost of agreement consists in satisfactions or aspirations which could have been achieved except for this relationship. Any concessions which the buyer makes with respect to the conditions of sale he originally imposed thus represents a reduction in the seller's cost of agreement.

First, in the matter of price, any change in a buyer's bid which creates or increases a price advantage over the bids of competing buyers or which more nearly approaches the offers of others necessarily has the effect of raising the seller's cost of disagreement on the buyer's terms (though not necessarily by an amount sufficient to induce agreement). The price advantage may be offered overtly, as at an auction, or covertly, if the buyer is hopeful of confining the added inducement to one of a number of sellers with whom he is dealing. The more advantageous offer may take the form of remembrances at Christmas time, the use of influence and contacts on behalf of the seller, special favors and entertainment, willingness to buy larger quantities than needed or to buy tie-in goods not wanted.

The seller's cost of disagreement can also be raised if the buyer is able to impose penalties on him for refusing to agree to the terms offered. The sanctions imposed may take the form of refusal of future purchases (in labor parlance, a lockout), use of influence on other customers to dissuade them from purchasing (organized boycott), or more generally any action capable of inflicting injury. The removal of such threatened penalties, no less than a price concession, represents an achievement made possible by the relationship.

The buyer's bargaining power can likewise be improved by lowering the seller's cost of agreement on his terms. There are two principal direct means by which the buyer can accomplish this: he can reduce the quality conditions which he originally demanded, and he can provide guarantees of his own performance. As examples of the first method, the maid can be granted two nights out instead of one, as originally specified, to induce her to stay; the house buyer whose bid for a house under construction is otherwise unacceptable can offer to take the structure with the second floor left unfinished; at the restaurant which declines to serve him dinner because it is after closing hours, the hungry traveler can offer to settle for a ham sandwich.

The seller who is reluctant to agree to the buyer's terms can sometimes be induced to do so by the second suggested means of lowering the cost of agreement, that is, lessening the seller's risk of being disappointed in the relationship. Underwritten credit, a reputation for fair dealing, and good will are all forms of such a guarantee. The seller who refuses to accept an unstable currency in exchange for his goods may be quite willing to accept the equivalent in dollars; an American Express check will be honored where a personal check is considered too risky; the buyer with a reputation for returning merchandise may be refused a purchase unless he agrees that the sale will be considered final; in contrast, a buyer whose bid is lower than another's may be accepted because he is known to be prompt in settling his bills and honest in presenting claims for adjustment.[5]

[5] Again it should be noted that the alternative method of calculating costs of disagreement and agreement (incorporating in the computation the relative advantages and disadvantages of the best alternatives) would require a different statement of the buyer's means of manipulating bargaining power. We would have to say that any price or quality change made by the buyer which offers some additional advantage not offered by others adds to the seller's cost of disagreement, while any price or quality adjustment which more nearly approaches the offerings of others lessens the seller's cost of agreement.

Finally, the buyer—like the seller—improves his position to the extent that his alternatives are increased. In the same manner that the seller can advertise to secure further customers, the buyer can advertise to obtain additional suppliers. By his publicized offer he may induce others to supply services which previously they did not supply (as housewives were induced to take jobs during World War II). The effect of such advertising is to raise the cost of disagreement of *additional* sellers (or to create a cost of disagreement, where none existed before), thereby lowering the buyer's own cost of disagreement on the terms of some original seller. By uncovering additional sources of the goods or services which he seeks, he reduces the risks involved in refusing to consent to the terms which some seller previously had sought to exact from him.

Both buyer and seller, then, have methods by which each can seek to manipulate the structure of aspirations and alternatives to their own advantage by actions which are directed at the symbiont. The effort is to make one's offering more attractive to the symbiont, so as to increase his inducement to agree on one's own terms. By seeking to conform one's offerings more closely to another's aspirations or to mold another's aspirations to conform more closely to one's offering, additional advantage may be gained, improving the prospects of agreement on one's terms because the terms are now more acceptable to the symbiont whose relationship is desired.

There is another way in which relative bargaining power can be modified, however. If a bargainer can influence the terms which are offered by his commensal rivals, he can thereby improve his own prospects by deteriorating the alternatives which face his symbiotic rival. If a buyer would like to effect a purchase, he can improve his bargaining power if he can see to it that other would-be buyers are prevented or dissuaded from making competitive offers; if a seller, he can improve his relative position to the extent he can insure that others do not undercut his terms in the same market. Let us examine these possibilities.

THE MANIPULATION OF BARGAINING POWER
IN COMMENSAL RELATIONSHIPS

Where a person is one of a number of commensal rivals for some symbiotic relationship, he can sometimes improve his position by taking actions against his rivals rather than by seeking to influence the symbiont directly. To the extent his actions succeed in weakening the symbiont's inducement to agree on the terms of his rivals or his rivals' inducement to agree on the terms offered by the symbiont, his own relative bargaining power is improved.

In general, a commensal's bargaining power (vis-a-vis a symbiont) can be increased to the extent that he can (1) force his rivals to alter their terms, raising the symbiont's cost of agreement with them or lowering the cost of disagreement, so that the rivals' terms offer the symbiont less inducement to agree, or (2) raise the rivals' cost of agreeing on the symbiont's terms, thus giving the former less inducement to agree, or (3) force his rivals to quit the field altogether.

These results can be brought about in a number of ways. There is no need to attempt a comprehensive catalogue here, but several methods may be mentioned by way of illustration. First, actual exclusion of rivals from a market may be accomplished by securing an exclusive governmental franchise. The grant may accord exclusive selling rights, as in the case of public utilities, or exclusive buying rights, as sometimes in the case of the development of public lands or resources. The exclusive franchise may run indefinitely, or as in the case of patents and copyrights, for a limited time.

Short of such outright exclusion of commensal rivals from a field, an individual may be able to influence the terms offered by rivals or the terms they are willing to accept. Such methods are sometimes extralegal or even illegal, but there are also a variety of legal ways of achieving this result. The seller who wishes to put a stop to price cutting by rivals or the buyer who wishes to prevent rivals from topping his bid may resort to threat of violence or retaliation or other forms of injury. He may also seek legislative limitations, as in minimum wage and fair trade laws or price and wage ceilings. If—through any of these means—rival sellers are forced to raise prices or rival buyers to lower their bids, the prospective symbiont's cost of agreement on their terms rises (or cost of disagreement falls), thereby lessening the attractiveness of their offerings relative to that of the manipulator.

A rival may be induced to share his quality advantage by threat of patent litigation or other forms of harassment, such as the questioning of property rights. Again, the symbiont's cost of disagreement on the rival's terms falls, since an advantage otherwise peculiar to him is now incorporated in the manipulator's offering. Unless they agree to restrict their competition, rivals may discover greater difficulty in securing needed supplies or an adverse turn in the terms of other bargains, if the manipulator can exercise economic influence; they may fear being subjected to legal actions if they believe the manipulator carries political influence.

If such methods as these sound gross, it should be remembered that they can often operate in subtle ways and that they are common to noneconomic as well as to economic pursuits. Interrival manipulations appear in political life, in courtship, in school, in a variety of other forms of social activity where a prize is sought and its achievement can be furthered by inducements to one's rivals to seek other prizes rather than this one or, if they insist on competing for this one, to do so on terms which minimize their advantage. Such manipulation of bargaining power affects the nature of the alternatives which are offered to the prospective symbiont, reducing the number and lessening the relative attractiveness of those relationships which might substitute for that offered by the manipulator.

Influence over the terms of the offerings of one's rivals is most readily achieved, however, through some form of commensal cooperation based on terms which are reached through commensal bargaining. We explore this method of manipulating bargaining power in the section which follows.

COMBINATIONS AND ALLIANCES

The matter of combinations and alliances can best be approached by considering certain characteristics of organizations. Additional characteristics of organizations will be explored in the chapter which follows.

Within any organization there are two major problems: (1) the definition of the common terms on which it or its members will enter into symbiotic relationships with others, and the consideration of the terms which are offered by those with whom the unit is bargaining (the terms of external agreement); and (2) the division among its members of the advantages and risks accruing to the group (the terms of internal agreement). These two problems are interrelated. The allocation of advantages and risks affects and is affected by determination of the terms of the organization's symbiotic relations with others. The resolution of these two interrelated problems involves the members of the unit in internal bargaining of a quite complicated nature.

At any time each member of the organization can be considered to seek the adoption of certain policies by the organization for the resolution of specific aspects of these two major problem areas. The policies which he advocates derive from the nature of his aspirations and his weighing of the alternative means by which they may be achieved within the organization. However couched in terms of benefit to the organization, the course of action which is urged always reflects the individual aspirations of the one urging it and, however subconsciously, is designed to further the person's own objectives through the medium of the group. The individual's associational life is simply one facet of his integrated time stream of aspirations. He is, in effect, competing with the other members of the group for a measure of control over the group, to assure that its resources and bargaining power are directed to the greater satisfaction of his personal aspirations.

We can thus picture each member of an organization as preferring that the group follow certain courses of conduct both in the definition of the terms of its external relations and in the allocation of the rewards and risks among its member, courses of conduct which appear to him most likely to realize his personal objectives. With respect to some types of action (say depreciation policy, in a business firm) only a few members of the organization may be concerned, only those who feel that the achievement of their aspirations is clearly involved; a majority may be apathetic. Other types of organizational behavior (say the determination of the wage and salary scale) may elicit more widespread interest within the organization and the expression of strongly held preferences.

As each individual strives to achieve the measure of his aspirations within the organization, to acquire sufficient control over its policies and actions to assure the fulfillment of his objectives (as they exist at the given stage in his time stream), he thus makes certain demands upon the other members of the organization and exercises his bargaining power to win the acceptance of those demands. His bargaining power, as we know, consists of the others' inducement to agree, which goes back to their costs of disagreement and agreement on his terms. The costs of disagreement are the advantages to each member, individually, which would have to be sacrificed if the terms were rejected. The costs of agreement constitute the risks and disadvantages, to each member of the organization, which would be incurred if the terms were accepted.

Although our attention in this analysis will be concentrated primarily upon the organization of the firm, the above remarks are equally applicable to the household. As will be developed in the next chapter, we treat the firm and the household as the two primary economic units outside of government itself. If more emphasis is placed on the firm than the household in these chapters, it is largely because we know less about the economic activities of the household than we do about those of the firm.

In the present context, however, it is apparent without extended argument that the household gives rise to internal bargaining by its members, each seeking to secure some measure of control over the disposition of its resources, in the accomplishment of the objectives which each prefers. The identity of some interests often disguises this elemental bargaining relationship, however.

The founding of a family involves the same kind of time stream of aspirations and bargains as we have already encountered. An individual may want a wife just as he would want travel and education, or he may want children just as he might want entertainment. Each of these involves initial expenditures and continued upkeep as a kind of capital investment (though perhaps it is wisest if we forego such terminology!). The important consideration, however, is that because wife and children are human beings, with aspirations of their own, he cannot control his expenditures on them as he would on other forms of consumption or investment. He may experience pleasure in seeing his wife decked out in new clothing as he would get pleasure in adding a shiny new gadget to his car, to be sure, but there enters a subtle distinction. He gets enjoyment from many expenditures on family *only because* the members of the family themselves derive enjoyment from the expenditures— as a car does not from the gadgets which are bought for it.

For some household expenditures, however, this vicarious satisfaction is not sufficient to create for the husband a cost of disagreement greater than the cost of agreement; the bargain would not have been made if the husband had followed his own judgment: he is glad that his wife likes her new hat but believes that she should not have spent so much on it. Obviously, the same judgments apply in reverse. The wife experiences a vicarious pleasure from the fact that her husband takes such a delight in his new set of golf clubs—but she doesn't think the expenditure should have been made when the children need new winter coats.

Despite the amount of vicarious consumer satisfaction which is characteristic of the household, then, there remains—and inevitably must remain, in the face of limited resources—differences in the aspiration streams of those who compose the household and hence bargains based on relative bargaining power as to how family income shall be derived and allocated.[6] We return now, however, to consideration of the firm.

Since organizations no more than individuals can follow two or more conflicting policies simultaneously, all members of an organization must be bound by the same policies and consent and conform to the same actions, willingly or unwillingly. Within a business organization, for example, there must be some common price policy and not one which is followed by some officials only, with others following a different price policy; only one individual can be promoted to a given job, only one wage and salary schedule can be in effect at a given time, and there must be consent by all the members in the unit, however reluctant, to a single decision in such matters. An organization thus requires a complex set of bargains, embracing all phases of its activity and binding all its members, the results of which are satisfactory to each member of the organization as a basis for continuing his association with the unit. At any time an individual is free to determine that the results of this complex internal bargaining are such that the costs of agreeing on the terms (policies) which emerge are greater than the costs of disagreeing, that too little of his demands have been granted by the others to warrant his continuing membership in the unit; he thereupon dissociates himself from the unit.

The costs of disagreeing or agreeing with a given policy or action

---

[6] Some tentative studies have already been made, particularly in England, concerning such family bargaining [for example, Michael Young, "Distribution of Income Within the Family," *British Journal of Sociology*, vol. 3 (1952), pp. 305–321]. After discussing the manner in which husbands are sometimes able to protect their expenditures on tobacco and beer while wives must scrape along on lower family budget allotments, in time of inflation, Young writes on p. 317:

"Indeed, there may be a tendency for wives to suffer, relatively to their husbands, in any period of inflation, and if full employment inevitably means some degree of inflation, in any period of full employment. A period of inflation is a period of rising earnings and of rising prices. Workers organized in strong trade unions can, in such a situation, protect themselves by forcing up their earnings fast enough to preserve their real income. Unorganized workers, in common with all groups with relatively fixed incomes, do less well. Since wives have no unions, each has to reach her own individual arrangement, or bargain, with her husband. Like other unorganized workers, their money income may not advance as fast as prices."

proposed by others within the organization are sometimes specific to an individual member, as when Jones must weigh the advantages and disadvantages of agreeing to Smith's promotion when he himself is seeking the same job. More frequently, however, the advantages and disadvantages of agreeing to a course of action proposed by another member or other members of the unit are felt less directly, through the expected effect on the organization and the organization's capacity to satisfy the personal objectives which are sought from it. Agreeing to Brown's proposals, for example, may be expected to involve the company in a program of forward purchasing which carries the risk of an enormous loss which would be sure to have repercussions on job or income security. On the other hand, disagreeing with Brown may mean the loss of the firm's principal customer if Brown should leave the organization. How one evaluates such advantages and disadvantages depends upon his perception of the effect on the organization—and through the organization, on himself—of choosing this policy over some alternative (consenting to Brown's terms rather than Jones's, perhaps).[7] Such perceptions differ among the members of the organization.

Suppose, by way of illustration, that there are ten partners in a business organization. One comes forward with the proposal that

[7] Richard Glenn Gettell in his essay, "Pluralistic Competition," appearing in Cox and Alderson (eds.), *op. cit.*, pp. 93–94, suggests the need for incorporating in the general study of economic competition an examination of competition within a firm, among its policy makers, in a manner which I interpret as according with the argument of the text.

Examples of this sort of intraorganization bargaining are easy to find in any journal of business. The *Business Week* issue of August 15, 1953, pp. 82–83, which is at hand as this chapter is being written, provides an excellent example. It describes the relation between Dore Schary, who in 1948 came to Metro-Goldwyn-Mayer (owned by Loew's Inc.) as vice-president in charge of production, and other members of that organization.

"The second crisis for Loew's directors in the Schary career came in 1951, when Schary locked horns with Louis B. Mayer, vice-president in charge of studio operations. . . . Mayer was bridling at Schary's kind of picture, and was putting obstacles in his way.

"Loew's had to decide (a) to look for a new vice-president in charge of production [cost of disagreement on Schary's terms] or (b) to give Schary his head. The latter course would involve buying out Mayer's 10% stock interest at a cost of $2¾ million [cost of agreement on Schary's terms].

"Loew's decided for Schary in a big way. They bought out Mayer, gave Schary the organization modify the nature of its activities (adopt a new product, build a new building, change the character of its relations with its external symbionts). Another of the ten opposes the proposal. The group is now faced with the necessity of making a collective decision one way or the other, thereby possibly redefining the terms of its own internal relationships. Whatever decision is made rules out the alternative (or if a compromise is effected the compromise rules out both proposals as originally made). If one's view is accepted, the other's must be rejected. Among the remaining eight members of the organization, perhaps six are indifferent, conceiving that the achievement of their aspirations is unaffected by the outcome, being willing to go along with any decision on the matter. Of the remaining two, one would prefer one proposal and one the other, as likely to have effects on the organization more nearly according with his aspirations.

In the effort to secure adoption by the organization of the policy which he advocates or prefers, a policy which is expected to advance his own aspirations more than the alternative course proposed, each of the "competitors" may seek to manipulate relative bargaining positions to his own advantage. To accomplish this he may resort to any of the techniques which have already been discussed earlier in this chapter. But the fact that he is participating in an organization is sure to induce another type of manipulation— an effort to form an alliance or to build a combination within the organization which will act as a unit in the matter. He will seek the support for his position of a number of other individuals within the organization, so that it is no longer he alone who demands the adoption of certain courses of action but a group of individuals within the organization, whose joint advocacy of some given policy increases (for the others in the organization) the costs of disagree-

---

a new 15-year contract at $200,000 a year, showered him with 100,000 shares of stocks, and added 'chief of studio operations' to his title."

(It may be noted, parenthetically, that by granting concessions above those which Schary had sought Loew's directors were increasing for Schary the cost of disagreement on their terms in some future policy issue.)

ment with that policy, as we shall see. The disadvantages of the policy to other members of the unit (the cost of agreement on his terms) are, however, likely to be unaffected by the creation of the alliance, so that the increase in the costs to others of disagreeing on the proposed policy represents an increase in their inducement to agree, which in turn is equivalent to an increase in the relative bargaining power of the policy proposers.

A combination or alliance can produce this effect when it succeeds in reducing the relative attractiveness of the alternatives available to those from whom concession is wanted. The rejection by some members of the organization of the action proposed by *one* individual means that they will face only the penalties which that one man can impose or lose only the favors which that one man can bestow. If, however, he succeeds in effecting a combination or alliance of members of the organization, all advocating the same action, rejection of the proposal by the other members of the organization now carries the threat of penalties or loss of benefits from all those in the alliance. The more individuals included in the alliance, then, the greater the cost of disagreement on their terms, and the greater the individual bargaining power of each member of the alliance, the greater the bargaining power of the alliance itself. A union of a company's employees familiarly illustrates these principles. The more employees in the union, the greater the cost to the management members of the company of disagreeing on their demands, and the more skilled and less easily replaceable are some of the union's membership, the greater the cost to the others in the company of disagreeing on the union's terms. The principle of strength through alliance is not restricted to rank-and-file employees, however. Almost every organization has its cliques which contend against each other for control over the organization and whose power lies in their collective ability to punish those who refuse to accept their terms and reward those who do.

The formation of combinations and alliances within an organization—the existence of lesser organizations (however ephemeral and informal) seeking to control larger organizations to their own advantage, in a fashion reminiscent of a holding company—is a phenomenon carrying several corollaries of economic significance. We shall observe three.

1. Because of the traditional emphasis upon the concept of perfect competition in economic analysis, we have often been inclined to regard anything smacking of combination as something atypical. We are aware that combinations exist but we tend to regard them as exceptional. In recognizing that combinations and alliances are not atypical but occur wherever people are gathered together, are in fact as common as society, we place the phenomenon in a more realistic light. Combination or alliance is a common—indeed, almost inevitable—method of manipulating bargaining power to one's advantage, which an individual, seeking to achieve his aspirations out of his position of scarcity and interdependence, is as sure to utilize as he is any of the other means of manipulating bargaining power. Whether the combination or alliance operates within an organization or between organizations involves a difference of scope (that is to say, of the specific content of the concept) rather than a difference in concepts themselves. Our corollary, then, is that the phenomenon of combination to improve bargaining power pervades the economy; it is not exceptional but an inescapable manifestation of competition, a means of improving one's competitive position.

2. It is not some organization "Standard Oil of New Jersey" or "General Electric" which makes decisions, but individuals with sufficient bargaining power to impose on others in those organizations a cost of disagreement on certain preferred policies greater than the cost of agreement on them. The price policy of a firm is not the consequence of the cerebrations of some designated officials charged with that responsibility. Price and other policies are hammered out by the bargaining of those members of the organization whose aspirations are somehow involved, and who exercise and manipulate their bargaining power within the organization to accomplish what satisfies their aspirations. Price policies and other corporate decisions are thus as likely to be a compromise of differing viewpoints as the imposition by some individuals on others of their

particular view. Such compromises of conflicting demands are as frequently to be found in *any* type of bargaining as in the buying and selling of an article of merchandise. As we have seen in previous pages, one improves his bargaining power by incorporating in his own product (here, the policy proposal) the advantages offered by competitors, as well as by reducing the terms which are sought. Compromise is simply a method of strengthening bargaining power or (to put it another way) of making one's bargaining power equal to the attainment of as much of what one is after as is possible.

3. In a previous chapter it was observed that bargaining power varied inversely with the degree to which personal aspirations coincide with the aspirations competitively sought by others. The larger the number of individuals who seek the same objectives, the less any individual's power to set the terms of the symbiotic relationship which makes the achievement of that objective possible. This conclusion holds, however, only if there is a *competitive* coincidence between one's own aspirations and the aspirations of others, so that achievement for one means less or no achievement for another, evoking a bidding relationship. In some instances, however, coincidence of aspirations may facilitate achieving one's objective. If competitive bidding is replaced by joint action to secure a common objective (that is, by commensal bargaining for commensal coöperation), then the chances of obtaining one's objective are likely to be increased. Thus, for example, the culture may encourage an aspiration for a higher income. In the absence of joint action, the widespread pursuit of this goal makes its realization more difficult for any individual, since he must compete with all others for every income gain. But if, as a wage earner, he joins forces with his fellows and organizes a union, their collective pursuit of the goal of higher wages helps instead of hinders one another in achieving it. Their goals are no longer competitive except as against those with whom they collectively bargain (or more accurately the competitive elements of their goals must first be bargained out among themselves so that they may present a united front to those with whom they collectively bargain). If people pool common aspirations, they are

jointly competitive against others whose aspirations are competitive with theirs. Our previous conclusion should thus be modified to read that bargaining power varies inversely with the degree to which there is competitive coincidence between the aspirations of bargaining agents, whatever their size and composition.

This does not mean, however, that competition will be wholly eliminated among those who unite in a common bargaining agency. As long as the scarcity relationship persists, so that more for one means less for others, the elimination of a bidding competition between them is likely simply to direct the burden of competition along other channels. If business rivals manage to reduce their price competition, the scarcity condition which still continues is likely to stimulate competition in advertising or product innovation. If workers organize to eliminate wage competition among themselves, this may exaggerate competition for the reclassification of jobs into higher wage-paying brackets or for a preferable seniority position. In all cases, then, it is necessary to isolate the competitive purpose of the collaborative effort, avoiding the erroneous assumption that a reduction of competition between individuals in certain respects reduces their competition in all respects. Combinations and alliances are directed to particular objectives, and increased coöperation to achieve these objectives may actually stimulate the remaining areas of competition among those in the alliance, where the underlying scarcity relationship persists.

If, in common with usage in the field of labor economics, we define the bargaining unit as the configuration (numbers and characteristics) of those on each side of a bargaining relationship, then it is clear that the bargaining unit is something which is manipulated to increase bargaining power. An individual's bargaining power is increased to the extent that he can ally with himself others who are potential competitors or whose symbiotic coöperation is sought by those with whom he is bargaining and to the extent that he can wean away from alliance with his bargaining competitor those who stand as alternatives to the latter or whose symbiotic coöperation is additionally desired. By allying himself with potential competitors all of whom agree on the terms of their offerings, he lowers the cost of agreement by others on his terms (since the cost of agreement no longer includes foregoing more favorable alternative relationships). By allying himself with those whose symbiotic coöperation, like his own, is desired by those with whom he is bargaining, he raises the cost of disagreement on his terms (since the cost of disagreement now includes the loss of benefits which others as well as himself can offer). In either case, the bargaining opponent's inducement to agree and therefore his own bargaining power are increased. By dividing a hostile alliance and thereby either making feasible commensal substitutes for the symbiont with whom the bargain was originally sought, or reëstablishing a symbiotic relationship independently desired, one lowers the cost of disagreement on the other's terms and raises his own bargaining power.

The more comprehensive the alliance, then (the more inclusive of one's commensal competitors or cosymbionts), the greater one's bargaining power. Under these circumstances there would appear to be a strong incentive for the continued expansion of organizations. The individual joins forces with other individuals to effect a more powerful bargaining agent, and this in turn can increase its bargaining strength by joining forces with other units, in a still larger alliance, and so on without end as long as there remain any outside the alliance whose goals are competitive with the goals of those within the alliance.

Simply to state such an hypothesis is to reveal its essential weakness, however. Alliances and combinations can themselves be formed only by bargains among those who would be party to the enlarged unit. As we have already seen, divergent views as to the desirability of a policy can always be expected, based upon individual perceptions as to how the policy will affect one's achievement of his personal aspirations. Even among workers in a labor union, for example, there often emerge disagreements as to the demands which will be jointly made upon the employer, depending upon how individual workers contemplate that the demands framed, in contrast to some other demand which might be made, will affect their achievement of their aspirations, and depending on their individual calculations of the cost of disagreeing on the counter terms offered by the employer. Older employees may prefer pensions to wage increases, in contrast to younger men. Skilled employees, on the one hand, or unskilled employees on the other hand, or female workers or those of some particular occupation, may feel that their demands are being slighted in the framing of the "package" of demands which all are to support, or that their conception of the costs of disagreeing on the employer's terms is given too little consideration. The less homogeneous are the members of the proposed alliance, the greater the disagreement that is likely to emerge in deciding on common terms to be offered to their bargaining opponent.

One reason why organizations experience a declining rate of growth or stop growing and even disintegrate is thus evident. Organization depends on a cost of agreement on the common terms, for all members of that organization, which is less than the cost of disagreement on those terms. The larger an organization, however, the more difficult to discover the common denominator—the internally consistent complex of bargains—which carries a higher cost of disagreement than agreement for all who are involved. Some individuals, with aspiration systems conflicting in important respects with others, inevitably discover that throwing in their lot with the larger organization offers less reward and carries more risk than dissociating themselves from the organization, perhaps embarking on a path of expansion which, too, in its day will break down from inability to discover that complex system of bargains (allocating rewards and risks, determining the organization's policies and course of conduct) which for all in the organization carries an inducement to agree greater than is to be found in alternative employments of one's time.[8]

[8] This is not the same thing as saying that monopoly can never be made effective. There is no assurance that the dissenters who leave the organization will be able to compete successfully with the organization from which they break away. Their alternative employment of their time may be in an unrelated field. Nevertheless, the difficulty which any organization is likely to experience in expanding

This result is all the more to be expected since the more comprehensive the organization the more important becomes the question of the allocation of rewards and risks within it (in contrast to the other question of determining the terms of relationship with symbionts external to it). The area of competition shifts more and more from relations between the organization and others to relations within the organization. Internal competition becomes more important than external competition, making the adherence of all within the alliance more and more difficult. The source of an organization's strength—comprehension of the additional and alternative bargains sought by one's bargaining opponent—is the source of its weakness as well. The closer it approaches comprehension of competing elements, the more does it simply transform the competitive struggle from one between itself and those outside its formal limits to one occurring within its own formal boundaries.

The process is the same in the economic sphere as that which has been witnessed for hundreds of centuries in the politics of nations. Internal cohesion is greatest when a nation is competing with others. When a nation, through conquest, expands to embrace its former competitors, in the expectation of strengthening itself in the competitive struggle with still other nations, it internalizes the competition previously external to itself. A nation that ultimately subjected all other nations, to rule the world, would thus carry within itself the same competitive struggles which formerly faced it from the outside. Formal organization is not determinative of bargaining strength. Alliances and combinations are necessarily transitory and shifting over time, depending on a constant recalculation by their members of the costs of disagreement and agreement on terms which are always changing.

The lesser the alliance, the more limited the policies and courses

---

to embrace *all* competitors is great, and if there is no assurance there is still a strong presumption that its bargaining power will be unequal to the task of inducing the agreement on its terms of all actual or potential competitors. Among such strong-willed competitors there are likely to be some who are capable of providing meaningful alternatives to others.

of action which are made common, the greater the chance for emergence and survival of the alliance. We are reminded of Professor Fellner's analysis of the oligopoly quasi agreement, which can be made workable with respect to limited areas, such as price policy, but fails of application to other areas, such as innovation and advertising. The lesser the alliance, however, the larger the area of competition which must be left external to the unit.

We conclude, then, that alliances and combinations (the manipulation of the bargaining unit) are one means of expanding bargaining power. The objective is to raise the cost of disagreement or to lower the cost of agreement on one's own terms, for those with whom one is seeking a symbiotic relationship. But the alliance can be formed and maintained only when, for each member of it, the cost of disagreeing on the common terms (which are always in the process of change) is greater than the cost of agreement.

There is one significance of the method of manipulating bargaining power by resort to combinations and alliances which should not escape us. As units expand through the cohesion of individuals seeking to strengthen their bargaining position, they limit the alternatives which are available to symbionts. Indeed, it is chiefly in this respect that the alliance can accomplish its purpose. As the enlarged bargaining unit thus augments its bargaining power vis-a-vis its symbiotic rivals, however, it is likely to evoke a counter-response. One typical reaction is countercombination, in which the symbionts—linking forces and themselves organizing into a single unit—limit the alternatives which are available to the alliance facing them.

The result of this maneuver is to establish two bargaining agents, each seeking a particular symbiotic relationship to which there are limited alternatives. The limitation on alternatives is a consequence imposed by each on the other. But because the relationship here is deemed so vital by the opposing party, because the achievement of its aspirations depends on it and alternate relationships are unsatisfactory, it will seek to compel the relationship by further manipulations of bargaining power, including—perhaps especially including—an effort to impose penalties of whatever sort on the other for disagreeing on its terms. The history of union-management relationships is replete with cases of such attempted manipulation, extending to the use of political influence, violence, and legal harassments, where no alternative relationship was possible to either party and each sought to coerce agreement on its terms by making disagreement more and more costly.

The expansion of bargaining units is thus likely to induce a shift in emphasis from commensal bidding for symbiotic coöperation to commensal coöperation for symbiotic competition.[9] Econo mists have been accustomed to associate the former situation (which approaches perfect competition as its polar limit) with "economic" relationships, and the latter (which approaches bilateral monopoly at the other extreme) with "political" relationships. Both situations are, of course, simply different aspects of the same phenomenon— the attempted achievement of one's time stream of aspirations by the manipulation of his bargaining power, to effect on more advantageous terms those symbiotic relationships which are important to him.

REACTION PATTERNS

Where combination begets combination, we have but one illustration of a more common phenomenon—the reaction of individuals

[9] This, I gather, is the purport of Kenneth Galbraith's argument in *American Capitalism* (Boston: Houghton Mifflin Comany, 1952), where he insists that it is simply the form of competition which has changed. While agreeing with most of his argument, I would prefer to rest the case on concepts more basic than his "countervailing power," since the latter is something (as I interpret Galbraith) which ceases to operate in time of inflation. I cannot conceive that symbiotic competition between expanded bargaining agencies ceases during inflationary episodes, even though the costs of disagreement and agreement on the other's terms may be radically altered. Galbraith seems to consider that countervailing power is present only when it is strong enough to accomplish some objective not clearly defined (but probably something like "defense of the consumer's interests"). Without adopting any such touchstone, I prefer to keep the emphasis simply on the constant and inescapable redistribution of bargaining power among the individuals in a society.

or groups to a modification of relative bargaining powers which is adverse to their interests.

The purpose of any attempted manipulation of bargaining power is to modify the structure of aspirations and alternatives to one's advantage—increasing the aspirations by others for the services one supplies, decreasing the aspirations by others for the things one desires, increasing the alternatives which satisfy one's aspirations, decreasing the alternatives for the services one supplies. The successful manipulation redistributes bargaining power, placing others at a relative disadvantage over the situation formerly obtaining. But this redistribution of bargaining power encourages a counter-manipulation by those whose relative bargaining position has deteriorated. This countermanipulation we refer to as a reaction. Reactions emanate from those whose bargaining power has been adversely affected by some change in circumstances; they involve actions precisely similar to those which have been discussed as manipulations in the preceding sections of this chapter.

The stimulus to *initiate* changes in relative bargaining power, through manipulation, comes from the structure of aspirations which is held, the achievement of which depends on relative bargaining power. In particular, the coercive comparisons which are relevant provide the most potent moving force for an individual to seek a readjustment of bargaining power to his advantage. The stimulus to react to changes in bargaining power which have been initiated by others derives from the same source—the attempt to achieve one's aspirations, in particular those which are subject to coercive comparison, which is possible only through one's relative bargaining power, which has now suffered.

Reactions may be evoked by changes in bargaining power not directly attributable to the manipulation of others. Thus a change in others' aspirations may leave one in a weakened bargaining position, inducing a reaction designed to restore at least a measure of the previous bargaining strength. Or a price reduction to strengthen the seller's bargaining power with respect to buyers will leave his employees in a weakened position, since the seller's cost of disagreement on their (existing) terms (the sales income which he would have to sacrifice) has fallen. They may respond with measures intended to restore their lost power. Or an employer may offer a wage increase to strengthen his bargaining power vis-a-vis the union with which he is negotiating, with the consequence that he raises his terms to his customers in the effort to maintain his own achievements, in the process necessarily weakening his bargaining power vis-a-vis them. He may thereupon seek an alliance with rival sellers in an effort to recoup his strength in his selling relationships. Or the racial prejudices of one's customers may affect one's bargaining-power relationship to workers of the race prejudiced, inducing a reaction on their part. In most such situations, however, the redistribution of bargaining power is in consequence of someone's efforts, in some relationship, to advance the achievement of his own goals, so that usually it may be assumed that reactions are responses to manipulations of bargaining power somewhere in the total system of relationships. Nevertheless, to put the matter in its most general form, we can say that reactions are responses to a deterioration in bargaining position designed to restore the lost position.

Reactions may be evoked by the attempts of one's *symbiotic* rivals to manipulate an improvement in bargaining position vis-a-vis oneself, either singly or in company with his commensals. Such symbiont reactions fall within the analytical framework which has already been set out. They affect directly the terms offered and the costs of disagreement and agreement on those terms, in the particular relationship.

Reactions may also be evoked by the attempts of one's *commensal* rivals to manipulate an improvement in their bargaining position vis-a-vis the common symbionts. These commensal reactions fall within the analytical framework developed by Professor Fellner.[10] Where the actions of one commensal (say X) importantly affect the

[10] William Fellner, *Competition Among the Few* (New York: Alfred A. Knopf, Inc., 1949).

achievements of another (say Y), the latter may be expected to react to the former's actions. Where X's action is unfavorable to Y's achievement, by reducing his bargaining power in important symbiotic relationships, the reaction from Y is likely to take the form of retaliation against X. The retaliation may be weak and ineffective or powerful and effective. X learns, over time, the limits with which he may set the terms of his symbiont relationships without evoking Y's unfavorable reaction, and he learns how to evaluate the effect of Y's retaliation. Similarly, Y's actions evoke X's reactions, and Y too learns what actions are likely to elicit an unfavorable response from X, and in what measure.

This relationship between X and Y is actually a type of bargaining relationship between commensals, in which each seeks to affect the other's terms of relationships with third parties, backed by a power to impose costs on the other for disagreeing on its terms. They seek an understanding (quasi agreement, in Fellner's terminology) as to the discretionary area within which each is free to manipulate his bargaining power to obtain further advantage in his relationships with symbionts.

In the oligopoly case, for example, rival sellers seek an understanding as to how much of a price reduction one firm may institute, to win customers, without subjecting itself to the retaliation of its commensal rivals whose bargaining power relative to consumers of its products has deteriorated because of the first firm's action. Failing such an understanding, they are likely to find themselves enmeshed in a price war in which the commensals succeed only in weakening each other's bargaining power relative to their common symbionts. To achieve an understanding or quasi agreement, which defines the limits of action without commensal reaction, the commensals bargain between themselves—not necessarily or even usually in open negotiation but by a process of learning by experience, each seeking to obtain a definition of permissible action which favors it.

This kind of a quasi-bargaining process, far from being an academic chimera, obtains wherever a small number of individuals (whether symbionts or commensals) importantly affect the achievement of each other's goals. Under such circumstances, each quickly learns within what limits he is free to pursue his own objectives without being subjected to retaliatory actions from the others. These limits are not fixed, but are subject to constant redetermination as the powers of retaliation of those within the group shift. Retaliation itself is, of course, subject to the check of inviting further reaction—not only from him against whom directed but against others who may be indirectly involved.

Thus in setting the terms of his relationships with symbionts the bargaining agent must be mindful not only of symbiotic reaction but of commensal reaction. Both symbionts and commensals, in reacting, may seek the support or alliance of others to implement their cause, including, as we shall see, the support of government.

Finally, the essential issue in all manipulations and reactions is the *relative* change in bargaining power which results. Absolute costs of disagreement may have increased for both manipulator and reactor, but the significant question is for whom have they increased proportionately more. It is the shift in relative bargaining power which determines the success of a manipulator's maneuver. But in calculating the relative shifts in position one must take into account the effect of a manipulation on (the reactions evoked in) *all* one's bargaining relationships and not simply in that relationship which was designed to be influenced.

There should now begin to emerge the conception of all the individuals within a society being bound together by a complex network of symbiotic and commensal relations, based on terms which are the result of relative bargaining powers, subject to change as bargaining power changes through shifts in aspirations and alternatives, shifts which are subject to manipulation, with each successful manipulation of bargaining power likely to evoke reactions from those whose position has thereby suffered. To gain an advantage in one relationship an alliance may be sought, which can be effected, however, only by making concessions to its other members which weakens bargaining power in another relationship. The strengthened bargaining power, in the one relationship, evokes reactions from others, both symbionts and commensals, while one's own weakened bargaining power in the other relationship excites an attempt at further manipulation to restore the lost advantage there. The web of relationships within the society is constantly subject to partial destruction and reweaving in new patterns, as each of the individuals in that web seeks to refashion it to the design of his own aspirations.

CONCLUSION

The terms of his bargains are the principal means by which an individual, in a society, is able to achieve his aspirations, a fact which leads the individual to seek to obtain the best terms possible. But the higher the seller sets his price, and the lower the buyer makes his offer, the lower is the bargaining power of each.

For a seller, bargaining power can always be increased by reducing the price demanded, and for a buyer by raising the price offered. These methods of manipulating bargaining power, however, necessarily involve some sacrifice of aspirations; they constitute a transfer of achievement, in the one case from seller to buyer, in the other case from buyer to seller. The particular interdependence relationship is established only through a less favorable resolution of the particular scarcity relationship.

The individual thus perpetually faces a dilemma in his bargaining relations: as a seller, if he sets his price high, or as a buyer, if he sets his price low, he risks his aspirations through loss of the relationship which he seeks, since his bargaining power is unequal to induce agreement; if he modifies his terms, his bargaining power may become capable of inducing the desired agreement, but only by reducing the degree of his own achievement.

One escape from this dilemma lies in concentrating efforts to manipulate bargaining power along lines other than the modification of price offers. If such an effort involves less of a cost (less of a sacrifice of aspirations) than would be involved in modifying the price asked or bid, it is obviously to be preferred. Such efforts involve two fundamentally different methods, one of limiting the alternatives which are available to others, the other of extending the alternatives which are available to others. By the first method, combinations may be formed embracing commensal competitors who would otherwise bid against each other, or powers may be used to impose hardship or penalty on those declining agreement on the proffered terms. By the second method, innovation or improvement in the nature of one's services is sought which, by more nearly satisfying the desires of symbionts, makes their disagreement on one's terms costlier, simply by denying them the "better mousetrap."

Which of the several methods of manipulating bargaining power will be employed depends on their feasibility and their prospect of success.

CHAPTER 9

Bargains and Flows: The Organizational Unit

IN previous chapters it was said that individual bargains are significant only in relation to a person's time stream of aspirations, and from the narrower economic interest, only in so far as they affect his income flows. We shall now examine this proposition more carefully.

Income flows (receipts and expenditures) reflect the continuing allocation of scarce resources in the economy, and are related to a person's time stream of aspirations by reason of the fact that the satisfaction of most objectives depends on scarce resources. A person's total aspiration structure determines his desire for income; some aspirations rely less on real resources for their fulfillment than do others. The individual whose leisure time is enjoyably spent in reading requires less income than the individual whose leisure time is given over to travel or golf or collecting rare autographs or night clubbing. Similarly, the individual whose aspiration structure emphasizes job satisfaction will willingly sacrifice income to achieve it. Nevertheless, for all individuals, whatever their aspirations, *some* scarce resources are necessary—food, clothing, and shelter, if nothing else. All individuals must rely on income for the satisfaction of certain of their wants.

Because some aspiration structure is continuous over a person's lifetime, we have referred to his wants as a time stream of aspiration, in which past and expected future are blended in the present. And because some income is necessary to the satisfaction of wants at every stage of this time stream, so too is income necessarily a continuous stream, in which present flows are also affected by past and expected future. The terms of individual bargains affect the size of the inflows and outflows of income, and are significant only because of this effect.

The revenue decision, we have seen, governs (in the present) one's inflows. The decisions as to how much of one's time shall be given over to working for pay and what emphasis shall be placed on income as opposed to job satisfaction in the choice of job (affected as these are by past and future in the form of assets and expectations) determine the flow of receipts. The budget decision governs (in the present, though similarly influenced by past and expected future) the outflows. But the revenue and budget decisions are not decisions at a single moment of time but continuing decisions which never cease being made. There is never a lining up of all the individual expenditures or potential expenditures, at a moment of time, to weigh their desirability against each other as well as against the foregone leisure or job satisfaction which gave rise or could give rise to each of them. In the household the cost of a single unit of labor is not measured against the utility of a single unit of consumer goods in a rational decision. Nor is the cost to a business firm of a single hour of a worker's time measured against the return to be expected from the sale of that hour's production. Such timeless or static decisions are both conceptually meaningless and operationally impossible where time goes on. It is the income flows (both real and money) which are important, the flows on whose continuity and direction and extent of change depend the achievement of one's stream of aspirations.

The validity of this proposition has been obscured by our efforts to break aggregates down into timeless elements. The assumption that income flows are composed of numerous price bargains leads us to assume that price is all that matters. The methodological isolation of a moment of time from all other moments, in a static system, leads us to operate as though time did not matter. But time is here the essential ingredient. At any given moment there *already* exists, for households and firms both, some flow of income permitting some level of realization of the ongoing stream of aspirations, and there exists too some expectation of future flows. It is only in their impact on these ongoing streams of income and aspirations that the prices of bargains have significance.

Income flows into the household in the form of earnings from the sale of services by household members, supplemented by savings out of past receipts and borrowings on the basis of future income expectations. It flows out of the household in the form of streams of payments for food, clothing, shelter, entertainment and family advancement, saving and investment, and so on. A change in any one of these streams, for whatever reason, requires some adjustment in one or more of the other streams, or in assets or liabilities. If the prices of food items rise, then some adjustment must be made to restore a balance, in a purely accounting sense. Either food purchases must be reduced, maintaining the volume of money flows constant though the real flow of food declines, or money flows for food increase, requiring a reduction in other expenditures or in savings or assets or an increase in income or liabilities. The *actual* effect of price changes on these flows is not wholly discernible or predictable at the time of change, since it will depend on choice among a variety of possible alternative courses of action whose relative merits are likely to change from one situation to the next— on substitution of goods whose price carries less risk to the household's achievements, or elimination of purchases which make the least contribution to family satisfaction, or determination of new sources of income which can supplement the old, or decisions whether income accumulations from the past or drafts on future income can fruitfully be used now in the light of such considerations as the changing productivity of family workers (increasing, decreasing), proximity to retirement, and so on.

Similarly income flows into the business firm in the form of sales (supplemented by assets and borrowings) and flows out of the firm as streams of wage payments, dividends, materials payments, investment, tax payments, and so on. A change in any one of these streams requires its compensation. If the wage *rate* rises, the significance of this lies only in its impact on the wage *stream,* and through it on other inflows and outflows of the firm. The impact on the wage stream is not certain, since it depends among other things on the rate of change of productivity (arising from changes in capital equipment, changes in morale and worker effort, changes in the product mix, changes in the level of activity), and consequently the impact on other flows is not certain. But over time it may become apparent that some adjustment must be made in product prices to increase the inflows to offset an emerging increase in the wage bill, or pressures may be applied to suppliers to modify the terms of their bargains in order to reduce the outflows to them, or efforts may be made to find new processes or materials which will curb outflows to labor or suppliers. Price changes, as part of the terms of individual bargains, are thus economically significant only in their effects on the income flows and asset position on which achievement of the stream of aspirations of those in households or business units depends.

We thus define *inflows* to include all current receipts (from the sale of goods and services, from past investment, from gifts, from borrowing) plus any assets used. We define *outflows* to include all current disbursements (for the purchase of goods and services, for investment, for gifts, for repayment of debt) plus any money savings. "Inflows" are thus roughly equivalent to the accountant's concept of "sources," and "outflows" to his concept of "applications." Since inflows and outflows include any changes in assets and liabilities, then at every moment an accounting balance must exist between inflows and outflows. For every household or business unit, every change in the rate of flow must have its offsetting entry. The sources-and-applications statement which firms cast up periodically could be prepared continuously, and for households as well as business units. Every increase in inflows must be offset simultaneously by an increase in outflows. If the former is accomplished by use of savings, the latter occurs through some purchase. If the increase in inflow comes through an enhancement of current receipts, then the increase in outflow takes the immediate form of an increase in savings. Every decline in inflows is likewise offset simultaneously by a decline in outflows. If current receipts fall off, savings must immediately decline. If the use of past savings is discontinued, purchases must simultaneously fall off.

These immediate adjustments, which require no decision but which preserve the balance between inflows and outflows, are followed by a rational rethinking of the revenue and budget decisions, which may evoke other adjustments. The real flow of goods into the household may be reduced as money outflows are curtailed, or additional family members may be put to work to increase inflows to their former level. The firm may reduce outflows by laying off workers and suppliers and cutting dividend payments, or efforts may be made to stimulate an increase in inflows through price reductions or product improvement or product innovation or entry into new markets or government subsidy. Such adjustments are designed not to bring inflows and outflows into balance, since they must always be in balance, but to bring them into a balance which permits a more satisfactory realization of the stream of aspirations of those whose flows have been affected.

Changes in income flows thus require adjustments which are commonly made through individual bargains; and changes in the terms of individual bargains have their effect on income flows. It is this interaction between bargains and flows which provides the central economic problem.

The problem of bargains has commonly been referred to as the problem of allocation—who gets what. The problem of flows has usually been spoken of as the problem of fluctuations—what determines the size of the pie to be allocated. The two have usually been analyzed separately and each has given rise to its own body of doctrine. But each is significant only in relation to the other. It would be only in a completely timeless society that the problem of allocation could be considered without respect to flows; it would be only in a Robinson Crusoe economy—in the absence of a society—that the problem of flows could be considered without respect to allocation. Economic theory which is to be tested for its reliability in explaining or predicting (on a probability basis) events in the real world cannot escape the relationship between bargains and flows.

THE ORGANIZATIONAL UNIT

Economic activity is commonly organized into units of more than one person. The three principal units of organization are the household, the business firm, and the government. We require a common conceptual framework within which to fit organizational economic activity, and we shall seek to develop one which will assimilate the single proprietorship no less than the large corporation. The concept which we seek is, however, relevant only to economic activity, so that we need feel no obligation to define the firm or the household in the same terms that a sociologist or political scientist might adopt.[1] For the moment discussion will proceed in terms of households and firms rather than governmental units, consideration of which will be postponed.

The elaboration of a concept of the organizational unit could fill a volume and distract our attention from the analysis which we have been pursuing. We have already examined certain of its aspects in the preceding chapter, and we shall now incorporate these aspects in a formulation which, while brief, should prove sufficient for our purposes.

The relevant characteristics of organizational units are these:

1. They bring individuals together in symbiotic relationships, whose activities are coördinated through a common revenue and a common budget decision. (These decisions, as has been pointed

[1] Our concept should not, however, *conflict* with concepts of these organizational units which are adopted for other purposes, if it is to permit some higher level of abstraction.

out, are always in the process of being remade.) The purposes of economic organization are subject to definition by the participants themselves, but in the nature of our foregoing analysis it is clear that a major (if not the primary) purpose *must* be to provide an income stream to the participants. Other objectives coexist, but the income objective is essential to their realization. Indeed, an organizational unit is something which is common to all fields of social relations, but it has economic relevance *only* when it affects income flow.

2. The coördination of a number of individuals in an organizational unit is achieved through a complex of bargains which is subject to two necessary conditions: (a) for each participant the cost of agreement on the terms offered must be less than the cost of disagreement and (b) the aggregate outflows which are the consequence of the terms of bargains must equal the aggregate inflows (including changes in assets and liabilities), which likewise are the resultant of the terms of bargains.

The nature of this organizational bargaining we encountered in the previous chapter. Each participant seeks to gain sufficient control over the organization (that is, to create a sufficient inducement to agree on his terms on the part of the other participants) to achieve a larger measure of his own aspirations. The objective and methods of the organizational unit are thus bent by the aspirations and relative bargaining powers of those who compose the unit, as these reinforce or contend against each other. But in this interplay of ambition and power (though the ambition may be ascetic and the power feeble), each individual is limited in his achievement by the necessity of allowing to others a sufficient share in the scarce resources accruing to the unit to induce their continuing adherence (creating a cost of agreement less than a cost of disagreement). And if the adherence prices *required* by all the participants add up to a sum greater than the resources available for distribution, the organization as it then exists must collapse, since the inflows do not permit outflows of this magnitude, and the necessary balance between the two flows cannot be achieved at the required level.

3. The function of coördinating the individual bargains among participants into a complex of bargains satisfying these two conditions belongs to a group of individuals whom we call management. Management *is* whatever individuals perform this coördinating role. The *terms* of the bargains struck (the decisions which are made in any area of operation of the organizational unit) are not peculiarly a function of management, however. Those terms are a function of the aspirations and relative bargaining powers of the groups involved. They involve the managerial function only to the extent that the terms of each bargain must not be inconsistent with the terms of all other bargains, in the complex of bargains which defines the unit's operations. (Thus, *whatever* decisions are made in the unit, *whatever* bargains are struck among the participants, the function of coördinating decisions and bargains remains, and is the function of management.) [2]

[2] This formulation represents a distinct departure from the conclusions presented in my book, *Union Challenge to Management Control* (Harper & Brothers, 1948), where I regarded the decision-making process as the management function, breaking it down into the four aspects of direction, administration, execution, and compliance. One corollary of the thesis there presented, which troubled some readers, was that it seemed to confer on the lowliest employee of a company some powers which would have to be called managerial. This corollary I myself was perfectly willing to admit, and indeed it seemed to have more meaning than any attempt to draw the line at some arbitrary level of employees (such as first-line foreman), asserting that all below that line were nonmanagement and all above it were management. The management *function* seemed to permeate an organization irrespective of such arbitrary lines. Moreover, I specifically took note of the fact that some writers had made coördination the chief management function, but went on myself to conclude that coördination was not a separable function, but was an ingredient of the decision-making process itself. In that book, the major conclusion derived was that unions were sharing in the managerial function, in the sense that they were participating in a variety of decisions within the firm and there was no logical ground for preventing their participation on an even broader front. To the extent that decisions on matters of wages, hours, promotions, workloads, and so on, were managerial matters before the unions entered, they remained managerial matters after the unions arrived, and the unions shared in their determination.

The present formulation, in the text above, so nearly reverses these conclusions as to preserve their significance! It now seems clear to me that precisely *because* decision making characterizes all participants in the organizational process, it cannot be called the function of any particular group. Decision making in fact is only the attempted or actual striking of bargains, as subsequent analysis will attempt to show more clearly. The decisions relate to the continual reformulation

In small units the coördination *may* be achieved by council of all the participants, but even in small units it is customary for some person to be recognized as having principal coördinating authority. It is to be stressed that the coördination here referred to is not simply a technological or supervisory role; only part of its concern is the integrating of specialized skills and abilities and tasks. Equally important for economic analysis, it involves the coördination of *bargains,* making consistent with each other the terms of many separate bargains, insuring that the promised allocations out of the given scarcity conditions of the unit do not exceed the resources available for actual allocation. (Scarce resources include both money, standing for economic goods, and prestige, but it is only the former about which the economist is concerned so that he need consider the latter only in so far as it affects the flows of income.)

4. In its coördinating role, management makes bargains not only with those whose demands constitute claims on the income stream (and who thus are party to the budget decision) but also with those who contribute to the income stream (and who thus are party to the revenue decision). The various parties to production within a firm—the employees, the capital contributors, the suppliers of raw and semifinished materials—cannot themselves strike bargains with the firm's customers. Instead, management serves as the control point in the flows of funds, to whom are channeled all receipts (the consequences of bargains with customers) and by

---

of the revenue and budget decisions. In this sense, then, they constitute the terms of relationship, and obviously all those who are related are in a position to affect those terms through the exercise of their bargaining power. But it is confusing to call this kind of bargaining "management."

Coördination, instead of being subsumed in the decision-making process, as I once thought, becomes the only *distinctive* function of an isolable group whom we call management. The number of individual (and group) bargains which must be made in an organizational unit do not organize themselves into a consistent complex; there must be someone to perform the function of maintaining consistency, by manipulating first one bargain and then the other. It is this function of coördination—inescapable and functionally isolable, as decision making is not isolable, which characterizes management.

whom are made all disbursements (the consequences of bargains with suppliers).

5. Conceptually, initiative can be exercised and innovations introduced by any of the participants to the complex of bargains. There is no theoretical reason why a labor union, for example, might not demand that an automobile company with which it has a bargaining relationship embark on research on the atomic powering of vehicles, or modify the design of its cars, or locate a new plant in an area where a number of the union's members are unemployed, producing a product unfamiliar to the company's present customers but familiar to the idle members' work experience.

In practice, however, there is a good reason why initiative and innovation are so peculiarly feasible for management (in contrast to other functional groups) that they may be conceived as management functions without losing much of conceptual reliability. Because of its coördinating function, management is the only group of functionaries in a position to realize the consistency of potential changes with the existing complex of bargains, and it is the only group functionally required to calculate the effect of change on the total existing complex of bargains.

This means that (1) whenever management sees the possibility of initiating actions which do not conflict with the terms of existing bargains, it is free to do so; it can raise new capital, hire additional employees, engage new suppliers, embark on new lines of activity in its own discretion, using the resources of the organization for this purpose, as long as such actions do not contradict bargains already struck; no other functional group is similarly equipped to act at its own discretion; (2) whenever management undertakes such actions, one inescapable consideration which faces it is the effect which the contemplated moves will have on inflows and outflows, that is, the level of activity at which inflows and outflows will be maintained in balance, on which depends the continuity of the organization as it then exists.

Even though, for these reasons, it is feasible to consider initiative and innovation as peculiarly functions of management, what motivates management to initiate and innovate must be sought in the aspirations of individuals, and beyond that, in the cultural conditioning of individual's aspirations.

6. Management is not simply a neutral agent which coördinates bargains in the interests of others. It is itself a party in interest in the bargains struck, and bargains against all other symbionts not only to perform its function of achieving a working organization through coördinating the relationships of others but to achieve its own aspirations as well. These aspirations relate to income and job satisfaction both.

7. The position and authority of the management (coördinating) person or persons is commonly underwritten in law or fixed in custom. In the firm, managerial authority derives from the ownership function. In the single proprietorship or partnership, ownership and management are commonly joined in the same people. In the corporation, management achieves its position by virtue of a legal relationship to the owner-stockholders, requiring their approval (however *pro forma*) as a condition of its exercise of authority. The legal presumption is that its power shall be wielded in behalf of the owners from whom it derives authority, but in fact as long as it can strike bargains with the owners, as with other functional groups, and satisfy the terms of the bargains struck, it can wield the power of unfettered initiation and innovation as discussed above.

In the household, it is the adult male who in western society is normally recognized as the managerial head. For some purposes this authority is recognized in law, as in the requirement of a husband's (rather than a wife's) signature on certain legal documents, and the nonlegal nature of contracts entered into by minors without parental consent. The small size of households normally minimizes the need for centralized management, however, and permits the sharing of the function in a family council. The lack of economists' interest in the economic management of the household has left this an area about which relatively little is known, empirically. It would appear, however, that the locus of managerial authority within the household and the nature of its exercise would prove almost as rewarding topics for investigation as their counterparts in the theory of the firm.

In the cases of both firm and household, managerial *authority* can of course be delegated. Junior executives and housewives alike are apt to operate within a budgetary framework, with power to effect bargains at their discretion within the limitations of the budget. Each may possess the authority to make capital expenditures below some stated figure. The *responsibility* which management (whoever it may be) cannot delegate, however, is that of coördinating all bargains with the income flows, of effecting such a system of related bargains that the resulting inflows and outflows—always necessarily in balance—balance at a level and reflect a quality of activity which permits the satisfactory realization of aspirations and the avoidance of risks of all those on whom the organization depends for its continued functioning.

The concept of the economic unit (firm or household) which is here adopted is, then, that of a center of authority for coördinating the bargains which together make up the revenue decision (inflows) and the budget decision (outflows). Whether those whose bargains are coördinated are to be considered part of the firm, or whether only the owners from whom managerial authority legally derives are to be construed as "the firm," or whether the persons exercising the managerial authority are to be so identified is a terminological matter of no significance for economic analysis. For economic analysis the important concept is that of the function of coördinating bargains to balance inflows and outflows at preferred levels, a function exercised by individuals whom (whoever they may be) we call management. The firm is simply the locus of the revenue and budget decisions.

CHAPTER 10

The Firm: The Balance of Flows and the Revenue Decision

IN exploring the relationship between bargains and flows in the organizational unit which we call the firm, we shall necessarily be concerned with the revenue and budget decisions, those continuing streams of choices as to the allocation of productive time and money resources. But the revenue decision and the budget decision are interrelated. The sale of services is governed by the expenditures which must be made; selling bargains are influenced by buying bargains. No less is it true that expenditure decisions are governed by the income which one receives, so that buying bargains are influenced by selling bargains. This interaction between the revenue and budget decisions we embody in the concept of the projected balance.

We have defined inflows as current receipts
+ any increase in liabilities
+ assets applied.

The projected balance is the planned contribution of each of these three sources, adding to an inflow sufficient to cover all the planned outflows at a satisfactory level of operations. This does not necessarily imply some precise figure (though in the larger firms, at least, the practice of budget planning is likely to set a quite definite goal) but rather a *condition* of satisfactory income flows. Nor does it take

173

into account only the level at which balance is achieved; the composition of the inflow and outflow streams, no less than the level at which they balance, is involved. The determination of the projected balance, while specific to a given period, is not arrived at in abstraction from the firm's time stream; it is governed by what the firm has been doing in the past and what it expects to be doing in the future. It constitutes the inflows necessary to permit a satisfactory achievement by all those on whom the organization, under its present leadership, depends for the fulfillment of the projected course of action. What is "satisfactory," both to management and the other participants in the firm, depends on their aspirations and alternatives (what they want to achieve and what their possibilities are for achieving it), which is another way of saying that deciding what is "satisfactory" involves one's continuing adjustment to his bargaining power position.

The firm's plans and the determination of the balance of flows necessary for their realization are the subject of internal bargaining (1) among members of management, and (2) between members of management and the other participants in the organization. In essence, the firm's projected outflows (based on such bargains) determine the inflow which is necessary to achieve a balance at a satisfactory level of operations. These projected outflows are accepted with various degrees of finality. Some expenditures must surely be made if the firm is to continue operations at all (wage obligations, for example). But expansion plans, contingency reserves, and dividend declarations are more tentative and can be adjusted as necessary to conform to what inflows make possible. The firmness with which such planned expenditures are held to determines the inflow needed and hence the projected balance.

The projected balance is realizable, however, only through the terms of specific bargains, and even more specifically, through the price component of bargains. This does not mean that firms are concerned only with price, since other elements than price determine the costs of agreement and disagreement of buyers and sellers, respectively, on which depends whether a bargain will be made at all and if so on what terms. It does mean that firms will seek to manipulate their bargaining power so that the price component of the aggregate of selling bargains will constitute an inflow adequate to cover the price component of the aggregate of buying bargains.

At any moment and at any level of operations the firm's inflows and outflows must, *ex post*, be in balance. But at the projected level of income flow the firm's receipts and expenditures balance *ex ante*, as planned, and therefore must be accepted as indicating the most satisfactory performance considered likely of achievement (though not necessarily the most satisfactory performance conceivable), given the existing structure of aspirations and alternatives determining the distribution of relative bargaining powers in the society.

It may become evident, during the passage of time for which the projection has been made, that the balance which is actually being realized differs from the projected balance. The deviation may reflect a performance superior to that which had been expected, so that management need only modify its projected balance without modifying its business behavior. But the deviation may also reflect a performance inferior to that which had been expected. Receipts from current production may be less than had been contemplated, so that if the desired level of activity is to be attained there must be an undesired transformation of assets from liquid reserves to inventories, or a greater application of assets than is deemed desirable, or an increase in borrowings. The same unpalatable contingencies may be faced if outflows prove greater than had been projected. Alternatively, the firm's level of activity may have to be readjusted downward to reduce outflows, resulting in a business performance which is less satisfactory both to management and to those whose incomes are adversely affected. A partial disintegration of the firm may occur, as it does, for example, whenever trained workers or accustomed suppliers and subcontractors are laid off.

Escape from these unwelcome alternatives may, however, be found in management's attempt to manipulate its bargaining power to modify the terms of either its selling bargains or buying bargains.

Its aim will be to achieve an inflow-outflow balance reflecting a performance superior to that which is actually being realized even if inferior to that which was projected. This new balance may or may not be accompanied by a change in the level of activity. It is likely to be set at a higher aggregate money level when outflows exceed inflows and are less susceptible to adjustment, and at a lower level when outflows exceed inflows and are more susceptible to adjustment. We shall call this new balance the preferred balance —preferred to that which is actually being realized. Choice of the level and composition of the preferred balance obviously depends on judgments as to where management's relative bargaining advantage is greater.

There are thus three balances with which we operate: first, the *projected* balance, the *ex ante* planning of inflows and outflows to balance (1) at an aggregate level and (2) with a composition that reflect the most satisfactory performance considered possible under the circumstances. This is followed by the *actual* balance which time reveals and which may be superior or inferior to that projected. Finally, if the actual balance is not accepted, a *preferred* balance is sought, one which represents management's attempt to adjust its bargaining power to achieve a performance superior to that which is being realized (the actual) even if inferior to that originally planned (the projected). The preferred balance thus becomes the new projected balance, which again—through the actual balance—time will reveal to have been warranted or unwarranted, leading to a new preferred balance which becomes the new projected balance, and so on, in continuous succession. This process of revision may be formalized, as in some firms where provision is made for quarterly review by an appointed committee, or it may be made informally, as by a single individual's "feel" of the situation.

Inability to realize the projected balance means by definition a poorer performance than had been expected. Inflows have proved inadequate to match outflows at the desired and anticipated level of activity, or such a balance is realizable only through an undesired shift in the composition of allocations (from working reserves to inventories, for example). Failure to achieve the projected balance thus affects management's bargaining power like a reduction in income. This means that initially its bargaining power is weakened in its selling transactions and strengthened in its buying transactions. The consequence is apt to be an attempted *manipulation* of bargaining power to restore its advantage in the production decision and an attempted *renegotiation* of the terms of bargains in the budget decision, where its power has been increased by its adversity. We consider only the former in this chapter.

The attempt to manipulate bargaining power in selling transactions is not, of course, limited to situations of failure to achieve the projected balance. A drive to ward off such an unhappy contingency often motivates managements to a continuing contemplation—even in periods when targets are easily realized—of how bargaining power can be manipulated to their advantage when, or before, the need arises. The manipulations in which we are principally interested are those involving current receipts from the sale of goods and services.

THE REVENUE DECISION

The revenue decision in the case of the individual involves his allocation of time and determines his present income. There are other sources of income than the sale of his services, to be sure, such as return on past investments, but for analytical purposes we incorporate such supplementary income in the revenue decision by viewing it as a determinant of how much of his time he will sell and under what conditions the sale will take place.

The revenue decision in the case of the firm is analogous. It involves the allocation of the firm's productive time (capacity) and determines its present income. As in the case of the individual, the decision as to the terms of sale of its goods (incorporating the services of its participants) will be affected by the existence of income from other sources. It will also be affected, as in the case of the individual, by expectations as to the terms on which future sales may be possible or as to anticipated income.

In our set of concepts, then, the revenue decision constitutes the continuing management of the relationship between the terms of selling bargains and the inflow stream. As we have seen, the size of the inflow stream which is set as the target is some (minimum) amount which will permit a satisfactory realization of the stream of aspirations of those whose adherence to the organization is necessary for the achievement of the goals of the present management. To realize this income the firm may seek to manipulate its bargaining power in the transactions which make realization possible.

Numerous devices are available to a firm for increasing a buyer's cost of disagreement or lowering his cost of agreement. The most important means of increasing the cost of disagreement are through changes in its line of products, through product differentiation, and through advertising and marketing practices.

LINE OF PRODUCTS

Economic analysis usually proceeds on the assumption that a firm produces only one product. In practice even small firms typically produce a number of products and a large corporation may carry several hundred. A company's receipts are thus normally derived from bargains involving the sale of a variety of items, opening up the possibility of manipulating bargaining power in a variety of situations to stimulate inflows. Product variety thus gives more than one string to a firm's bow: a decline in the sales of certain products, whether a secular or cyclical or seasonal decline, will have its adverse effect on the size of the inflow, but this adverse effect can be at least partially offset if other products have been chosen to yield— or can be made to yield—a concurrent increase in sales.

A secularly declining demand for product A (say radios), reducing receipts, can be met by the secularly rising demand for product B (say television). Product innovation is thus important. A cyclically declining demand for product X (say machine tools) might be disastrous if that were a firm's only product; the inflow necessary to hold together the organization would melt away. But at least the heart of the organization might be maintained if the company also produced products Y and Z (say firing mechanisms for military artillery and components for road-building equipment), the demand for which might be stimulated by countercyclical governmental expenditures. Product diversification is thus also a safeguard.

More generally, a company can never anticipate all influences which might operate to reduce its bargaining power in particular markets, cutting down the minimum inflow needed to maintain the organization's value as a going concern. A multiproduct line allows management to choose those products most amenable, under the given circumstances, to a price or quality treatment to increase bargaining power to restore diminished income.

By the judicious management of its product line a firm thus not only maintains alternatives which, because more desirable than other alternatives in its own or in its rivals' lines, carry a higher cost to the consumer of disagreement on the firm's terms; by substitutions or additions to the product line a firm likewise lessens its dependence on the consumers of any one of its products, thereby lowering its own cost of disagreement on their terms below what it would be if survival depended on that product only. A styling fiasco in the Pontiac car would be less damaging to General Motors, since it could continue to count on Chevrolet, Buick, Oldsmobile, and Cadillac, not to mention its numerous nonautomobile products, than such a misstep would be to an independent automobile company which relies on its single line of cars.

In addition to its insurance value, a multiproduct line offers the possibility of expanding a firm's size. If firms were limited to the exploitation of one market, the size of most would be severely restricted. Beyond some point corporate growth depends on branching out into new product lines.

The judgment as to which collection of product alternatives provides a firm both insurance against unfavorable price bargains (whether because of changes in the aspirations, alternatives, or incomes of its customers) and opportunity for growth (if this should be sought), is roughly equivalent in the household unit to a worker's choice of occupation. Just as in that instance the choice may be haphazard and unplanned, so too in the case of the firm's decisions as to its product line. But as in the case of the worker, the opportunity for planning exists and constitutes a fundamental means of manipulating one's relative bargaining power to his advantage.[1]

PRODUCT DIFFERENTIATION

Closely related to management of the product line is the differentiation of one's products from the competing products of other producers. The two problems, indistinguishable if a differentiated product is considered the same as a "different" product, can be distinguished if one considers the stages in the decision-making process. We can conceive of a management deciding to add air-conditioning equipment to its sales line, as a means of supplementing the sales of other electrical appliances or of taking the place of some item the sales of which are faltering, without at the same time reaching any decision as to the kind of air conditioner it will put

[1] To pursue the analogy further by presenting its contrasts, however, a firm can be multiproduct in a way that workers can scarcely be multioccupational, and a firm can change its line of products in a way that workers can scarcely change their occupations. Moreover, new products can be devised and held in readiness for a need not presently felt more easily than workers can develop new skills in anticipation of a future obsolescence of those now relied on.

On this last point, we shall discuss the research expenditures of firms more fully in the next chapter. But an example from *Business Week* of September 12, 1953, underscores the manner in which product development is regarded as a bargaining weapon in the business community. "Reichhold Chemicals, Inc., . . . announced that it has developed a synthetic resin metal finish that uses plain tap water as a solvent. . . . If this new resin (called Hydrophen) is all Reichhold says it is, it'll mean tremendous savings for many industries that put clear or colored finishes on metal. . . . Major paint companies are frankly skeptical about Reichhold's new product. It'll take at least a year, they say, before Hydrophen can be tested thoroughly enough to prove its worth. . . . Though Reichhold's announcement left paint companies unconvinced, it didn't leave them cold. As a result of Hydrophen's debut, at least three paint manufacturers are ready to come out with new products of their own—products that they have been nursing along in secret, ready for a rainy day."

on the market. This is a line-of-product decision. The choice of *type* of product with which it will compete against other air-conditioning manufacturers is a matter involving the differentiation of its product. The product-styling decision can be changed again and again without disturbing the product-line decision.

The nature of product differentiation is too well known to warrant any extensive discussion. It is designed to assure consumer agreement on one's terms, whether or not the price asked is higher than a competitor's. If the quality characteristics of one product cannot be duplicated in another, to the extent they are desirable they raise the cost of disagreement on one's terms and improve his bargaining power. This kind of bargaining tactic is so universal in the American economy that it is taken for granted. To pick examples at random, the Kelly-Springfield Tire Company advertises that "you'd be amazed at the number of tire deals completed on the basis of price alone," and then urges: "Look, not for just a 'minus' in price, but for a 'plus' in mileage." The Elwell-Parker Electric Company advertises trucks that are "built up to quality, not down to price." The Crane Company reminds its public that "It's not what you *pay*—it's what it costs" that is important. "There probably isn't a thing you buy that you couldn't buy cheaper," but the wise buyer looks for differences among products and foregoes "merely price-tag buying."

There is another aspect of product differentiation than distinguishing one's product from his competitors'.

The introduction of new products into the American economy involves two simultaneous movements: (1) a gradual reduction in the relative price of the good, as mass production methods permit the tapping of mass markets; (2) an increase in the number of models of the good (from "economy" to "deluxe") as producers seek to develop a complete selling line of the particular good, with each model representing a different level of quality for different income groups. In this second movement we encounter product differentiation of a different variety than that which is regarded primarily as a weapon against one's business competitors, the means by which one producer can win greater success than another, the method by which he might reduce the effectiveness of any price competition of rivals. Here product differentiation arises not from competition among producers but from socially induced comparisons among consumers, the desire of upper social and income groups to distinguish themselves from others. Product differentiation may thus be introduced by a single seller who is oblivious to the competition of other firms in order to enable him to enlarge his market by appealing to consumers of differing incomes on a quality basis. Few manufacturers of consumers' goods content themselves with producing a one-quality, one-price item. They customarily deal with a spectrum of quality characteristics and a corresponding spectrum of prices for the same generic good.[2]

If we consider demand curves not for the generic good—automobiles, for example—but for the differentiated products—Buicks, Chryslers, Fords—the aggregate effect of a price change is likely to be as the price analysis suggests, but in some instances the mechanics may be very different. Instead of a price decline leading present consumers of that article to demand more or inducing others *in addition to* present buyers to become consumers, it may *tend* to drop that article from the consumption schedule of one social-income group and to add it to the consumption schedules of the group next lower on the social-income scale. Since in the latter group there are always more than in the former group, the result is likely to be an expansion of the market in the long run.[3] But the high-income group is not left unsatisfied. A new species of the good, of superior quality, is developed to meet the demand for "something better,"

[2] ". . . manufacturers of many articles in common use divide products into classes which may be called price classes. Products falling within each of many price classes are supposed to sell only to certain roughly demarcated income groups of the community. Allowance is made for the fact that there is overlapping at the margin and that an appeal to marginal buyers is always desirable." C. Clive Saxton, *The Economics of Price Determination* (Oxford University Press, 1942), p. 40.

[3] The Hicksian income effect of a price decline may thus be quite significant. For important classes of goods, price changes can act as income changes, particularly in the long run.

at the old or perhaps even a higher price. The quality spectrum of consumer goods is expanded to meet the psychological compulsion for distinguishing one's position in society by consumption standards. Such a pattern of consumer response is limited to those goods which have status significance, but as the sociologists would tell us this covers considerable ground.

The same considerations lie behind the phenomenon of producers' "upgrading their products." As consumer income rises over the years, low-quality items tend to drop out of the budgets even of the (relatively) low-income receivers. Even the latter can afford merchandise of superior quality. With rising income there thus tends to be an upward shift of the quality spectrum; not only do more individuals move into upper income brackets, but those in the lower brackets have more to spend and can afford goods of better quality.

Product differentiation is one of the most important methods by which sellers can improve their bargaining power vis-a-vis particular groups of buyers, distinguishing their offerings not only from the alternatives which other sellers are offering to the same group of buyers but from alternatives which they themselves are offering to other groups of buyers.

Modification of the product line and differentiation of the product as means of a firm's improving its bargaining position relative to buyers can perhaps be joined in the single concept of the product cycle, which proceeds in four stages. First must come the innovation, the new product, which at the start usually commands a premium price (at which, however, the firm may or may not make a profit, depending on developmental and production costs). In the second stage there is imitation by rivals with a consequent fall in the price. Product differentiation among competitors enters. This is followed by a period in which the weakest of the rivals are weeded out and those remaining develop a price line of products—differentiation within the firm to meet the quality demands of varying income groups. In the final stage prices drop and quality improves over time in response to technological changes in the product and the production process, and the competitive drive by sellers to improve their bargaining power by lowering cost of agreement or raising cost of disagreement on their terms; the low-end items tend to drop out of the picture with rising per capita income. A firm can break into this product cycle at any point, and its competitive behavior (its effort to manipulate its bargaining power to increase its advantage) is dictated by the stage at which it breaks into the cycle.

Advertising and Marketing Practices

Little need be said concerning this method of influencing bargaining power. Through advertising and promotion sellers seek to affect the aspirations of consumers or their evaluation of the alternatives facing them. Through such marketing devices as full-line forcing and exclusive dealerships they also seek to influence the amount of dealer selling effort which is put behind their products. By these methods they hope to increase an already existing cost of disagreement or to create one where none previously existed by persuading the buying public of the special advantages of their products.

Pricing

If modification of the product line, product differentiation, and promotion constitute the major methods of influencing customers' costs of disagreement on the firm's terms, it is through the manipulation of price that firms can most easily affect buyers' costs of agreement. The familiar "elasticity of demand" is simply a measure of the extent to which a firm's bargaining power improves as it drops its terms, thus making the buyer's cost of agreement lower (relative to an unchanging cost of disagreement).

There is no basis, however, for viewing price as of special significance in the bargaining process. It is simply one manipulable variable, like product differentiation and promotion, designed to influence the relative bargaining powers of buyers and sellers. The bargain is entered into not only because of price but because of other elements such as the quality of the good or service. The relationship between price and quality is such as to preclude one from saying whether price or quality is more important to the bargain. Obviously, at *some* asking price the buyer would refuse the symbiotic relationship, since the cost of agreement would exceed the cost of disagreement, and in this sense price is determinative. But equally obviously, with *some* different set of product characteristics the buyer would also have refused the relationship, since the cost of disagreement would have been less than the cost of agreement, and in this sense nonprice elements are decisive.

Price is thus no more significant in the bargaining relationship than any other variable affecting the costs of disagreement and agreement. It warrants the economist's special interest only because on the price component of the totality of a firm's bargains depends the balance between the money inflow and the money outflow, depends the relationship between its revenue decision and its budget decision. Price has no more influence than any other variable *in determining the individual bargain*, but in an exchange economy it is the *flow of prices*—resulting from the total number of individual bargains—which determines the level of activity of the economic unit. The nonprice elements of a firm's activity do not require any objective equality between inflow and outflow as a condition of the unit's operations; indeed, we have no objective measure for such "real" costs and utilities. But the money elements of a unit's operations *must* be balanced as between inflows and outflows, and the manner in which and level at which this balance is achieved are determinative of the firm's life and growth. Regardless of the extent to which nonprice variables influence the terms of a firm's bargains (product characteristics in its selling bargains, job satisfaction in its bargains with labor), money inflows must balance money outflows, and the level of and method of achieving the balance are important.

Satisfactory price bargains are thus necessary to a firm's operations, but this does not mean that price necessarily *induces* the bargains which a firm makes. The manipulation of price affects both relative bargaining powers in the immediate bargain and the flow of income, but the same manipulation may not serve both ends equally well. The price offer required to conclude a bargain may not satisfactorily maintain the flow of income needed to keep operations at the level where such bargains can afford to be made. Or to maintain the flow of income necessary to operations at a desired level, price may be raised, though this reduces the firm's bargaining power. Firms which are caught between the millstones of rising costs and declining sales are thus faced with the dilemma of whether a cut in prices designed to increase their bargaining power vis-a-vis the buying public will at the same time produce a sufficient increase in total revenues to create a balance of receipts and expenditures at the required level of operations, or whether an increase in prices designed to offset rising costs will so reduce their relative bargaining power as to limit the number of sales and hence of total revenue to a figure which would balance outflows only at an unsatisfactory level of operations.[4]

Because of the relationship between price and income flows, we might expect that (as long as it produced at all) a firm would set its price as high as possible without at the same time creating a

[4] This dilemma will not always be resolved identically by the competitors in an industry. In the fall of 1953, for example, the wool carpet industry showed divergent managerial decisions. The price of carpet wools had been rising, reportedly by as much as 15 percent within a four- or five-month period. Mills were reported to have absorbed this added cost because of "sluggish" sales of carpets, but—said one management—"there is a limit to cost absorption for any reason." On September 29, Mohawk Carpet Mills announced a 3 to 6 percent increase in mill prices, to become effective October 15. The following day James Lees and Sons cut prices by an average of 6 percent, because of "realistic competition" (presumably lack of consumer interest). On October 1 Alexander Smith, Inc., while maintaining its price schedule, sought to maintain a satisfactory balance between inflows and outflows by cutting back production and laying off 600 of the 4000 employees at its Yonkers mill, a move explained as one "to keep inventories of finished goods at proper levels in view of generally low sales in the carpet industry during the summer months." With the rest of the industry failing to follow its lead, thus weakening its relative bargaining position vis-a-vis the consumer, Mohawk at that time reversed its action and rescinded its price increases. *The New York Times*, September 30, October 2, 1953; *Business Week*, November 21, 1953.

cost of agreement on its terms greater than a cost of disagreement. This would assure the bargain, on which inflows depend, but would also insure that the inflow stream ran at as high a level as was possible under the circumstances. Such a formulation would hold, however, only if a firm could segregate its bargains, dealing with each customer individually and setting whatever price met the above conditions in each instance. Unfortunately for the firm, it cannot always segregate its buyers so neatly, and the terms offered to one often must also be offered to another.

Nevertheless, there are some opportunities for most firms to discriminate among buyers. Those selling in more than one region may lower their price in an area where their relative bargaining power is weaker, to induce agreement by lowering the cost of agreement, without changing price in other areas. Prices may be set differently for different *classes* of buyers. Professor Joel Dean has listed the net prices resulting from the schedule of distributor discounts allowed by the manufacturers of spark plugs, ranging all the way from a price of 6 cents per plug to the automobile assemblers (for original equipment) to 65 cents for a single plug to the individual car owner, with a variety of prices inside this range to national distributors, mail-order houses, secondary jobbers, retailers, and garages.[5] In some instances price differentials may be allowed on an individual basis by such devices as shading list prices, applying discounts, absorbing freight costs, or negotiating trade-in allowances. In the period of surplus stocks of automobiles in the latter part of 1953, one automobile dealer was reported to have granted a trade-in of $640.87 on a goat!

In contrast to such opportunities for price discrimination, prices are often quoted publicly. In these instances the firm is faced with the necessity of calculating for how many consumers, at the quoted price, the cost of agreement is lower than the cost of disagreement and whether the income so derived is satisfactory relative to the outflow contemplated, and how many more or fewer bargains

[5] Joel Dean, *Managerial Economics* (New York: Prentice-Hall, Inc., 1951), p. 521.

might be made at a lower or a higher price and whether the income so derived would be more satisfactory relative to the outflow required or contemplated than the first position. It is this kind of decision which is pictured in the usual marginal analysis of economic theory, but typically such analysis takes the situation as determined for the firm rather than something over which it has some (but an indeterminate) control.

There are some types of operations in which price constitutes a firm's most manipulable variable in its effort to improve its bargaining power relative to commensal rivals. These are the bidding relationships in which the services of goods offered are relatively homogeneous, usually because of standards or specifications imposed by the buyer and enforceable under contract law. Construction is an example of a field in which price may become the only determinant of which seller gains the relationship, once the competition has been narrowed to those which can meet the specifications imposed.

Where product differentiation (quality differences) is important, however, and this embraces most of manufacturing activity, or where the number of rivals is sufficiently small so that the actions of one can be expected to influence the behavior of the others, there is a marked tendency for the attempted manipulation of bargaining power to be confined, in the short run, largely to the nonprice elements of style changes and advertising and promotion. There is substantial evidence that except in the cases of homogeneous products and a field of many sellers firms customarily regard price cutting as a last-resort means of increasing bargaining power. Moreover, price increases as a means of augmenting income are also likely to be last-resort methods except in periods of unusual demand (as in the postwar automobile market) or in the face of general price increases, both cases where there is no fear that price advances will adversely affect one's bargaining power.

The emphasis on short-run price stability has several explanations. Two reasons are dominant, however.

1. In manipulating bargaining power by promotion or by making quality changes, price need not be tampered with. A successful

manipulation usually permits more sales at the same price and sometimes even at a higher price, thus giving rise to an augmented inflow. Outflows are not necessarily increased proportionally or even at all, since the appeal of product styling or innovation is not correlated with cost of production.

In manipulating bargaining power by modifying the price, however, management necessarily accepts the risk that—even should more customers be induced to buy—the result may be worse than the situation it was designed to correct. The additional revenue from new customers may not offset that lost from the price reduction to former customers.

Price manipulation affects (or profits from) the relative bargaining powers of buyer and seller in *particular* transactions, but where such transactions cannot be segregated (where price discrimination is not possible), the effect of price changes on the *aggregate* of bargains must be determined by the firm before it can assess the costs of agreement and disagreement on the terms of any *one* buyer. For price changes to be effective on the aggregate of bargains they must have a downward elasticity and an upward inelasticity. Price cuts increase the total outflow (as production expands) and simultaneously lower the per unit inflow. Whether they are successful depends on whether the number of transactions at the lower rate not only make up for the lower per unit return on the original level of sales but also cover the additional costs incident to increased output (and if the manipulation was designed to improve a bad situation, make a further net contribution to the inflow stream). A 10 percent reduction in price must be met not simply by a 10 percent but by a greater increase in sales, except in those rare instances where the additional output involves no additional cost.

On the other hand, a price advance reduces total outflow (as production contracts) and increases per unit inflow. Whether it is successful depends on whether the smaller number of sales, even at the higher rate, is sufficient to cover costs, even at the lower total. While something more than a 10 percent decline in sales can be tolerated in response to a 10 percent increase in prices without worsening the profit position (except in those rare instances where a reduction in output involves no reduction in cost), the difference cannot be great, since the decline in costs is less than proportionate to the decline in output, due to fixed costs. If the price increase was designed to augment the inflow, then certainly a relatively inelastic demand is required.

Most producers uncertain of the price elasticity of the demand for their products would be inclined to prefer other methods of increasing revenue which, even though involving additional outlay, do not threaten the existing inflow by tampering with the per-unit rate.[6] It is primarily in the absence of other alternatives (as notably in the case of small businesses) that price manipulation is resorted to. In particular, we may expect that in those years when per capita income is rising (so that consumer expenditure on any article carries less threat to standards of living), managements will regard as good strategy quality improvements rather than price reductions. The latter can be postponed to the lean years, when the relevance of individual expenditures to the consumer's standard of living is more apparent, or to the long run, when cost-reducing methods of production remove the risk element from cutting the per-unit rate of return. When to this attitude is added the frequently alleged belief on the part of large numbers of firms (for reasons discussed below) that their demand curves are inelastic downward and

[6] Price manipulation thus necessarily carries two risks: (1) whether the lower price will attract more customers (the bargaining power consideration), and (2) assuming that it does, will it add to inflows (the income consideration). Quality changes require an answer only to the first question, since more customers automatically add to inflow.

Where quality changes entail costs over and above those that would have been incurred in the absence of change, then indeed it is necessary to ask a second question, comparable to that required by the price case: whether the additional revenue will offset the additional cost. But the cost increase bears no functional relation to the increased sales appeal, in contrast to the price-reduction case, where the price cut is necessarily functionally related to the increased sales appeal; quality changes thus give management a greater degree of freedom to manipulate bargaining power without risking the preferred balance. Price manipulation is therefore likely to be reserved for situations where quality changes are not possible or where quality changes alone are considered inadequate.

elastic upward—the opposite of the conditions for effective price manipulation—then it is understandable why price stability is preferred to price variation.

2. Where the number of sellers is sufficiently small so that the effort of one to manipulate bargaining power to its advantage has a measurable effect on the others, such manipulation is almost certain to invite reaction. The most common reaction takes the form of retaliatory price cuts—a form of commensal bidding. As Professor Fellner has shown,[7] the probable consequence of such a close-knit relationship is a kind of quasi bargaining among the rivals. Each is anxious to avoid becoming caught in a price war in which its income will be squeezed, endangering the stability of the enterprise. Over time the commensal rivals will therefore feel each other out to find within what limits price changes may be made without evoking retaliatory action. The result of this quasi bargaining (commensal quasi agreement for individual symbiotic bargaining) will be to narrow the uses to which price may be put as a bargaining device, emphasizing the nonprice variables which may be manipulated without fear of a retaliation that threatens the income stream. Sellers in such circumstances view themselves as facing a demand curve which is inelastic downward, since price cuts designed to increase their bargaining power with consumers simply evoke counteraction by their rivals that leave them roughly where they were vis-a-vis the buying public. (At the same time there is no confidence on their part that price increases will be matched by competitors, with the consequence that the firm increasing its price fears that it will lose much of its trade to its rivals—a conception of upward price elasticity.)

This limitation on the use of price as a means of manipulating relative bargaining powers in situations where the number of rivals is small enough to permit a predictable effect and reaction, was illustrated by a former president of the International Paper Com-

[7] William Fellner, *Competition Among the Few* (New York: Alfred A. Knopf, Inc., 1949).

pany in testimony before a committee of the House of Representatives.[8] Speaking of the market for newsprint, he related the manner in which the several rivals were driven to match each other's price reductions, sometimes with ruinous results:

I was saying that [newsprint] manufacturer B has a contract under which he can collect $45 from his publisher, his customer, but manufacturer A is supplying the competing publisher at $40, and I have said that under those circumstances, where the competing manufacturer is supplying newsprint at $40, the competing publisher is getting newsprint at $40 from a substantial manufacturer, that the manufacturer who has a right to collect $45, if he uses good judgment, is certain to waive that right and collect no more than his customer's competitor is paying.

After all, publishers are the only customers for newsprint and the years have been few in which there have been enough publishers to go round. The result? Manufacturer B falls in line and charges $40, too. Not because he has agreed with A, whom he may detest—and that is not an overstatement—not because $40 is a fair price, not because he can afford to sell at $40—not because he does not wish he could afford to enforce his contract—not because he dared to enforce his $45 contract, but simply because as a practical matter he feels that he must sell as cheap as his competitor if he is to succeed in the long run. I do not recollect a single case where a North American manufacturer charged more than the market—and he has had plenty of opportunities recently.

I have already indicated, but I want to repeat that does not necessarily mean every manufacturer's price cut is met by all the others. But in the typical case, in the case where a substantial manufacturer cuts the price, the chances are that all the others will feel they have to meet it regardless of their contracts. Of course, that is what was done time and again throughout this period.

So much for manufacturer B collecting more than the market. How about manufacturer A selling for less than the market? The 12-year decline and the bankruptcy of a large part of the industry is a monument to the hopes of many manufacturers A that they could do just that and so fill their mills with orders while their competitors wept. I won't say it never worked, but it worked very seldom. Ordinarily manufac-

[8] Testimony of Archibald R. Graustein, in *Study of Monopoly Power,* Hearings before the Subcommittee on Study of Monopoly Power, Committee on the Judiciary, House of Representatives, Eighty-first Congress, second session, Serial No. 14, Part 6A (1950), pp. 554–559.

turer A finds out that his competitors meet his lower price and that instead of selling at less than the market he has merely lowered the market price. The instinct of self-preservation in most cases tells the other manufacturers that they must meet A's price, and the sooner the better, because if they meet it right off, they hold their business. If they do not lower their price, they lose the customer and they are likely to find pressure from other customers is too great and then they lower the price.

The consequence is to cause the manufacturers of newsprint to take into account the likely price retaliation of rival manufacturers, should they seek to increase their bargaining power relative to a publisher by price cutting:

If [the publishers] want to get paper at a low price they will shop around among the manufacturers for it. The manufacturers say to themselves, "Can I afford to give them paper at that price?" In deciding whether they can afford to give them paper at that price, they have to take into consideration what effect it will have on the general market for paper if they do it. If the Consolidated Paper Co. or Abitibi should come in here or go into New York and drop the price of paper any number of dollars a ton, at least when there is not a seller's market, it is practically certain that the rest of the industry would have to follow, and the price would be uniform again.

The fear of price retaliation thus acts as a brake on price competition. It would appear from the testimony of this former company executive that the newsprint manufacturers, while freely competing among themselves for newsprint contracts, were careful to keep their price concessions within a narrow "zone of tolerance" where price action did not elicit price reaction:

In the ordinary market these newsprint manufacturers keep expensive sales staffs on the job all the time trying to win a customer away from a competitor. . . . I can assure you as a matter of fact that uniformity of price is a practical necessity. Substantial uniformity, I do not mean down to the last dollar. In 1938 I think it was, or in some years, the Great Northern was $2 below the rest of the industry, and in another year it was $1 below, and the Great Northern is a big company, but it always had a tendency to—it has in the past, I do not think it does so much today—it has had a tendency to pride itself on being somewhat below.

In order to arrive at such a quasi understanding as to the limits of price competition, no collusion or formal agreement is required. Nothing more need be involved than a young suitor's understanding—gained in practice—of how late he can stay at his girl's home without arousing her father's ire, or the politician's experience with how far he can go in mudslinging to woo the voter without bringing on a retaliation in which his own reputation would suffer more than he is willing to accept.

For these two reasons—the risks to the income stream of manipulating price, due to fear of the uncertain symbiont response or the more certain commensal response—there is a considerable reluctance among many firms to use price as a bargaining device in the short run. The prevalence of this attitude or practice should not be overstressed, however. In the first place, the quasi-bargaining relationship makes possible price leadership, so that price manipulation may be resorted to by all rivals simultaneously, to strengthen their bargaining position vis-a-vis their total public. In the case of small numbers, a certain amount of price cutting may be accepted as a promotional device, available to all without fear of retaliation because carrying no threat to the income stream of any; the bargain sales of department stores fall in this category. Price reductions may be resorted to in order to clear inventories, particularly where style or model changes outdate them, as in the case of clothing and automobiles; again, such practices may be accepted by the trade and generally used without initiating a price war. Where there is a large number of rivals, so that the price actions of any one do not impinge significantly on any of the others, price remains an effective bargaining tool; cut-rate drug stores thus rely on price appeal, without sufficiently affecting their higher-priced rivals to invite retaliation. And—what should not be forgotten—the fear of retaliation, even among a small number of rivals, arises only when one's price cutting is exposed; as long as concessions are shrouded in secrecy, they may be used to advantage.

Nevertheless, price as a means of improving a firm's position in bargains with customers, in order to maintain or improve its income position, is primarily a long-run device. It is encountered chiefly as part of the long-range strategy of organizational growth rather than as a one-shot tactical maneuver to achieve this year's projected balance. In the American economy it is the expansion of the consumer market which is primarily relied on to expand a firm's income stream. In some instances this requires time for consumers to become acquainted with a new product and for the product to become generally accepted as part of the standard of living to which consumers aspire, so that over time the cost of disagreement rises. But more importantly the building of a mass market depends on a declining product price, so that cost of agreement is falling at the same time that cost of disagreement is rising. Technological improvements push down on costs of production, lowering the outlay required for a unit of output, making possible a lower price, a larger number of selling bargains, a greater money inflow, and growth of the organization.[9] In their competitive struggle for mass markets, firms over the long run cannot escape reliance on price reductions to increase their bargaining power vis-a-vis the buying public. But such reliance requires, as we shall see, a continuing downward pressure on costs of production, on the budget side of the income flow.

We conclude, then, that price constitutes an important variable in the manipulation of bargaining power, to affect the income stream, but that its importance is greater in the long run than in the short run.

The *equivalent* of a price reduction may be resorted to in the short run, however, by raising the profit margin or discount which is allowed to dealers, wholesale and retail. Average revenue to the firm is reduced, and although the reduction does not serve directly to stimulate consumer buying by lowering the cost of agreement,

[9] "GE always takes a long range price view. In 1923, it got together reports on refrigerator prospects, decided the thing to do was plan on year-by-year price cuts until 1933, when the price should be 37% less than it was in the beginning. GE finally entered the field in 1927 and, 10 years later, the price reduction was 43%. Profits went from a $5-million loss in 1927 to a $5-million net in 1930." From *Business Week*, April 18, 1953, p. 143.

it is intended to have the effect of a promotional effort. The dealer, it is hoped, will be induced to influence customer estimation of the alternatives facing him by "pushing" the high-margin item or by directing consumer choice.

Let us summarize briefly what has been said about the bargains of the revenue decision, in their relation to the income flow. To improve the terms of selling bargains (and hence to improve its chances of achieving the projected balance), management manipulates the variables which determine relative bargaining power in its customer transactions. At the risk of oversimplifying, we may associate efforts to increase the buyer's cost of disagreement with quality changes and promotion, while efforts to lower the buyer's cost of agreement are linked with price reductions. Firms are not limited to only these methods of manipulation—the imposition of penalties for not buying, the formation of larger bargaining units through combinations and alliances to reduce the buyer's alternatives, even bribery and political influence are other resorts. But style, promotion, and price changes are more common instruments, and their use can be expected on a probability basis. Again at the risk of oversimplifying, style changes and promotional efforts appear to be relied on most heavily by individual firms in the short run, and product innovation and price in the long run.

Due to multiproduct operations the number of possible manipulations is vastly increased. Some prices can be adjusted down and others up. New products can be added, old ones dropped, style changes made in those still carried. Promotional emphasis can be shifted from one product to another as seems desirable to stimulate the flow of revenue.

At times the projected balance is easy to achieve, and this circumstance tends to strengthen management's bargaining power in its selling transactions. Because the firm expects easy achievement of its objective it is under no pressure to make concessions to any buyer. Efforts to manipulate bargaining power to its advantage are likely to be desultory under the circumstances. This effect is heightened if there are expectations of continued prosperity and a strong asset position. At other times the inflow sought appears more and more difficult of realization, weakening management's hand in its selling bargains and giving greater urgency to attempts to modify the structure of relative bargaining powers. Expectations, if pessimistic, heighten this effect, as does a poor asset position.

We have been talking about a firm's manipulation of bargaining power in its revenue decision, as a means of achieving its projected balance. We turn next to its alternatives of manipulating its bargaining power in the allocation of revenues.

CHAPTER 11

The Firm: The Budget Decision

WE have defined the projected balance as the planned contributions of current receipts, borrowed funds (based on expectations), and assets (the contribution of the past), adding to a total sufficient to cover projected outlays at a level of activity which management deems satisfactory in the light of its aspirations and alternatives. To phrase it differently, management's objective is to bring inflows and outflows into balance at a level of activity which, *ex ante*, is regarded as a satisfactory use of its existing bargaining power relative to its buyers and sellers.

Failure to achieve the projected balance acts upon bargaining power like a decrease in income. Until the firm's operating program is revised in the light of the actual balance being realized (incorporated into a preferred balance, which becomes the new projection) there is a dearth of income relative to planned needs. As we know from previous analysis, the result is to weaken bargaining power in selling transactions (since the need for income is great) and to strengthen it in buying transactions (since each individual expenditure represents a greater threat to the total stream of activity).

The firm's situation need not be taken as given, however. In both buying and selling relationships management may seek to manipulate bargaining power to its advantage. It may achieve its target if it can increase inflows, particularly receipts from current production. It was the possibilities of achieving this result that were explored in the preceding chapter. It may also maintain the desired level of real activity, even in the face of a reduced money stream, if it is able to secure more favorable terms in its buying bargains; it is this possibility which we shall explore in the present chapter.

In the area of the budget decision, the allocation of its inflow, the firm confronts two possibilities for improving its performance: (1) in the event of failure to achieve its projected balance, it can seek to renegotiate agreements with those having claims on its income stream, since its bargaining power has increased through its very misfortune; (2) at any time, whether of adversity or ambitious expansion, it may seek to manipulate its bargaining power to improve the terms of its relationships with income claimants.

We shall proceed on the hypothesis that the firm's manipulation of bargaining power in its own buying transactions takes time, involving such techniques as the formation of employers' associations, the creation of a vertically integrated producing organization, the merger with competitors, the discovery of raw material substitutes or more efficient methods of production. In the short run an improvement in its position as buyer is more likely to stem from renegotiation under conditions of stress.

In general, we assume that when a firm's bargaining power relative to buyers is strong or when its manipulation of relative bargaining power has been successful, the projected inflow can be put high and readily reached, and so cover with ease the projected outlays. In this event no modification of its own buying transactions is called for, and such transactions need not be watched so closely. (Loose and wasteful practices then become more prevalent, for example.) On the other hand, when the firm's bargaining power relative to buyers is weak or its attempted manipulation of relative bargaining powers has been unsuccessful, the projected inflow must be kept realistic—that is, low—and even then may be difficult to achieve, so that outlays must be guarded closely and pared to the bone.

We shall in this chapter be less concerned with the specific techniques of renegotiation and manipulation of power relative to each of the several claimants of the firm's income than with the more general indication of how the outflow stream may be modified in volume by varying the rate of flow of one or more of its components. We shall divide total outflow into two major categories, current production costs and the costs of continuity and growth. These categories and their components are subject to all the difficulties attending any system of classification, as will become evident. The general basis for distinguishing current costs from costs of continuity is that in the short run the former are more largely nondiscretionary, the latter more nearly discretionary. The former deal with factor payments on which current output is conditioned, the latter with savings and investment on which future production is conditioned.

CURRENT PRODUCTION COSTS

By current production costs is meant all expenditures made in the present for present output, whether for immediate sale or for inventory. They are roughly equivalent to factor costs. The distinguishing characteristic of this category is that its components represent the *kinds* of expenditures which are unavoidable for current operations; they constitute the outlays necessary to satisfy (sufficiently to secure their continued adherence to the firm) the aspirations of those on whom management depends for the current level of performance. We cannot speak of these as nondiscretionary expenditures in any strict quantitative sense, however, since as we shall see their amount is discretionary within limits, but they are discretionary only as to size and not as to whether they shall be made. We include in this category (1) the wage bill; (2) the bill for materials suppliers and subcontractors; (3) capital-use costs; (4) distributed profits, and (5) taxes.

THE WAGE BILL

The size of the wage bill is variable within economically significant limits for any given level of output. The most direct approach is, of course, through a change in the rate structure itself. The recurring collective bargaining contests in organized firms have focused attention upon this primary determinant of labor costs. At times when a firm is experiencing difficulty in achieving its projected balance, it may seek maintenance of the *status quo*, if competitors in the labor or product markets are increasing their rates, or a rate reduction if competitors are only maintaining the *status quo*. Such action carries a threat to employee morale, however, and may be difficult to carry off if the firm faces a strong union which seeks to enforce a pattern or if it is a member of a multiemployer bargaining unit whose other members are not experiencing similar difficulty. Normally employers would prefer to obtain a reduction in the wage bill by other means than a wage cut—a resort which is bound to create a chillier climate in the industrial society of which the employer himself is a part and which does not redound to his credit in the larger society. Unions too will normally, however unhappily, prefer to go along with alternative cost-reducing devices if they are convinced that only in this manner will they preserve a rate structure which they have attained with considerable effort and sacrifice over the years.

There are a variety of alternative means for reducing the wage bill on a given output. An increase in workloads is one possibility—either a stretch-out of a worker over a greater number of machines or an upping of the number of pieces to be turned out within some time interval. A substantial saving can sometimes be made through more effective quality controls which reduce spoilage and scrap; laxness of standards, previously tolerated, can be penalized, or more efficient procedures introduced which might previously have been protested. These two paths to lowered production costs are likely to yield appreciable results in themselves, but other devices are also available.

The amount of unnecessary work can be reduced, with employees so released assigned to more productive jobs. Job descriptions can be made less circumscribing and jobs restudied, permitting the addition to some existing job of tasks formerly assigned to another carrying a higher rate of pay. Where rate ranges exist, in contrast to a single job rate, the granting of in-grade or merit increases can be slowed down. Discipline can be tightened to reduce the amount of time clipped at either end of the workday. Hours can be re-scheduled to avoid payment of overtime, and nonworking time previously paid for can be reduced either through elimination of some such payments (cutting out rest periods and coffee breaks, for example) or through a tighter administration of such provisions.

Such devices as these are not simply one-shot resorts which can be used by a company in one period of stress and whose potentiality is then exhausted. With the alternation of periods of prosperity and adversity, the looseness and tightness of labor standards themselves tend to alternate. The wage bill which has all water (and some blood) squeezed out of it at times when the projected balance is difficult of realization is likely (to change the metaphor) to accumu-late a good deal of fat during an ensuing period when inflows accrue so easily as to permit some softness in the cost structure.

MATERIALS SUPPLIERS AND SUBCONTRACTORS

Much of what has been said with respect to the wage bill is ap-plicable, too, to the bill of expenditures for raw materials and for any subcontracted semifinished parts, finished parts, or services. Materials costs are adjustable by a variety of expedients.

The firm may seek an improved bargain with its suppliers or from substitute suppliers, stiffening its negotiating tactics inversely with its ease in achieving its projected balance. It may ask for a better price or for a better product (greater uniformity, less waste, for example). It may also seek to reduce the amount of materials required per unit of product by devices such as improved scrap con-trol procedures, materials substitution, and most importantly, prod-uct simplification. It may reduce its expenditures on some facilitat-ing services, such as advertising.

In attempting to reduce the materials bill by renegotiations with suppliers, firms are often aided by the number of the supplying firms from which they purchase. Large corporations such as General Motors and DuPont buy from literally thousands of other businesses, and even smaller firms purchase from an amazing number of other firms. This complex of relationships provides a number of points at which bargaining pressure may be applied to improve the terms on which materials are obtained. In general such pressure is most effective on those suppliers who are faced with a number of competitors, to whom they fear losing their customer's trade, and particularly if such supplying firms themselves obtain their materials from other firms facing a similar competitive situation, and to whom at least part of the income loss may be passed.

The importance of adjustments in materials costs as a means of reducing the income necessary to sustaining a given level of operations has been underscored by Ernest R. Breech, who as executive vice-president of the Ford Motor Company, once commented: "An automobile is not a single product, but a whole symphony of products. In a Ford DeLuxe six, four-door sedan, for example, there are over 10,000 separate pieces, counting every nut and bolt and washer which we buy or manufacture. . . . Cutting two or three cents from a part—or better yet, eliminating a part—is an achievement of greatest importance when you are dealing in terms of a million or more cars." [1]

Capital-Use Costs

These consist of the obligations incurred in borrowing funds, namely, interest payments and payments on the principal. Both of these items can at times be renegotiated. Callable bond issues

[1] Ernest R. Breech, "The American Method of Pricing," an address before the American Marketing Association, New York City, June 11, 1947. Such a saving would not be wholly attributable to materials cost reduction, of course, if the part were made in the company's own plant, since it would then be partly attributable to a reduction in labor costs. On subcontracted parts the savings would be wholly chargeable to the materials category, and on internal production, partly chargeable. (Product simplification is thus another means of reducing the wage bill.)

or those maturing may be replaced by new issues at a lower rate. Sometimes outstanding debts can be consolidated to advantage. In some instances the debt itself can be extinguished by a substitution of equity rights, but more frequently such obligations are shiftable in time rather than in amount by postponement or anticipation.

DISTRIBUTED PROFIT

Profits have played an ambivalent role in economic theory. They have been viewed as a factor cost which must be met in the long run but as a residual in the short run. No other factor is so treated. It may therefore seem anomalous to include under nondiscretionary current costs a factor return which in the short run is conceived as a residual, a condition which implies virtually complete managerial discretion in determining the share going to owners in contrast to other factors.

This treatment is adopted because *distributed* profit is here recognized as a category distinct from *retained* profit. The latter is relevant to business savings and investment, not factor returns. The question of management's discretion in the distribution of profits thus relates to the extent to which profits are adjustable against savings and investment, the answer to which depends on management's relationship with the owners. Even though management may possess almost total discretion in adjusting profit returns vis-a-vis other factors, since profit in the short run is considered a residual,[2] there are circumstances under which it has virtually no discretion in adjusting distributed profits vis-a-vis retained earnings.

This is indeed the case with the owner who is his own manager and with the owner who controls a hired manager. In both instances the owner's decision as to how much of earnings shall be retained

---

[2] There is ample reason for believing that management does not view distributed profits as wholly discretionary even against other factors, however. Failure to earn a profit may make management's tenure of its position difficult, so that it is led to bargain more sharply with other factors in order to show a profit sufficient to insure its position.

in the business is binding upon management. At the other extreme is the large public corporation, whose stock ownership is widely dispersed and whose proxy machinery management controls. Between these two extremes lie a variety of situations in which owner control over management, and management control over owners are blended.

We assume that while owners recognize the necessity of retaining some portion of earnings in the business for reinvestment for continuity and growth, as well as for precautionary reserves, management would normally (an exception will be noted later) prefer to retain more than would the owners. With respect to stockholders, mangement's sole interest is to satisfy their property claims with least cost to the ongoing activity and the achievement of its own aspirations. Stockholders, like employees and suppliers, constitute claimants upon the income stream with whom bargains must be struck by management, and whose bargains must be made consistent with the total complex of bargains. A conflict over the firm's scarce resources thus exists which essentially is similar to that between management and other factor groups. The decision as to the allocation of the firm's receipts is a matter of the relative bargaining power of management and owner.

Even in the case of, let us say, the small family-held enterprise, management is not wholly without bargaining power. The cost to the owners of refusing to agree on his terms as to the amount of earnings to be left in the business may be his resignation. In the case of the large public corporation, management may have difficulty even in assessing the demands of owners unless faced with a proxy fight. It cannot afford to assume, however, that stockholders, because less vocal and often less effectively represented, in fact have no demands.[3] They constitute a group which, like employees and

[3] In the 1954 proxy fight between the groups headed by Robert R. Young and William White for control of the New York Central, the contestants appealed to the self-interest of stockholders in order to gain the proxies which they sought. On February 17, 1954, *The New York Times* reported:

"The statement made on Monday by Robert R. Young, who is seeking to elect

suppliers, must be satisfied if management is to retain its position; while under the circumstances their bargaining power is weak in direct relations with management, they have (as we shall see in a later chapter) some indirect power over management through their direct access to government regulatory bodies—legislative, judicial, and administrative. Particularly in the case of those corporations whose widespread holdings place management in a dominant position, management policies which are unsatisfactory to large numbers of individuals may lead to pressure for legal curtailment of management powers, a threat which carries a high cost of disagreement to management on the stockholders' terms. In those corporations where stock ownership, while spread among many, has a measure of concentration in a few hands, these large minority interests may give effective representation to all owners by constituting a potential nucleus for opposition of which the management must remain conscious.

There are times when management must consider not only its position with respect to present owners but also with respect to prospective owners. This is the case when additional equity financing is contemplated because earnings, even if retained, do not provide funds sufficient for the desired expansion and where the ratio of equity capital to indebtedness is already sufficiently low as to make the terms of further borrowing onerous. Under these conditions management is likely to maintain a generous dividend policy

---

his own board of directors at the annual meeting, to the effect that Central ought to pay $7 to $10 a year in dividends, was branded as 'hokum' by Mr. White.

"'I consider it a very unfair thing to do to stockholders,' Mr. White continued, 'to hang before them bait, like a big increase in dividends, when we know it can't be produced, at least in the amounts Mr. Young talks about.'"

John Brooks, in "The Great Proxy Fight" (*New Yorker*, July 3, 1954), comments on p. 28: ". . . In the case of the New York Central ruckus, management seemed to be admitting once and for all that the public—or at any rate the not inconsiderable portion of the public that holds stocks in railroads—has become so influential as to make damning it inconsistent with keeping one's job. Devices that in the past had been applied chiefly to political elections, revival meetings, and tent shows were used to beguile the Central's forty-one thousand stockholders. . . ."

in order to encourage the purchase by present owners or others of additional shares of stock. The high rate of return increases management's bargaining power vis-a-vis prospective shareholders by increasing their cost of disagreement on any given terms of stock sale.

In sum, to the extent that management must face the bargaining power of this factor group and reach some agreement (however *pro forma*) as a condition of retaining its position as management, to this extent there is a nondiscretionary element in the determination of distributed profits. Some agreement is necessary if management is to be left in charge of current operations. But to the extent of management's bargaining power in its relations with the owners it is in a position to adjust the flow of profits out of the firm.

TAXES

While tax expenditures automatically adjust to the tides of business fortune, this is a category which ordinarily is not subject to much manipulation to reduce outlay at a given level of activity. There are, it is true, minor ways in which the tax obligation can sometimes be reduced, such as charging off certain capital items to current expense instead of amortizing them, where either practice is allowed, but generally there is little leeway for renegotiating tax liabilities with the government.

COSTS OF CONTINUITY AND GROWTH

Not all income accruing to the firm is distributed in the form of claims incurred through current operations, under one of the categories discussed above. Some portion of inflows is generally allocated, at least over time if not in every year, with an eye to the firm's future. Such allocations fall under the categories of investment and saving.

Without much sacrifice of conceptual reliability, such allocations may be regarded as management applications, outlays directed by management in accordance with its time stream of aspirations after the demands of current operations have been satisfied. To be sure, the factors whose income claims depend upon the firm's continuity recognize and accept the necessity of diverting some portion of receipts to new investment and to saving, in order to assure the firm's survival. A management which made inadequate allowance for the depreciation of assets might well be subjected to demands by owners that applications of business receipts be somehow readjusted to permit such provision. Employees have sometimes accepted wage reductions to permit the firm to invest in new equipment which seemed to be necessary to the firm's continued existence.

Nevertheless, the drives which we have come to associate peculiarly with American management—the expansion of the business by plowing back earnings, the development of new products and new technological processes to gain superiority over competitors, the erection of impressive home offices, the struggle for market share or market dominance, these drives yield satisfactions to management which are seldom shared by the factors and which can be satisfied out of the inflow only after all current production expenses (including dividends) have been met, as long as management remains within the framework of its bargained obligations, and which give to management an interest greater than is held by any other participant in expanding the firm through investment and making it secure against catastrophe by the accumulation of financial reserves.

Management can thus accept profit as an immediate objective, but the profit sought by management is not the same as the profit sought by owners. The latter seek dividends, the former retained earnings. It is only through distributed earnings (or the promise of them) that owners benefit, but it is through the undistributed profit that management commonly achieves its objectives. This does not imply that all investment must come out of retained income, but except in those relatively rare cases where expansion is financed consistently through sale of additional shares, the retention of earnings in the business—even if not adequate to support all the planned investment—facilitates investment. It does this by adding to the assets which act as security for borrowed funds. The disbursement of profit as dividends can be justified from a management point of view as necessary only (1) to retain or strengthen its managerial position, or (2) to make company stock more attractive to prospective owners when equity financing is contemplated.

As suggested above the costs of continuity and growth may be broken down into the two categories of investment and saving.

INVESTMENT

Investment in turn may be viewed as either capital replacement or capital expansion.

The depreciation *account* is an amount set aside, as a cost item, which is intended to recover—over the useful life of the plant and equipment—its original value, its replacement cost, its earning capacity, or some combination of these. The estimate of the proper depreciation rate is a judgment influenced by the conservatism or optimism of the management, by its income position (how much *can* even a conservative management write off in light of its inflows and other outflows?), by the tax laws, and by the choice of one of a number of possible accounting procedures.

In tracing investment flows, however, we are interested not in the amounts set aside (which as long as they remain set aside constitute savings) but in the sums actually spent on replacement of obsolete plant and equipment and on maintenance of plant and equipment still in use. These sums are adjustable. Actual replacement may be postponed by continued maintenance, at less expense, of the existing equipment.[4] Old tools may be made to do a little

---

[4] The British productivity teams which visited the United States in the period following World War II are reported to have discounted "the notion that Americans are constantly scrapping good machinery for better. On the contrary, they frequently found high rates of production achieved with old machines ingeniously adapted to new tasks, and maintained systematically with a care the English seldom attempt." Robert W. Smuts, *European Impressions of the American Worker* (New York: King's Crown Press, Columbia University, 1953), p. 39.

longer and judgments as to the need for replacement can become more conservative as circumstances dictate. There are also areas of business operation where management is influenced by the same factors that influence a household's decision to trade in the old car which, while still functioning satisfactorily, is no longer abreast of automobile fashions; there are fashions in factory equipment and practice as well.[5] The up-to-dateness of the company's trucks, the appearance of its buildings, elevators, grounds, cafeteria, the furnishings of its offices, the streamlining of its equipment, even the fashionableness of its location are among the items that may influence replacement decisions when investment funds are readily available. The consequence is to create an area of latitude within which depreciation expenditures may be adjusted downward, if necessary, to facilitate the balancing of inflows and outflows at a preferred level, if the original projected level proves impossible to achieve.

Capital expansion involves investment in excess of that needed to maintain the firm's earnings. Thus replacement involves the firm's continuity, capital expansion involves its growth.[6] Despite these apparently meaningful distinctions, it is pointless to attempt to identify any given investment expenditure as something intended either for replacement of capital goods or for their expansion. In dealing with firms which change their product lines and technologies and markets over time, the only replacement which is of significance is a replacement of earning power rather than of any specific plant or equipment. Because the replacing equipment may be superior to the equipment it replaces, at no increase in cost, a

---

[5] Nor are such fashions confined to factories. In 1953, when farm purchases of tractors and power machinery were falling off, the major farm equipment companies were reported to be concentrating on style changes designed to influence farmers (in their depreciation policy) in the same manner as automobile manufacturers have influenced their consumers.

[6] The importance of replacement—of continuity—depends on whatever time stream is relevant. In the case of a small unincorporated enterprise the relevant time stream may be the life of the proprietor, while in the case of an "immortal" corporation it may be an indefinite time stream, generations of individuals following each other in continuous succession.

circumstance which, however, cannot be anticipated at the time that depreciation allowances are computed, there can be no direct tie between the size of the depreciation account and the earning capacity which it can purchase.

The only method by which expansion can be distinguished from replacement is through the expenditure of sums in excess of those needed to maintain earning power—*net* real investment. Such net real investment may be financed out of the depreciation account no less than from undistributed profits, new equity capital, or borrowed funds. We shall therefore not seek to distinguish between replacement and expansion in terms of the form which investment takes: the tooling up for a brand new product, for example, constitutes replacement if it is made only to maintain the firm's earning power, while in those periods when there is net new capital investment it is literally impossible to distinguish as replacement or expansion the purchase of a piece of equipment which physically replaces an identical piece which has been worn out and the addition of another plant in a new location. It is only the sum of investment which determines whether expansion has taken place.

The decision as to whether and in what amounts investment shall be made in new products or additional capacity or cost-reducing technologies or in industrial research depends on a number of variables, among the most important of which are how much remains to management after the terms of the complex of the firm's bargains (with factor and consumer) have been satisfied, how much of borrowings and assets management is able and willing to apply, and management's judgment as to whether the firm's bargaining power can be improved more through one form of investment than another.

In the case of new product development, management is faced with calculations of an uncertain nature: whether sufficient demand can be elicited, over time, so that at any of a range of possible prices it could recover sunk costs as well as the direct costs of producing; whether, if it fails to produce the new item, competitors will, and whether consumer demand is trending in such a direction that it will thereupon find its competitive position weakened; whether product development has reached a stage where there is a reasonable basis for expecting future changes not to make obsolete expensive equipment which had not yet been amortized, and so on. Such uncertainties make decisions of this sort highly speculative. Small firms probably tend to leave product innovation to larger firms wealthy enough to entertain the risks involved, restricting their own activities in this field largely to product differentiation. Research expenditures probably follow similar lines.[7]

In the case of cost-reducing investment, uncertainties are still present but of a much less serious sort. The decision-making procedure is relatively standardized in many companies.[8] It begins with a computation of the likely savings from the new equipment. The

[7] It is sometimes argued that most research expenditures are concentrated in the large corporation. This is probably true in the same sense that most sales and most employees are concentrated in the largest corporations. The more difficult question is whether the research expenditures of large corporations are *proportionately* greater than the research expenditures of small businesses. On this point there is no conclusive evidence, since the research expenditures of small firms have never adequately been appraised. It seems quite likely, however, that the proportionate difference, if any, is quite small. The large appropriations for industrial research of a DuPont or a General Motors would, to maintain proportionality relative to sales or assets, require only minuscule absolute expenditures by a neighborhood shop or family enterprise.

The real significance comes in the absolute expenditures, however. The large corporations *appear* to have a monopoly on industrial research because the huge sums available to them will buy the equipment and research time necessary to achieve spectacular results—the development of modern miracles, while the small sums in the hands of a small firm are generally sufficient only to develop small quality distinctions or style changes. Numerous exceptions to this latter hypothesis can be found—the instances where the ambitious entrepreneur kept plugging away in his spare time finally to come up with some major discovery. However, if we distinguish the lone inventors from the small entrepreneurs, and include product development as part of industrial research, it seems doubtful that, on a probability basis, we should as readily expect new products from small firms as from the large ones. Five hundred separate small firms may collectively spend as much on research and development (if only in styling) as one large firm having the equivalent in assets, but five hundred separate small research projects are unlikely to permit a depth of investigation or a cumulation of results which are important to major achievement.

[8] Lloyd Reynolds has described it concisely in *The Structure of Labor Markets* (New York: Harper & Brothers, 1951), pp. 179–182, based on interviews with a number of managements in a New England manufacturing community.

prospective monthly saving is then divided into the cost of the equipment to ascertain the pay-out period, which is then used as a measure of the desirability of making the investment. Plant and sometimes heavy machinery of a basic kind are considered in a category apart from the general run of equipment. The alternative cost-reducing investments available to the company are then ranked in a rough sort of way by length of pay-out period. The funds available for capital expenditures determine how far down the listing projects will be approved, although exceptions to such a simple rank ordering are sometimes made, and in the smaller companies individual equipment purchases are sometimes considered on their own merits as they come to the attention of management and can be fitted within the budget allowance.

The maximum pay-off period which is allowed to any approved project appears to be quite short in most American firms. A survey conducted by the McGraw-Hill Company in 1949 among large corporations, primarily in industries where capital investment per worker is highest, revealed that most firms required a write-off period of no more than five years for nonplant equipment and of ten years for plant. Emphasis on a quick amortization of capital expenditures has been confirmed by other investigators as well.[9] The reason for such rapid write-off appears to be a rather high weighting of the risks of poor judgment, obsolescence, and illiquidity of assets. These precautionary motives will reveal themselves again when we consider managerial applications of income to the savings category.

There appears to be a close correlation between such minimum pay-off requirements and the size of allocations for investment. If fewer investments meeting the minimum requirements are available (as in a depression period, when demand is slack so that capital costs must be spread over fewer units), the funds appropriated for

[9] The McGraw-Hill Survey is given in *Business Week,* January 22, 1949, pp. 54–60. Supporting evidence is provided by Ruth P. Mack, *The Flow of Business Funds and Consumer Purchasing Power* (New York: Columbia University Press, 1941), p. 297, and Joel Dean, *Managerial Economics* (New York: Prentice-Hall, Inc., 1951), p. 123.

capital expenditures are reduced. As the number of favorable investment outlets increases, capital expenditures likewise rise. But it is equally true that smaller sums are available for investment in times of depression, when the pay-off period tends to lengthen, and that larger amounts are available in times of prosperity, when the possibilities of an early write-off are greater. To a considerable extent, then, both the availability of investment possibilities meeting the minimum pay-off requirements and the availability of investment funds are influenced by the same causal factor, the underlying demand conditions.

Depending on the size of actual inflows relative to outflows, management can and usually must adjust its investments upward or downward, as the circumstances require. Such adjustments do not usually affect the level of the firm's current productive activity. They can be expected to have some, but an uncertain, effect on the firm's operations over time.

We assume that failure to achieve the projected balance acts like a reduction in income and thus increases the bargaining power of management relative to those from whom it purchases. The result, in the case of the investment category, is to place pressure on the sellers of investment goods to reduce their bids or to redesign plant or equipment more economically. If actual income falls appreciably below that projected, the firm's cost of agreement on the terms of the investment goods sellers will rise sufficiently to preclude or cancel agreements which have not yet been executed.

Financial Savings

The set-aside of liquid reserves to be drawn on as need dictates safeguards management against the unexpected calamity, protecting its achievement. Such resources may be held in the form of cash or securities. The management concern for financial security appears to be at least as great as the management drive for growth and expansion. Professor Robert A. Gordon has concluded: "The fear of bankruptcy and the even more widespread fear of temporary financial embarrassment are probably more powerful drives than the desire for the absolute maximum in profits. In my own investigations, which have dealt only with very large firms, I have been impressed by the extent to which the 'banker mentality'— leading to the sacrifice of probable profits for the sake of an impregnable financial position—is found among top executives. My impression is that similar financial considerations also play an important role in smaller scale enterprise." Oswald Knauth, both a businessman and an economist, corroborates this judgment. "Large cash reserves reckoned as a part of costs are the only safeguard against chance misfortune. How large they should be depends upon the temperament and judgment of the management. It is difficult to say where prudence ends and timidity begins." [10]

Like investment, the amount budgeted for savings can be adjusted as the actual or preferred balance necessitates. If realized inflows prove greater than outflows, savings can be allowed to expand; if less than outflows, savings can be permitted to shrink. We should be in error to conclude that any adjustment is first made in savings (or even in savings plus investment), however. Savings may be cut, but not to zero before cuts are made in wages, and certainly in distributed profit. It constitutes an application of inflows that management can be expected to defend against factor claimants.

We have now considered the chief components of the firm's outflows. There are current production costs, which include the wage bill, the bill for materials suppliers and subcontractors, capital-use costs, distributed profit, and taxes. There are costs of continuity and growth (managerial applications) which consist of investment ex-

[10] The first quotation is from Robert A. Gordon, "Short-Period Price Determination in Theory and Practice," *American Economic Review*, vol. 38 (1948), p. 271. The second comes from Oswald Knauth, *Managerial Enterprise* (New York: W. W. Norton & Company, 1948), p. 102. It is perhaps worth noting that the use of depreciation reserves appears to follow a cyclical pattern. They are more likely to be spent in years of prosperity than in years of depression; in the latter periods they are frequently held as a kind of safety reserve. Mack, *op. cit.*, p. 236.

penditures and financial savings. Each of these items (with the usual exception of taxes) is susceptible to adjustment or manipulation so that total outflows may be brought into a preferred balance with total inflows, both with respect to level and composition. Aggregatively they exhaust the aggregate inflows, necessarily achieving an *ex post* balance with them.

CHAPTER 12

Interrelation of the Revenue
and Budget Decisions

SINCE inflows must be projected in the light of outflows, and out-flows in the light of inflows, the *ex ante* adjustment of inflows and outflows must occur simultaneously. The revenue and budget decisions are each based on the other. The outcome of this process of adjustment is the projected (or preferred) balance, which we have already encountered.

Ex post a similar simultaneous adjustment of inflows and out-flows—both their level and composition—must occur, resulting in the actual balance. Any change which is made in any of the flows composing the firm's receipts and applications necessitates—both *ex ante* and *ex post*—a simultaneous change in other component flows. In this chapter we are concerned with this interrelationship between the production and budget decisions in the firm, and in particular with the influences determining the level and composition of the projected or preferred balance.

In line with our analysis we should expect that managements would translate changes in prices or rates—anticipated or actual—into changes in the magnitude of the relevant component of the income stream. In the light of the resulting imbalance *ex ante* they would then consider alternative actions restoring a balance. The alternatives would include possible adjustments in the terms of other bargains, possible adjustments in the level of current savings and investment, and possible changes in the level of existing assets and liabilities, and these in any combination. Two examples will be offered of such income management, following actual changes or in consideration of prospective changes in the terms of bargains with employees. The first presents certain findings of a field study involving approximately 50 manufacturing companies in a New England community of about 350,000 population. In his examination of the operation of a local labor market, Professor Reynolds was interested in ascertaining the considerations which prompted managements' response to demands by employees for a wage increase.

There are two starting points for management reasoning on ability to pay. The first is the conception of a "normal" or "safe" rate of profit. This is invariably expressed as a percentage of sales, but the percentage regarded as normal varies with the circumstances of the industry. An industry which turns over its capital more rapidly, i.e., has a higher ratio of annual sales to capital investment, can afford to be content with a smaller profit on sales. The rate of return on capital thus enters indirectly into businessmen's conceptions of a normal profit.

The other starting point is the income statement for the most recent accounting period, usually a calendar quarter. Some attention is paid also to earlier periods in order to determine the general trend of sales and profits, and there is some tendency to assume that the trend will continue in its present direction. If the fourth quarter of 1948 was below the third quarter of 1948, the most probable estimate is that the first quarter of 1949 will be below the fourth quarter of 1948.

The next step in estimating the impact of a wage change is to compute the probable addition to payroll costs. Management says "This increase will cost us $150,000 a month," or whatever the figure may be. By inserting this figure into the most recent income statement (or the projection for the next quarter), it is possible to estimate the effect on the profit margin. The result may be to reduce the margin below what is regarded as a normal or safe level. The next question which arises, then, is how the profit margin can be restored to a proper level. In management parlance, "where is the money (to pay the wage increase) coming from?" Can it be obtained from greater physical volume of sales, or higher prices, or both?

The estimate of prospective sales volume is particularly strategic. A marked drop in volume can very quickly push a plant below its "break-even point." On the other hand, an appreciable increase in volume may enable the company to absorb a wage increase with no change in selling prices. It is very difficult, however, to estimate prospective sales with any degree of precision. Some of the larger companies in the area set up sales and production budgets for a year in advance, but little reliance is placed on figures beyond the quarter immediately ahead. When conditions are changing rapidly, estimates may have to be revised within the quarter. Most of the smaller companies do not even attempt systematic budgeting or forecasting. They rely on current reports from salesmen in the field, trade gossip, the tone of voice which their customers use in placing orders, and other straws in the wind which they interpret on the basis of past experience.

A similar uncertainty attaches to the future course of prices. This may be uncertainty as to how prices themselves will behave (in industries which are subject to strong price competition), or uncertainty as to whether higher prices will mean a reduction in sales volume (in industries where prices are relatively well controlled). Altogether, then, prospective ability to pay is highly uncertain, though the degree of uncertainty varies with the general business situation. It was much greater, for example, in the midst of the 1949 recession than it had been during 1946–1948.

Uncertainty has a twofold effect on management's conception of a proper wage policy. First, most managers believe that you should not try to pay wages as high as you might be able to pay on the basis of budget forecasts, for if these forecasts prove erroneous you may be in a bad situation. This amounts to weighting the possibility that your revenue estimates are too high more heavily than the possibility that they are too low. The effect is to reduce the present worth of anticipated future profits. As one employer said, "We try to be very conservative in calculating our ability to pay. We want to have enough safety margin so that we know any increase we make can be maintained." Another company said, "We have always followed a conservative financial policy. We want to make absolutely sure where the money is coming from before we start handing it out. Unless we have rather definite assurance about future income, we won't even consider an increase in wages." Still another management man said, "It's a very dangerous thing to try to anticipate your financial returns. The safe thing is to make your profits first and then hand them out, instead of trying to hand them out in advance. We figured on a twelve million dollar business last year. It turned out to be a lot less than that. If we had made our wage increases on the basis of this twelve million dollar figure, we would now be out of business."

The second effect of uncertainty on management's wage policy is to produce a desire for flexibility. The time horizon of most businesses seems to be quite short. Production and sales plans are rarely viewed with much confidence for more than three months ahead. Businessmen therefore dislike committing themselves on wages for a year in advance, and if they must commit themselves for a year, they are reluctant to make as large a commitment as they would make for a shorter period. As one employer remarked, "I would have made a larger increase last spring if I could have reconsidered it after three months. But with the union, any increase I make is with me for at least a year. So I had to play safe."

So much for what management thinks it ought to do. What does it actually do? Are estimates of ability to pay a governing consideration in wage changes? The situation differs materially in union and non-union plants. In union plants, many managements were obliged during 1946–1948 to raise wages faster than they considered wise on economic grounds. Again and again one encountered the statement, "Well, we gave an increase—but we shouldn't have done it," or "There wasn't any economic basis for the increase we just gave." In the spring of 1949 profits were declining and uncertainty was so great that many managements believed wages should actually be reduced as a safety measure. This conviction did not extend to the point of being willing to stand a shutdown, however, and in most cases contracts were renewed at the same wage level. It is important to note that when management gives an increase larger than it "should" give, it is not concerned merely over the reduction of prospective profits; it is concerned also with the reduction in the company's safety margin. The union does not allow as large a discount for uncertainty as management would like. Union pressure on the wage structure, in other words, forces managers to assume a greater degree of risk than they would be willing to assume voluntarily.[1]

In this synoptical statement of business practice in the community investigated, we observe the effect of a prospective change in the terms of one bargain (the wage bargain). The prospective change in wage rates is translated into a change in the wage bill, and its effect on the profit flow is determined in the light of other expected flows. If the result is to shrink the profit stream below a figure which permits the achievement of management aspirations

[1] Lloyd Reynolds, *The Structure of Labor Markets* (New York: Harper & Brothers, 1951), pp. 163–165.

and protects past achievements (current position), there follows a reconsideration of the likelihood of favorably influencing the terms and number of selling bargains. In all such calculations, the risk element induces an overestimate of outflows and an underestimate of inflows. Not until such calculations are made can management meaningfully determine the costs of agreement and disagreement on the union's wage demand. This is an example of simultaneous adjustment of the production and budget decisions *ex ante*.

The second illustration of managerial efforts to reach a new *ex ante* balance after the previous projection had been disturbed by the terms of a new union agreement comes from a statement of Mr. Enders M. Voorhees, who, as chairman of the Finance Committee of United States Steel Corporation, was defending before a congressional committee the corporation's price increases of December, 1949, in a period when the nation was still inflation conscious and therefore sensitive to price advances.

It is my purpose briefly to describe the financial facts and factors behind the increase in steel prices, averaging about 4 percent, recently announced by the steel-making subsidiaries of United States Steel.

Behind the 4 percent price increase are many financial facts. But there is one simple central fact that dominates all other facts. It is this: There has been a large and continuing increase in the cost of producing steel in America.

The price changes are primarily the resulting effects of employment cost increases. I confess to some difficulty in understanding how anyone can reasonably condemn the effects while condoning the causes. If, however, one should approve the increased cost but disapprove the cost-covering price increase, I can only conclude his attitude to be that someone other than the person who actually gets the higher cost steel should foot the bill for that higher cost. Who should that other person be? The too easy answer is, of course, that the increased cost, whatever it is, should come out of the owner's profits or losses, whatever they are. . . .

For these reasons, I think it very important to look for a few moments at the facts that bear on the proposition that the increased costs with which we find ourselves confronted should be absorbed rather than passed on to the buyers of steel to the extent that they may be competitively willing to pay the higher prices involved. For such an examination, we need two sets of facts. The first set of facts is the increases in costs with which we are confronted. The second set of facts is the flow of cash received from customers through the Corporation in order to consider the consequences of "nicking" some of those flows, so that the flow of buying power to and for employees may be enlarged. . . .

Mr. Fairless has told you of our cost increases in the period subsequent to the third quarter of 1949 and up to the December 16 price increase. I should now like to tell you what happened to some of our costs during 1949.

As you may observe in the accompanying tabulation, we have an increase in annual employment costs of 70.9 million dollars when 3.4 million dollars for further Federal old-age benefit taxes is added to the new pension and insurance cost of 67.5 million dollars.

During 1949, transportation cost on an annual basis increased 17.3 million dollars because of the freight rate increases.

SUMMARY OF COST AND PRICE CHANGES DURING 1949 [1]

		Millions of Dollars	Per Ton
Changes in cost:			
Employment costs:			
Pensions and insurance		67.5	
Federal old-age benefits tax		3.4	
Total		70.9	$3.88
Products and services bought:			
Increases in coal (3-day week effect)		19.9	
Increase in freight costs		17.3	
Decrease in scrap, tin, and fuel oil	−17.8		
Decrease in other purchases	−14.1		
		−31.9	
Total		5.3	0.29
Total above cost increases		76.2	$4.17
Price increase of December 16, 1949		69.7	3.82

[1] Based on yearly shipments of 18,250,000 net tons of steel to the public.

The added cost of coal, because of the 3-day week limitation on production and the resulting necessity of purchasing millions of additional tons of coal in the open market, adds 19.9 million dollars to annual costs.

During 1949 United States Steel had a gross decline of 31.9 million dollars in the cost of purchases. This total comprehends reduction in the annual cost of scrap, tin, and fuel oil of 17.8 million dollars and an annual decline of 14.1 million dollars in costs of other products and services bought.

Giving full weight to the lower current costs of certain of the items purchased the net effect of both additions and reductions is an increase of 5.3 million dollars since the beginning of 1949 in our annual costs for products and services bought.

If to this net increase in products and services bought there be added the 70.9 million dollars increase in employment costs, the result is a cost increase of 76.2 million dollars. This total exceeds the estimated additional revenue from the price increase by 6.5 million dollars. . . .

So much then for the fact of substantial cost increase. I turn next to the other set of financial facts that we need—that is, the flows of buying power through United States Steel.

I am sure that everybody understands, in the first place, that the only continuing source of money that any business has with which to pay the bills it incurs in the course of production is the receipts that it gets from customers in exchange for the goods and services it sells to them. That is as exactly true of United States Steel as it is of a corner drug store, the butcher, the candlestick maker. All businesses and all individuals have no way in the long run of paying out more than they take in.

Next I suppose that most people understand that there are certain main categories of expenditures that virtually every corporation experiences, and which must be covered by the receipts from customers if the corporation is to continue to do business.

With this in mind, I now give you the cash flow figures for United States Steel. I give them to you for the period January 1, 1946, to September 30, 1949, and also show the aggregate data reduced to an annual average basis. [See next page.]

You will note from the tabulation that in the postwar period from January 1, 1946, to September 30, 1949, we received cash from our customers in the amounts of $7,971,000,000. In the same period we paid out cash amounting to $3,365,000,000 to or for our employees. In order to conduct the business we bought products and services from others in the amount of $3,285,000,000. We spent $818,000,000 in the purchase of tools of production—largely for replacement and modernization of plants and equipment. We paid taxes in the amount of $325,000,000. The cash used to pay dividends, including a small amount of interest, amounted to $273,000,000, and we also spent $17,000,000 to repay money we had borrowed. Adding these up, we find that our total cash disbursements in this period amount to $8,084,000,000 or $113,000,000 more than we received from our customers.

These figures which I have just given you represent the actual flow of cash—of buying power—into, through, and out of the corporation. I have recast the conventional financial statements of the corporation in

TOTAL CASH RECEIPTS AND DISBURSEMENTS, JANUARY 1, 1946,
TO SEPTEMBER 30, 1949
[in millions of dollars]

	Total	Annual Average
Receipts from customer—the public	7,971.0	2,125.6
Disposed of as follows:		
Employment costs	3,365.1	897.4
Products and services bought	3,284.6	875.9
Expenditures for property additions and replacements	818.0	218.1
Taxes	325.4	86.8
Interest and dividends	273.4	72.9
Repayment of borrowed money	17.2	4.6
Total	8,083.7	2,155.7
Deficit in cash	112.7	30.1

order to give you these flows of hard cash through the corporation for two reasons: In the first place, we are dealing with the fact that hard cash—not book entries—must actually be paid out to or for the benefit of employees. Therefore we need to know what cash there is coming in and to what purpose and for what end it is already actually being used. Secondly, I have already referred to the widespread misunderstanding of the true significance of accounting terminology. I think those who do not understand that an undistributed profit represents buying power that has already been distributed can have a better basis for forming judgment by looking at the facts of cash income and outgo. . . .

I have now laid before you the financial facts with respect to, first, the increase in our costs, and, secondly, the flow of cash—the flow of buying power—into, through, and out of the corporation. The committee is now in possession of the same set of basic financial facts that we had in considering the alternatives that were possible with respect to what to do about the increased cost with which we are confronted.

If we consider only the large and continuing employment cost increases, we find, as I have set forth, that they amount to approximately $71,000,000 a year. Just where are we going to find that cash within the framework of these financial flows, assuming for the moment that customers are not to be charged for the products as much as they may competitively be willing to pay? Let us consider the possibility and consequences of "nicking" the other flows of cash through the corporation to secure the required addition to employment costs.

To make the added annual employment cost figure comparable with the recent 9 months' flow data which I have mentioned I could take three-quarters of it. Alternatively, I can compare the annual cost increase directly with the annual average cost flow data for the 3¾-year period I have just described. I have done both and the resulting conclusions are the same. Since pensions and insurance are long-term affairs, it is preferable to use the longer-term basis.

Using the annual averages for the 3¾-year period, then, our problem is to hunt through the cash flow data to find $71,000,000 to be added to our $897,000,000 annual employment costs.

First, could our $876,000,000 cost of goods and services purchased from others—our second biggest cost—be reduced [by] $71,000,000? With regard to that, we are up against an interesting and even dismaying fact: It has been United States Steel's long experience that whenever a significant employment-cost increase—whether in wages, pensions, or insurance—gets started in one of the country's industries, that increase of employment cost tends to spread to all industries. This is indeed evidenced by the fact that wage levels among the industries tend more nearly to parallel each other than to be diverse in their changes. It is also given popular recognition in the phrase "rounds of wage increase." The effect of those spreading increases in employment cost finds its expression in cost-covering price increases for the things which United States Steel has to buy in order to do business. This applies not only to the current goods and services we purchase, but it applies also to the purchases of construction, machinery, and equipment which must be bought if the business is to be maintained. The point of this is that it is almost an historical certainty that sooner or later the increase in our employment costs will be nearly matched by an increase in the cost of goods and services we purchase from others. The cost increases we must ultimately contemplate are, therefore, not just the $71,000,000, but substantially greater amounts. . . .

Well, let us turn next to our purchases of the tools of production.

Such purchases averaged $218,000,000 annually in the period being used as an example. Could we squeeze the needed $71,000,000 out of that $218,000,000? Here, it is true, we have some elasticity in our choice. We could, in fact, greatly slow down or stop the purchase of the tools of production, aside from those most urgently needed to keep production lines in operation. We could let our tools wear out and become obsolete without undertaking to replace them. Suppose we did that. What are the consequences, and would they be in the public interest? Let me list for you those consequences.

The first obvious consequence would be to curtail the modernization program we have under way and, if carried far enough, this course of action would serve to erode United States Steel's existing capacity to produce steel and provide jobs. . . .

Careful scrutiny of the consequences of attempting to provide the increased benefits to our employees by cutting down our purchases of tools of production leads to the conclusion that it is financially possible but is not in the public interest or in our interest to do it that way if it could be achieved otherwise. From the point of view of national security, it does not seem wise to slow down or reverse the trend toward replacement and modernization of steel facilities. From the point of view of employment in this country, it does not seem desirable to bring about disemployment. . . .

Getting back now to the listed flows of cash in our hunt to find the needed $71,000,000, we come next to the item of taxes. It is $87,000,000. Taxes, their amount, and the means of their calculation are determined by the several taxing bodies. There is nothing we can do about them.

There remains, finally, out of the entire receipts of cash from our customers, only one last item—the $73,000,000 paid in dividends to our stockholders. Could we squeeze the $71,000,000 out of that? Well, of course, we could do so if it were absolutely necessary; and, indeed, there have been periods in United States Steel's history when the cash flows into the corporation have not been sufficient to leave anything to be paid to the owners. . . .

Based on a current rate of $2 annual dividends per present share, with a book value of $60 per share, there is but a 3⅓ percent return to common stockholders, and this in a period of near capacity operations. Any attack on the size of such dividends—that is, upon what the owners are getting out of the business that they have created—is comparable to killing the goose which, though underfed, continues to lay the golden egg. . . .

Please consider for a moment why anyone ever spends or lends or invests his money to buy tools of production. Is there any other incentive that commends itself to good judgment than that he hopes and expects thereby eventually to get back enough to compensate himself for his self-denial and the risk of loss he takes? In the case of savings loaned, the compensation is interest; in the case of savings invested, the compensation is, for corporations, termed a dividend.

The interest and dividend compensation is the cost to the community of having the tools of production, and if that cost is not covered by receipts from customers there will be no further savings voluntarily forthcoming for investment in tools of production. Of these two incentives, that of dividends after personal income taxes is a major key to progress. Loaned capital is not available unless equity capital has first been supplied to cushion the risk the lender would minimize. . . . If we want ample tools of production and the jobs their presence creates, we had best set up and maintain in America a social atmosphere endorsing rather than condemning ample dividends and the profits which make them possible. . . .

I have now described each of the major flows of cash through the corporation and accounted for all the dollars that have come into the corporation in the given period. I have considered the possibility of and the consequences of subtracting from some of those flows of cash through the corporation in order to meet the required increase in the flow of cash to or for employees. As a result of that analysis, I think you will agree with me that there are only two places in which we have any practical discretion. First, we can reduce our buying of tools of production, which would tend to bring on unemployment in the tool-producing industries. It would also reduce productive capacity beyond what it might otherwise be. The second place where we have discretion is to reduce or eliminate the dividends to owners, concerning the consequences of which I have just given you my views.

This completes my examination of the proposition that payments to or for our employees should be increased but that someone other than the customers who get the higher-cost steel should pay for that higher cost. This brings me to borrowing as a source of money with which to purchase tools of production, thus freeing money from that expenditure to provide increased benefits for employees.

It is my opinion that a manufacturer should be able to recover out of the sales dollar, through depreciation and through income remaining for reinvestment after equitable dividends, amounts sufficient to replace and keep modern his plant and equipment so as continuously to retain his productive capacity on a competitive basis. By depreciation I mean depreciation on either a replacement or an accelerated basis, whereby sufficient dollars are recovered currently to provide the same purchasing power as so-called normal depreciation dollars commanded when they were initially expended. It is only for expanded capacity that there is justification for borrowing or new capital. . . .

To finance increased capacity a durable-goods manufacturer should, if possible, use equity securities; and whether or not new equity money can be obtained depends upon the earnings of old equity money already in the business. A durable-goods manufacturer should avoid incurring fixed interest or dividend obligations except as a last resort, for it means in times of reduced business volume the fixed charges and principal payments will be very hard to meet. . . .

Since United States Steel has been engaged far more in a modernization and replacement program than in expansion of basic capacity, its financing must, to the extent possible, lie within the policy I have just described. This brings me finally to a consideration of the price of our products as a source of the needed $71,000,000 increase in our employment costs.

With regard to the general prices of steel products, the first thing to note is that those prices, as compared with the prices of other major groups of commodities, are not high. On the contrary, they are low. It is a fact that advances in the prices of steel products have been markedly laggard rather than in the vanguard of the great price inflation during the past 10 years. . . .

May I, in the second place, point out that we possess a distinct realization, which I trust will not be regarded as too naive in this environment, of the vigorous competition that prevails among and between the buyers and the sellers of steel products. Our customers are our policemen. They are on the job every day, and there is absolutely no way in which we can force them to pay any higher prices for steel products than they believe those products are worth in the light of what other competing buyers are willing to pay to secure those products for themselves. Short of true emergency periods, characterized by sudden large and necessitous demands for steel, there isn't any possibility of getting steel prices too high except as we abandon the principles of competition as our standard of judgment. . . .

Let me now summarize. We find ourselves confronted by the hard financial fact of a large and continuing increase in our employment costs. I have revealed to you the entire disposition in expenditure of all the cash coming in to us from our customers, and I have surveyed all the alternative ways of trying to find the cash to meet the increased costs. That reckoning has revealed that, without going outside the corporation to find the needed sums, the only places in which we had any practicable discretion were, first, to reduce expenditures for tools of production with the double consequence of bringing about disemployment, primarily in the tool-producing industries, and simultaneously slowing down or reversing our program of replacement and modernization toward more efficient production of ever-better steels; or, secondly, we could restrict or eliminate dividends with, we believe, devastating consequences to public confidence in American industry.

We then considered going outside the corporation either to the capital markets or to the steel-product markets to find the additional cash required. To go to the capital markets we found to be outside those financial policies which we believe fundamentally sound for manufacturers of durable goods.

This left only the buyers of steel products. It was decided that it was entirely appropriate for those who actually got and had the benefit of the higher-cost steel to pay, at least in part, for that higher cost to the extent that they were competitively willing to do so. Should this proper referring of the matter to the democratic judgment of the competitive market place prove to have been the wrong course of action for us to have undertaken, I think that we can all be very sure that it will very soon be self-evident and self-curing.[2]

The above statement by Mr. Voorhees was couched in terms of fairness and equity, phrases which perhaps were more persuasive with the Congressmen, but it might more realistically have been based on bargaining power relationships, with steel consumers chosen as the most likely prospects, in this postwar period of continuing high demand, for being "nicked" (to use his term) to restore *ex ante* a balance which the additional labor costs had upset. Presumably for purposes of persuasion, too, he reasoned as though any simultaneous adjustment necessitated by an increase in the wage bill must come wholly in some other single flow item, though obviously partial offsets might have been made in all the flows, both into and out of the firm. He summarily dismissed the question of whether the proportion of the $818 million of property expenditures which went for expansion—even if "far less" than that going for modernization and replacement—was still of a magnitude that could hardly be financed out of current receipts.

[2] *December 1949 Steel Price Increases,* Hearings before the Joint Committee on the Economic Report, Eighty-first Congress, second session (1950), pp. 60–70.

Nevertheless, the fact remains that a change in the terms of any bargain can be presumed to affect the magnitude of the relevant money *flow*. Once any flow is affected, other flows are necessarily involved in the adjustments leading to a new balance, both *ex ante* and *ex post*.

Ex ante such adjustments do not occur automatically, however (as they do *ex post*)—they must be planned, by definition. The planning of adjustments in the various flow items—the projection of the balance—requires a determination of the level and composition of that balance. This determination is, as we know, a product of the relative bargaining powers of those symbiotically related in the company's operations, the terms of whose bargains are coördinated by management. But in the process of coördinating the bargains that make up the firm's operations, management achieves whatever degree of discretion it is to have, and its exercise of that discretion gives direction to the firm's activity. Through its discretionary control over the income remaining after the claims of all other participants have been satisfied, it is in a position to accomplish—meanly or greatly—some measure of its aspirations. The managerial applications arise from its residual control over the firm's flows.

In an earlier chapter we have already set forth the proposition that individuals are motivated by a variety of considerations, which for convenience we grouped under the two categories of consumption objectives and job satisfaction objectives. In the case of management, job satisfaction may involve the creative satisfaction of developing a new or superior product or of building an enterprise, the competitive satisfaction of becoming the largest firm in the industry or the nation, the social satisfaction of being known as a fair employer or a leading citizen of the community, the political satisfaction of wielding authority over others, and so on. Each of these types of satisfaction, if it could be isolated in its purest form, would have associated with it a succession of proximate goals and intermediate objectives, related in a time stream of aspirations. The creative urge to develop a new product meeting some recognized consumer need may, for example, call for the proximate goals of increasing the amount of profit and retained earnings, with the intermediate objectives of expanding the allocation for research and hiring a capable research staff. The competitive urge to be recognized as the largest firm in the industry may suggest the same proximate goals but with the intermediate objectives of obtaining newly developed equipment which will permit lower production costs and prices. The social satisfaction of being recognized as a considerate employer may dictate the proximate goal of expanding the product line with the intermediate objective of stabilizing employment.[3] The balance of inflows and outflows which management projects will reflect the proximate goals associated with its time stream of aspirations.

Because individuals are not singly motivated but seek a concomitancy of satisfactions, however, the balance which management projects will normally reflect some combination of goals, a balance of satisfactions. Profit will be sought if that is the instrument for one satisfaction, but not to the point where it requires such a sacrifice of gross sales as to weaken the firm's position in the industry hierarchy, if that is the instrument for another satisfaction. Employment will be maintained in a time of recession, but not to the extent of sacrificing all profit or requiring an excessive application of assets. The projected balance will reflect, moreover, managerial judgments as to the nature and degree of risk to management's aspirations inherent in any course of action. One balance may be preferred over another because it permits a higher level of saving or investment, or saving instead of investment, as precaution against future uncertainty.

The balance which is projected thus reflects the aspirations of the management. It does not reflect management's aspirations alone,

---

[3] The aspirations of some managers are considerably more limited. In describing the father-and-son enterprise run by William F. Koch of Haverhill Corners, N.H., makers of the musical instrument the recorder, *Business Week* of Sept. 19, 1953, p. 122, reported: "Koch ships his output to Schirmer once a month, does practically no bookkeeping, and declines to expand by hiring workers. 'It's nice just as it is,' he says 'If I can make a good living, that's all I want.'"

however, since management must meet in some measure the objectives of those on whom it relies in order to secure some measure of its own objectives. But because of its coördinating role in setting the terms of the complex of bargains necessary for current operations, and in particular because of its residual discretion in determining the firm's behavior once the terms of such bargains are met, management aspirations are peculiarly strategic.

PROFIT AS AN OBJECTIVE

It was previously argued that the balancing of satisfactions appears to be a more useful motivational concept than the maximizing of some single variable. It would be, then, only on the supposition that all satisfactions sought by management, however balanced, could be best achieved through the proximate goal of corporate profit that we could treat *maximum* profit as being the criterion by which management projected the firm's balance of inflows and outflows. If, instead, we adopt the more likely hypothesis that management pursues multiple objectives, not all of which can be achieved through the instrument (proximate goal) of profit, then *maximum* profit cannot be regarded as the criterion used by management in determining the projected balance.[4] Nevertheless, profit appears to be the most important proximate goal by which management seeks to achieve its longer-run aspirations.

This is true because in the American cultural environment size confers prestige and growth represents achievement; the process of expansion conveys some of the same creative thrill that the architect and artisan acquire from the construction of a building. But growth occurs and size is gained largely through earnings which are "plowed back" into the business, the retained profits. At the same time the security of what has been achieved, the very continuity of

[4] The term maximum profit is here used in the sense in which it has traditionally been employed—as an objectively identifiable rate of output at which the profit earned is greater than that which would accrue at any other rate of output. Formally, it is the point at which marginal revenue equals marginal cost.

the business, depends importantly on liquid reserves which can be drawn upon to meet emergencies, and these too come from profits which have been left in the business. Thus undistributed profit becomes one of the most important means by which the costs of continuity and growth (the allocations which are peculiarly "managerial applications") can be met.[5] In the case of small businesses, where management and ownership tend to be united in the same person, this union of interests means that the entrepreneur reaps a reward from *total* profit, the distributed earnings satisfying his income requirements as head of a household unit, the undistributed earnings providing him satisfaction as head of a business unit.

SHARE OF THE MARKET AS AN OBJECTIVE

We can, then, accept an improved profit position as being one and probably the most important immediate objective of management. For some managements, particularly in the large corporations, there is another proximate goal which subsumes but is not identical with profits—market share. Market share as an objective involves *comparative* achievement, using competitors as a standard by which to gauge the quality of one's own performance. It too is linked to continuity and growth of the firm. Maintaining its relative position in an industry is frequently an important condition for holding to-

---

[5] The other two principal sources are borrowing and equity financing. Each of these methods places greater limitations on managerial discretion than does the use of undistributed profits. All are used and all have their special usefulness, but retained earnings constitute the source allowing greatest managerial freedom.

The relationship between earnings and management objectives was revealed in the testimony of A. B. Homer, as president of Bethlehem Steel Co., in his testimony before the congressional committee investigating the December 1949 increases in the price of steel, the same hearings from which the previously quoted testimony of Enders of U. S. Steel was taken. In explaining why his company had gone along with the price increases Homer said, "If . . . there is an opportunity of being able to maintain your business and still keep at the market level on your prices [a market level now raised by the price action of U. S. Steel], you certainly would meet that particular market level, would you not, when your earnings are not sufficient to do what you want to do?" *December 1949 Steel Price Increases,* pp. 513–514.

gether the organization.[6] Increasing the firm's relative position in an industry represents an important personal achievement for its management. The "beat Chevrolet" spirit which pervaded the postwar Ford Motor Company and the effort on the part of the Buick Division of General Motors to wrest the No. 3 position in the industry from the Plymouth Division of Chrysler (even though the latter two do not compete in the same income class) almost suggest, too, that the growth and survival spurs to the struggle for market position are supplemented by a spirit of rivalry for its own sake.[7]

Just what is meant by "share of the market" is a matter for each management to define for itself. Definition first requires a decision as to what market is to be shared, a decision which can be expected to change over time. There is no security even in a dominant share of a secularly declining market, and a firm which seeks simply to maintain its absolute level of activity may find itself under the necessity of having to expand its field of operations. If the radio market begins to decline, the radio-manufacturing firm may be forced into producing television sets or air-conditioning equipment to preserve the value of its assets as a going concern. The firm with $50 million of assets may find a single industry sufficient for its scope of operations for a time, but with changes in tastes it may find it necessary to branch out into other industries to keep its

[6] This latter for at least two reasons. (1) The abler men in the organization may be lured to the expanding firms, setting a lower cost of disagreement on the terms of others in their organization in view of the organization's relative decline and the dimmer prospects it therefore provides for their future. At the same time, in a declining organization, the cost to others of agreeing on the terms (presumably higher, over time) of such abler colleagues will increase if the relative decline is also associated with an absence of absolute growth. (2) In oligopolistic industries share of the market is an important determinant of the relative strength of a firm's bargaining power in the quasi-bargaining relationship, thus affecting a firm's ability to maintain the competitive conditions (vis-a-vis symbionts) most favorable to it. William Fellner discusses this latter matter at length in his *Competition Among the Few* (New York: Alfred A. Knopf, Inc., 1949).

[7] Professor Frank Knight is one who has suggested that organized economic competition may have its base in the competitiveness of play, in *Freedom and Reform* (New York: Harper & Brothers, 1947), p. 41. "No empirical classification of activity into play and work is possible; it would be hard to find any concrete activity which may not be one or the other, depending on 'circumstances'" (p. 388).

assets employed, or new product lines may be necessary if it is to continue to grow.

In *whatever* industry or industries the firm operates, however, it will be concerned with the proportion of total sales it is able to capture. This is its share. What share of the product market or markets it sets for itself is determined by management aspirations for growth, its risk consciousness, and the firm's present assets. An enterprise which starts in one industry, in which its share is perhaps 20 percent of sales, may find it advisable to expand its operations into some developing field. Here its present assets, organization, and bargaining power may permit only a 10 percent share of total sales. Other firms with which it is now competitive may, however, have larger shares, or it may fear that other newcomers will expand to capture larger shares, motivating it to seek to increase its share for security and strength. By "market," then, in the term "share of the market," we mean an identification of certain product markets which provide adequate scope for a firm's operations, and by share we mean the proportion of total sales in those markets falling to the firm. Markets change, and as they do shares are likely to change too.[8]

The share of the market concept, over time, is thus intimately related to decisions as to line of products. It sets a goal which, to achieve, requires expenditures of given magnitudes (for production, for promotion), and hence influences the projected balance. In multiproduct firms (the typical case) the expenditures on a product

[8] John M. Hancock, who in his lifetime has served as both chief operating executive and board member in a number of large companies, has been quoted as saying that when he moves into a company as a director he wants to know just three things: (1) How do we stand compared with our competitors? (2) Where ought we to stand? (3) How do we get there? (*Business Week*, January 17, 1953). Here Hancock is presuming that the identification of a firm's competitors constitutes the identification of the "market," leaving the further question of what share of that market is a reasonable goal for the firm's best interests. Hancock has identified as the three factors determinative of the structure of his firm's economic relationships and therefore its projected balance: aspiration (where ought we to stand), comparative achievement (where do we stand), and methods of manipulating bargaining power to reduce the gap between the two (how do we get there).

being pushed may for a time exceed the revenues from that product, being covered by the firm's receipts from other operations. There is no requirement, however, that receipts and expenditures balance for each product but only for the firm as a whole. The firm's projected balance relates to total inflows and total outflows, and the two totals may be disproportionately affected by the several activities of the firm.

We have now set up as two likely proximate goals influencing the level and composition of the projected balance a satisfactory profit showing and a satisfactory market position. These two objectives may supplement each other but they may also in some degree supplant each other, requiring compromise. Even though the market-share objective is sought at least in part for long-run profit, as a *present* objective it may displace (in some degree) the drive for profit. The effect of such displacement is of course discernible in the balance sought, both its level and composition. As production grows to increase market share, outflows to employees and materials suppliers must increase. If the terms of selling bargains must be reduced to increase sales, or if advertising and marketing expenditures must be substantially increased, the immediate result may be a smaller profit flow on a larger volume, a result considered acceptable because of the superior market position which has been gained in the process, a result which is viewed as satisfactory not only because of its long-run profit potentiality but because in itself it represents business achievement and perhaps security.

EXPANSION AS AN OBJECTIVE

There is a third objective which appears sometimes to take its place with the two already mentioned—the expansion of the firm. Let us initially consider this objective as one which is simply designed to improve management's bargaining power over time. There are three ways in which a firm's growth adds to its bargaining advantage.

1. Size may be sought to improve the firm's bargaining power

in its selling transactions. It may do this by making possible technological advances which permit price reductions, decreasing their customers' cost of agreement,[9] or by absorbing rivals (either directly through merger or indirectly by taking over their customers by a variety of devices), thereby limiting their customers' alternatives and raising their cost of disagreement.

2. Size may be sought because it confers bargaining advantage in relations with suppliers. In bidding relations with smaller commensal rivals, the large firm's assets reduce its cost of agreement on the symbiont's terms, assuring it of a successful bid. At other times the magnitude (actual or potential) of its purchases increases the supplier's cost of disagreement on its terms, in contrast with the terms of rivals.[10]

[9] The technological advance may come through improved means of production or in the form of superior products. The relationship of size to such technological advances may lie not simply in the fact that some production processes are possible only on the grand scale, but also that large-scale operation is necessary to accumulate the sums which support research leading to new developments. This is the basis for the behavioral sequence to which Professor Schumpeter gave the name of the process of creative destruction.

Research and development are, to be sure, viewed not only as a means of growth but as security and "insurance" (a cost of continuity). The continuity aspect was stressed by Harlow H. Curtice, as president of General Motors, in an address, "The Business Outlook for 1953." "Further tangible evidence of our confidence in the country's future—in its long-range future—is our investment of more than 100 million dollars in the General Motors Technical Center in suburban Detroit. This may seem like a tremendous sum to invest in such facilities. It is, but we feel that every penny of it is being well spent. This investment is in the nature of an insurance fund—insurance that guarantees, to the extent possible, our continuing leadership in technological progress in the years ahead."

[10] When the fire at General Motors' Livonia, Mich., plant in August, 1953, wiped out so much of its capacity for manufacturing automatic transmissions as to prevent it from marketing certain of its makes of cars for a period which originally was expected to run to several weeks, the restoration of production hinged largely on replacing or rebuilding the expensive and intricate machine tools which had been destroyed or damaged by the fire. *Business Week*, September 12, 1953, p. 33, reported: "For the average machine tool shop, with a regular production schedule to maintain, GM's rush repair orders have thrown a big strain on capacity. Many grouse that GM is demanding too much service too fast. . . . Some of these have sidetracked regular production schedules to make way for GM's renovation job. Others are frantically trying to fit the extra load in somewhere. . . . The first week or so, many a machine tool builder got nettled at GM for its management of the situation and for the pressure it put on." A small company could not have exerted such pressure. To General Motors, this power meant millions of dollars in sales that would otherwise have been lost.

An enterprise which is big obtains from its sheer magnitude a special kind of power, based upon the fact that it can spend money in large amounts. If such a concern finds itself matching expenditures or losses, dollar for dollar, with a substantially smaller concern, the length of its purse assures it of victory. In encounters with small enterprises it can buy scarce materials and particularly attractive sites, inventions, and facilities; can preëmpt the services of the most expensive technicians and executives; and can acquire reserves of materials for the future. It can absorb losses that would consume the entire capital of a smaller rival.[11]

3. Size achieved through vertical integration improves the possibility of securing the projected balance by increasing the number of points at which bargaining power may be manipulated for advantage. By integrating forward to the consumer, the producer gains direct control over marketing; by integrating backward, he gains control over his raw materials. In either case he gains greater discretion and advantage by the power to rule out rivals from access to the supplying or marketing organization on which he depends, as well as by the power to effect cost economies and price advantages both backward and forward in the production process.

The expansion of the firm may thus be sought, in a variety of ways, with the objective of improving the firm's bargaining power. If this is the purpose, however, then growth is simply an instrument of achieving some other objective such as a more favorable profit or market position; it is a proximate goal in the achievement of an intermediate objective. At the same time we are aware that one aspiration which has characterized American managements has been the prestige which is associated with size and that profits have been sought so that they can be plowed back into the business to achieve the growth which is desired. In this context, profit is the proximate goal for the intermediate objective of business expansion.

There is nothing anomalous about this relationship between profit and growth as business objectives, in which each serves as

[11] Corwin D. Edwards, "The Conglomerate Enterprise," paper delivered before the Conference on Business Concentration and Price Policy sponsored by the National Bureau of Economic Research, 1952.

an immediate goal in the achievement of the other as intermediate objective. The fact is that growth is sought both as an objective in its own right and as a device for increasing profit, and profit is sought in order to facilitate expansion (both as an end in itself and to increase profit still further) as well as for other objectives, such as reserves to assure continuity.

Three proximate objectives are thus suggested as characterizing American management: a satisfactory profit, a satisfactory market position, and a satisfactory growth. What is satisfactory in each instance depends on the relative bargaining powers of all those involved. As we have seen, these three goals are not identical but are interrelated. All three may affect management's projection of the balance of inflows and outflows, or one may be dominant. Nor are they exclusive: we have recognized that a satisfactory rather than a maximum profit must be accepted as a management standard because (among other reasons) managements like everyone else have concomitant aspirations, not all of which can be achieved through the instrumentality of profit. We posit only that these three goals are sufficiently dominant, prevalent, and persistent to be conceptually reliable.

The significance of this conception of management motivation, in contrast to the traditional conception of profit maximization, lies in this resulting conclusion. Once we abandon the idea of some single, unique, objective maximum profit as management's goal, we are forced to abandon the idea of some single method of achieving it, since the "it" itself is now ambiguous and uncertain. The controversy over whether firms price by marginal cost or average cost, over whether they conform to the marginal productivity theory of wage determination or some other is revealed as a misleading statement of the problem. With hundreds of thousands of firms in this country, there is good reason for supposing that examples could be found supporting almost any theory of price and wage determination.

A looser but more reliable conception of management's purposiveness recognizes the greater discretion permitted to management in the simultaneous adjustment of the items composing the balance. As long as (theoretically) profits had to be maximized, management's discretion was limited to the finding of the single best way. If now managements are viewed as seeking not some single, unique point of most return but an objective which must be staked out much more roughly, a variety of procedures may be used to adjust the bargains which influence the flows which affect the balance that management projects. The problem becomes one of determining whether there are conditions under which the probability is greater that one procedure will be used rather than another.

There is, however, this one inescapable and overriding consideration in any context: management's job is to coördinate, in a never-ceasing succession of adjustments, the complex of bargains in the firm in order to achieve a preferred balance of inflows and outflows.

A NOTE ON MAXIMIZATION

For many years the argument has raged whether maximum profit constitutes the businessman's objective. It now appears that this argument is fairly well resolved, and its prolongation involves only the flogging of a dead horse.

In the absence of perfect knowledge and in the face of uncertainty, there is no objectively identifiable maximum. Uncertainty, as much as any other element, makes purposive maximization literally an impossible ideal. Because the future is unknown, because the present involves so complex a set of determining forces, no individual can operate with certain expectation of the consequences of the courses of action which are open to him. In the face of such uncertainty, each possible course of action has not a single possible outcome but a distribution of such outcomes, as has been shown by Gerhard Tintner in "The Theory of Choice under Subjective Risk and Uncertainty," *Econometrica*, vol. 9 (1941), pp. 298–304, on whose argument Armen Alchian has relied in his related "Uncertainty, Evolution, and Economic Theory," *Journal of Political Economy*, vol. 58 (1950), p. 212.

The businessman who has a variety of decisions open to him—whether to increase output and by how much, whether to raise or lower price and by how much, whether to alter the product itself, or expand his advertising, and so on—is thus faced with a number of distributions of potential outcomes equal to the number of alternative courses of action he may pursue. Moreover, the distributions overlap, so that the *same* outcome may be a possible result of several different courses of action. For example, a shift in advertising expenditures and a shift in price may each have, in their distributions of potential outcome, some same outcome. Associated with that same outcome will be other potential outcomes, however, which make the two actions not equally acceptable. One may carry with it greater risks but also the possibility of greater gains, the other fewer risks and smaller gains. Which of these two (or more) actions that might be taken can be said to maximize profits?

If one chooses that action which includes in its distribution of potential outcomes, the maximum profit, from among *all* the distributions of potential outcomes, that same action may involve as well the possibility of maximum loss. It will not necessarily therefore prove to be the profit-maximizing course. A course of action carrying the chance of smaller profit but less risk *may* prove, in the event, to be more profitable. Profit maximization thus serves as no guide to action. One can only ask which course of action is preferable to the businessman, considering his subjective reaction to risk and uncertainty.

If maximization is not feasible on the basis of objective data, what of the chance of maximizing by trial and error? This possibility would exist if in fact society were static—if all the underlying conditions were fixed once and for all, with unchanging demand for all products, unchanging technology, unchanging population. Under these circumstances the businessman might seek that combination of price and output which, by experiment, he found to yield a maximum return. To state the necessary conditions for maximization by trial and error is to indicate the infeasibility of this method. Experience and experiment provide the only secure basis for a firm's actions, to be sure, and they are a sound means of making profits; they are not adequate for maximizing profits, however. For the firm would never know whether the experience of a previous period was so precisely relevant to the experience of the present (or the future, for which planning must be currently undertaken) as to assure maximum profit, even if that experience provided reasonable grounds for expecting merely profitable operations.

The absence of this static quality, the presence of the effect of the movement of time, like uncertainty renders maximization in any objective, measurable sense an unrealistic goal. For if profit-making over time requires different guideposts than profit-making in a static system or in the immediate present, it is equally true that profit maximization within an *indefinite* time span becomes objectively meaningless. Only if maximization within some delimited time period is sought is the problem even conceivable. But there is no basis for any such segmentation of time.

It is thus uncertainty and time, the former a product of the latter, which precludes maximization in the time-honored sense of some ascertainable point of most profit.

If the argument of Edith T. Penrose in the *American Economic Review*, vol. 43 (1953), pp. 606–607, can be accepted as at all representative of those who espouse profit maximization as a concept, the common meeting ground for those who have fought out this argument is discernible. The traditional usage of maximum profit as a unique and objectively identifiable point of most return is described there as an "inappropriate use" of the term. It is enough to assume of businessmen "that in general they tend to try to make, if they think they can, a bit more profit than they are making."

This formulation can be readily accepted. It seems quite likely that a conception of American management as motivated by the proximate goal of a better profit showing is one that can be accepted by most schools of economic thought. This formulation, however, undercuts much of the foundation for the marginal price analysis, whose rationale lay in the logical necessity of individuals moving to some ascertainable point where marginal cost equalled marginal revenue. If we now assume that management does not seek maximum profit in this logical sense, but only a bit more profit, there is a much greater variety of managerial behavior compatible with the new assumption than with the old. The ineluctable behavior of the old-time maximizer gives way to the discretionary behavior of the profit seeker.

A NOTE ON PRICING

There is some indication that one of the most prevalent pricing procedures followed by American managements is that called "average-cost pricing" or "full-cost pricing" or "cost-plus pricing." Alfred Oxenfeldt, in *Industrial Pricing and Market Practices* (New York: Prentice-Hall, Inc., 1951), p. 162, concludes that this method is used universally in the distributive trades and frequently in manufacturing. He estimates that "well over one-half and perhaps as high as three-quarters" of all goods are priced in this manner. The procedure itself varies, but the following provides a generalized description. It will be observed that what is termed a pricing process is actually part of the process of projecting a balance.

Firms which are engaged in continuous production for the general market typically operate under a production plan covering a period of time which may vary from a month to a year. The plan may be highly articulated or may constitute nothing more than the mentally coördinated fragments of information accruing to an individual proprietor.

On the basis of experience, the reports of its salesmen in the field, its advertising plans, the analysis of market-research specialists, and the hunches of its responsible officials, management assumes some "normal" or "standard" output. On the basis of accountants' estimates and trade conventions, the management of a multiproduct firm (the typical situation) allocates some share of fixed costs to the product under consideration. By dividing this allocated share of the burden by the standard output, an average fixed cost is determined.[12] To this is added the estimated unit variable cost to arrive at average total unit cost. This costing process is admittedly imprecise. As Oswald Knauth, an economist and manager, has written in his *Managerial Enterprise* (New York: W. W. Norton & Company, 1948), pp. 104–105, "By its allocations [of costs to specific outputs], management can rationalize almost any course of action or justify any extravagance. . . . An estimate of costs is a valuable but slippery tool."

On the basis of its estimate of average cost for the expected output, management can proceed to the determination of product price. It will be noted that average cost in the sense used by the businessman (and as used above) differs from the average cost of the economist's price analysis in that it includes no allowance for normal profit. That allowance must be added by the businessman in the form of a standard markup.

The set of marked-up prices for a multiproduct firm cannot be expected to be adopted as they stand, however. They constitute only a first approximation, requiring an adjustment in line with the competitive situation. Products facing a more intense competition may have their prices shaved, while those having a competitive advantage may be adjusted upward to carry the weaker members of the product line. Where the number of rivals is small, the quasi

[12] "The 'burden' used in standard costs is based on an allocation of fixed costs to a level of output for which there is reasonable expectation of achievement on the average over the future. This, at least, is the prevailing practice, although some firms have used simply the technical capacity of the firm as a basis for standard burden costs. For instance, out of 177 replies to a questionnaire of the National Association of Cost Accountants, 138, or 78 percent, based the normal or standard burden on ability to produce *and* sell while the remaining 39, or 22 percent, used only capacity to produce. Furthermore, these 39 firms were concentrated, for the most part, in industries with fairly stable demands. When actual rates of operation in a period vary from the average of expected rates, this difference is frequently written off to profit and loss through an underabsorbed and overabsorbed burden account. The important thing to be noticed about these standard costs for the present purpose is that they are not strictly historic costs; they involve a standard of expected performance." Committee on Price Determination, *Cost Behavior and Price Policy* (New York: National Bureau of Economic Research, 1943), pp. 25–26.

bargain limits a firm's discretion in price determination to some range which experience has shown will not invite retaliation. The upward and downward adjustments are designed to provide the firm with an overall operating profit which is satisfactory in the light of its aspirations and alternatives. "Under no interpretation is the price named the only one under which a managerial enterprise could operate," says Knauth (op. cit., p. 124). "The choice of practicable policies is wide and management has considerable latitude in the emphasis it places on each policy. . . . There is ample room for argument, tests, and differences of opinion."

A smaller firm often withholds the announcement of its price until some dominant firm—the price leader—has published its price for the coming planning period. If the small firm's calculated price bears some normal relationship to that of the price leader, it can be maintained without fear of loss of competitive position. If the two prices deviate significantly from their customary relationship, however, some adjustment will have to be made by the smaller firm if it is to protect its share of the market. In the latter event, some adjustment in cost may also be necessitated if the firm's profit position is to be protected as well. As we know, this can sometimes be done through renegotiation with suppliers, or a tightening of labor standards, or improvement in efficiency and elimination of waste or luxury, or some tinkering with the quality of the product. Despite such efforts, however, the profit ratio may have to be sacrificed (the markup shaded) as the price of preserving the firm's competitive position in the market. Cost adjustments must then be deferred to the future, when a more decisive manipulation of bargaining power can be attempted.

Once the price has been announced, it is customarily maintained for the duration of the planning period, except under the most unusual circumstances. A frequent fluctuation in price is regarded as destructive of buyer-seller relationships, except on the impersonal organized commodity exchanges. "The business man will assume that his sales estimates will be wrong to some extent, but he is almost certain to be prepared, within a considerable margin of error on both sides of his sales estimate, to maintain his price during the period for which plans are made. . . . As time now elapses within the planning or price-quoting period, the unknown demand curve . . . may shift frequently or may remain below or above the level implied in the estimates made at the beginning of the period." [13] Despite such fluctuations the price will be defended.

Every other expedient is tried before prices are tampered with. When surplus stocks have to be worked off, the objective is to create as little disruption to the price pattern as possible. Goods may be marked as seconds and offered at lower prices. A new outlet apart from the regular market, such as Filene's bargain basement or a cut-rate store is sought. Or a new brand name is put on the goods so as to break the connection with the established brand. Surplus articles may be dumped abroad. Special inducements such as rapid delivery, deferred payments, thirteen to the dozen, extensive advertising, and mammoth displays may be offered. Such concessions never get into the records. Not until management is sure that the old price pattern is no longer possible does it build a new balance around a new price.[14]

The measure of the firm's short-run success is the extent to which its expectations are fulfilled (or overfulfilled) in fact. If the expected sales materialize and if its cost estimates have been reasonably accurate, it will realize the full amount of the hoped-for profit. If its sales exceed expectations, its profit likewise will exceed expectations as long as marginal costs remain constant or do not rise by more than actual fixed costs decline. On the other hand, if sales fall below the estimate, the projected balance (and therefore the profit component) will not be realized and a loss may even result (since average cost had been allocated over a larger output in the pricing decision than has been realized in fact).[15]

---

[13] Robert A. Gordon, "Short-Period Price Determination in Theory and Practice," *American Economic Review*, vol. 38 (1948), p. 283.

[14] Knauth, *op. cit.*, pp. 129–130.

[15] To guard against this latter contingency some firms calculate average fixed cost on a lower volume than the normal output, perhaps the volume which represents the break-even point (the point at which total costs are just equalled by gross income). If the planned sales do not materialize, then, fixed costs will still be recovered as long as output is held at or above the break-even point. Unless profit margins are adjusted, this would result in a higher price than would be obtained if average cost were calculated on the basis of the planned output.

Figure 2 shows the possibilities. Suppose that the firm has chosen Q_n as its normal output, setting price P equal to average production cost at that output plus a profit markup. It should be noted that marginal revenue is always equal to average revenue, since the firm maintains a constant price regardless of fluctuations in output. The shaded area indicates the possible profit. Short of the expected out-

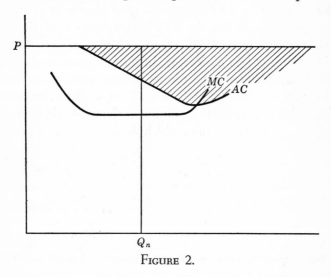

FIGURE 2.

put profit declines rapidly. At greater outputs total profit increases substantially.

It would be rare indeed that a firm's results would conform to its plans. Such a result would be highly coincidental, in view of the firm's lack of control over such conditions. The relationship between plans and results, however fortuitous or however much due to able use of such data as are available, is the basis on which business performance is rated. The most rational calculations may go astray because of changes in the economy which could not be foreseen or controlled, and the rashest behavior may prove "justified" for exactly the same reason.[16]

[16] In an address entitled "The American Method of Pricing," delivered June 11, 1947, before the American Marketing Association in New York City, Ernest

Even in such an average-cost pricing procedure, producers use, to be sure, whether implicitly or explicitly, marginal calculations. The concept of elasticity of demand is involved in even the roughest estimates of how output is related to price and how in consequence revenue varies with output. A comparison of average cost data for two or more possible outputs has implicit in it a marginal cost calculation, that is, the additions to cost from change in output. But such marginal calculations are not the same thing as maximization, and the statement sometimes made that marginalism is nothing but maximization is at best misleading. In the first place, in the pricing process described there is no precise output and price at which a producer can be sure that profit is maximized. But even more important, no effort is made to set output at the point where marginal cost equals marginal revenue, which is *the* marginal calculation,

---

R. Breech, as executive vice-president of the Ford Motor Co., described his own company's policies in terms which are reminiscent of the above description of average-cost pricing, even though there may be substantial differences between Ford practice and the generalized statement of the text. Said Breech:

"All the way through this process of designing, engineering, purchasing and manufacturing to a cost pattern we have to arrive at some reasonable, anticipated volume of sales in relation to productive capacity. The term we use to describe this is 'Standard Volume.' Expressed simply, it is the average or normal return of production, generally about 80 per cent of capacity, calculated on a two-shift basis.

"We take the design cost of all our cars and develop a price study, showing the probable return on investment at this volume. By this method we can test whether a proposed operating program has reasonable expectancy of attainment.

"The idea of standard volume is a useful one in price-setting, for it is directly related to the profit we expect to average over a period. This 'standard return' is the rate required at standard volume for the company to cover its risks, to meet its obligations, and to continue to grow soundly. Further, this method of pricing assures the customer that he will not pay for idle plant facilities if standard volume is not realized.

"Such a price is obviously only a 'standard' in the sense of being used for comparative purposes. It is a useful guide to judgement, but the actual price set may be lower. The final prices are, of course, determined by the competitive situation. Whether or not we are able to attain a standard return on investment at any one time is chiefly influenced by how good business conditions may be, how efficient our production may be—or it may depend on the appeal of our cars. We find that the standard price offers a good measuring stick for financial purposes, but we know that the real test of our pricing—and of all our policies—comes finally in the market place. And back of all our pricing decisions is ever present the principle that lowest possible prices bring reward of larger volume."

and the only one, which can be identified with maximization. For the average-cost pricing procedure does not permit of such a purpose.

That average-cost pricing cannot be used, purposively, to arrive at the MC-MR equality can be shown. Average revenue (price) is greater than average production cost if the markup is excluded and equal to average cost plus markup. Within the range of planned output average cost (with or without markup) is greater than marginal cost, as long as the latter is relatively constant, as appears often to be the case; hence average revenue is also greater than marginal cost. Since marginal revenue is always equal to average revenue (due to constant price), marginal revenue under these conditions must necessarily be greater than marginal cost. They cannot be equal.

It is true, of course, that average revenue as determined by the businessman is not likely to mirror actual demand conditions, since the actual demand curve can be assumed to be sloping over some range of output while the businessman's price remains constant. It is therefore possible that, at the output which materializes, actual marginal revenue (unknown to the businessman) *may* equal marginal cost. But this possibility has no significance. The businessman has no way of knowing whether this result occurs, and there is no relationship between his actual pricing practice and this abstract possibility which would permit him to believe that one leads to the other. Average-cost pricing is not purposive of maximization.

Average-cost pricing, where used, is simply one aspect of projecting a balance of inflows and outflows, the level and composition of which satisfy the aspirations, in the light of their alternatives, of management and those whose bargains it coördinates. As we know, in the process of projecting such a balance management need not take most of its data as given, but has the option of seeking to improve the terms of its bargains by manipulations of the sort with which we are already familiar.

Such manipulative efforts may be directed at modifying not the current balance, however, but, rather, the one for the succeeding planning period or even one five years in the future. Management, like others, operates within a time stream in which present actions influence future behavior, and plans for the future affect present conduct. In the face of an unsatisfactory actual balance, management may thus forego steps to change present relative bargaining powers, concentrating its efforts instead on measures which, while requiring more time for their fulfillment, can be expected to modify more drastically, to management's advantage, the structure of future bargaining powers. And its own present bargaining power will be affected by the expectations it holds of the future success of its efforts.

CHAPTER 13

Households, Bargaining Agents, and Bargaining Units

THE HOUSEHOLD

THE household as an economic unit has basic similarities to the firm as an economic unit. Each requires a revenue and a budget decision, and these two decisions are interrelated through simultaneous adjustments. We shall therefore summarize only briefly some of the major considerations relevant to the household.

The revenue decision of the household involves primarily the allocation of its members' time. Some have the tasks of working outside the home to earn income. Others have as their working assignment tasks within the household, the performance of which by someone outside the household would require payment. Still others (chiefly the young) must spend most of their days at non-remunerated tasks such as schooling. Often a member will allocate some portion of his time to paid employment (part time or full time), some portion to nonpaid employments around the house (such as washing and ironing clothes or mowing the lawn or building shelves in the kitchen), and some further portion to non-paid tasks outside the home (such as evening instruction in some

251

occupation or profession to which advancement is sought). Usually the time remaining to a household member after the discharge of his obligations to it is left to his own use in whatever form of leisure activity he prefers. The revenue decision of the household thus involves a determination of who works at what for how long. But this determination requires, too, some answer to the question, for how much income? In order to decide which members of the household will seek paid employment and at which kinds of jobs and for what hours, there must be a decision as to the household's income objective and there must be some knowledge of the wage bargains which can be expected, on the basis of which the family's time can then be allocated.

Since in this analysis our attention is centered on income flows, we have agreed to treat the revenue decision as determining the inflow of funds. We allow for the time element by including in the inflows any assets which are currently applied (the fruit of the past) and any borrowings (the fruit of expectations).

The household's budget decision involves the allocation of its inflows. As in the case of the firm these may be broken down into the two categories of costs of current operations of the household (= consumption) and costs of continuity and advancement (= savings + investment in the household + investment outside the household).

Finally, as in the case of the firm, the revenue and budget decisions are interrelated. A change in any inflow or outflow item necessitates a simultaneous adjustment in other flow items, *ex post*, and a further adjustment *ex ante* as soon as the individuals in the household rationalize their activities under the changed conditions. If inflows (including the use of assets and borrowing) decline, outflows must necessarily decline simultaneously. If outflows for consumption increase, then other outflows must decline or inflows must increase accordingly. *Ex ante*, some portion of the time of additional members of the household ("secondary workers") may be allocated to paid employment to permit a higher level of expenditure than would otherwise be possible, or a decision may be made to apply some portion of assets.[1]

As in the case of the firm, the job of management in the household is to coördinate buying bargains and selling bargains to achieve a preferred balance of inflows and outflows. In doing so, however, the household is not required (any more than is the firm) to take conditions as given. It is free to manipulate its bargaining power as it can to achieve a more advantageous position.

In this chapter we shall not attempt to examine in detail the components of the household's revenue and budget decisions and the methods by which one or more component flows may be adjusted in response to change in some other flow item. Instead, we shall make use of the household to introduce the concepts of the bargaining agent and the bargaining unit.

BARGAINING AGENTS

The manipulation of bargaining power in its wage bargain or bargains constitutes one method of improving the household's income position. The labor union is one instrument designed for this purpose. The employees of a given industry or trade band together to improve their bargaining power in transactions with the employer. In this process the union serves as the *bargaining agent* for all those households represented by its members. The union is the creature of the household, a means of strengthening its position in its selling bargains. It has no significant function other than this agency role.

Like the firm and the household, a bargaining agent may be an economic unit in the sense that it requires management of an in-

---

[1] The patterns of adjustment of flows in households can best be explored by statistical analysis. A good deal of study has already gone into and is currently being undertaken in such matters as labor force attachment, job movement, and family budgeting. Future research—particularly if the time variable is included—will prove even more rewarding as we continue to achieve a clearer understanding of the questions concerning the household's economic behavior which need answering.

come stream for its functioning. In the case of unions, it has its official managers who must coördinate its inflows and outflows in an effort to achieve a preferred balance. The inflows are derived chiefly from the initiation fees, dues, and assessment of its members; the applications are for expenses of office operation, for organizing drives, for strike benefits, for savings, for investments such as a headquarters building. In this respect, the union as a bargaining agent must be managed in the same way as other economic units.

In distinct contrast to the firm and the household, however, a bargaining agent derives no income from those *with* whom it negotiates but only from those *for* whom it negotiates. The union draws no income from the companies with which it bargains, but only from its members for whom it bargains.[2]

The labor union seeks to secure more advantageous terms for its members by modifying the company's costs of agreement or disagreement on its terms, by the variety of devices which we have already encountered. There is no need to do more than mention here the chief weapons at its command: strike, picketing, and boycott to increase the firm's cost of disagreement on its terms; promise of increased coöperation in improving productive efficiency to decrease the firm's cost of agreement. There is, however, another means at its disposal of accomplishing its objective—the manipulation of the bargaining unit to influence the relative bargaining powers of the two parties.

BARGAINING UNIT

In any negotiations between union and management, there must be a prior determination of what employees the union speaks for,

[2] On this definition, any salaried salesman would qualify for the title of bargaining agent, as he should. He derives no income from the customer to whom he sells but from the company for which he sells. His discretion may be limited by his employer, as sometimes in the case of a union by its members, or he may have wide discretion in negotiating terms, or he may be required to submit for company approval the terms which he offers to a customer, just as a union must commonly secure from its membership approval of a negotiated agreement.

and what company unit or units management speaks for. The configuration of employees may be of a craft nature, embracing only workers who possess specialized skills or who perform particular functions. A craft unit is usually a splinter group of a larger body of employees. Examples of such groups are the maintenance electricians in a chemical plant, pattern makers in an automobile plant, molders and coremakers in a foundry, truck drivers in a packing house, engravers in a textile printing and dyeing establishment. On the other hand, the employee group may be comprehensive, embracing most or all of the employees on a payroll, without respect to their skills and functions. It would therefore include all the employees in a chemical plant, or an automobile plant, or a foundry, or a packing house, or a textile establishment, regardless of their duties or training.

The company unit or units in collective bargaining negotiations range all the way from a single department or shop to an entire industry. In terms of the management groups who do the negotiating the distinction is usually drawn between single employer and multiemployer bargaining. The terms are virtually self-explanatory: in single employer negotiations, the company management speaks only for itself (whether it is dealing with a craft or comprehensive group in a single department or in the whole company). In multiemployer negotiations, a number of employers (from two to all in an industry) negotiate jointly, signing a single agreement with the union, the terms of which are binding on all the employers. There must thus be prior bargaining among the employers of such a group before they can arrive at a decision as to what proposals or counterproposals they shall jointly offer to the union. In multiemployer bargaining, the employers may have their own bargaining agent in the form of an employers' association, corresponding to the union which represents their employees.

The bargaining unit consists of the configuration of the parties on both sides of a single bargain. A bargaining unit in labor relations may thus be of a craft-single employer nature or craft-multiemployer; it may alternatively be comprehensive-single employer or comprehensive-multiemployer. It is not a matter of indifference to union or employer, however, as to which of these types of bargaining units is adopted. The choice of the bargaining unit affects their relative bargaining power, so that at any time both union and management are likely to have some preference as to the scope of the unit. The size of the unit itself becomes an issue—a demand made by one or the other of the parties, supported by its existing bargaining power, with the objective of increasing that power.

Skilled employees may prefer a craft unit in the belief that their strategic skills, if withdrawn by strike, would require the shutdown of the whole plant, imposing on the employer a severe cost of disagreement on their terms, while the fact that their numbers are small means that even a substantial wage increase will add only a little to the firm's total wage bill, so that the cost of agreement is low. Employers, on the other hand, may prefer a comprehensive unit in order to avoid the danger of a series of plant closings which they would face if their work force was fragmented into numerous craft units, in each of which a strike could be called. In quite different situations, however, mass production technology may have so diminished the need for special skills that the employees' only strength is to be found in a comprehensive unit since their employer, even if able to replace some category of workers, would find it more difficult to replace the whole force. And in other situations an employer may prefer several craft units to a comprehensive one if the crafts come under the jurisdiction of stable unions known for their responsibility and if the establishment of such craft units so fragmentizes the body of employees as to make impracticable the formation of any residual comprehensive unit, the jurisdiction over which would fall to a union known for its radical leadership.

Similarly, a union may prefer a multiemployer unit in industries where competition in the product market puts constant pressure on the wage rates, in the expectation that it can improve its bargaining power if it is able to stifle price cutting by precluding competitive wage cutting. On the other hand, a firm may prefer the single employer unit where its competitive position is sufficiently weak that it can expect to get concessions from the union, concessions that would not be allowable under a multiemployer agreement. But where the union runs into a solid wall of resistance from an employers' association, it may seek to split off from the association, into single-employer units, those firms that it believes can be brought to sign on its terms. And at times employers who have grown tired of being picked off one by one and of being whipsawed may press for a multiemployer unit which would make a strike more costly for a union, thereby reducing its relative bargaining power.

Over a period of time it may be to a party's advantage to shift from a unit of one scope to a unit of different extent, and perhaps back again later. The United Mine Workers seeks an industry-wide agreement in one year, as this suits its advantage, and seeks to split the southern operators off from the northern operators in another year, as strategy dictates. Playing the unit becomes a means of manipulating bargaining power.

Unions as bargaining agents thus direct the bargaining power which comes from organization against managements to secure an improvement in the terms of their bargains, and employers' associations similarly bring their organized power to bear upon their employees to secure favorable bargains. There are some objectives, however, which cannot be secured through this private bargaining. No firm is capable of guaranteeing employment to its workers in the face of a widespread depression, for example. No union is capable of assuring a firm that the productivity of its members will be so high as effectively to meet all foreign competition. Governments can provide such guarantees, however. Governments can undertake public works programs to sustain full employment; they can impose tariffs and quota restrictions on imports from other countries. The same kinds of organizations which act as bargaining agents in making private bargains can act as bargaining agents to secure such desired terms by striking bargains with governments. Depending on the objectives sought, the bargaining unit in these instances may be the municipality, the county, the state, or the federal government. And as with private bargains, so with bargains with governments it becomes a matter of strategy to determine in what unit one's bargaining power with respect to some objective is strongest.

The labor union which negotiates a wage increase from General Motors is, at the most elemental conceptual level, no different from the farmers' bloc which exacts a price support program from Congress. Both are bargaining agents, both seek bargains benefiting the income position of their members. They are merely operating in different bargaining units.

CHAPTER 14

The Economics of Political Bargains

GOVERNMENTS, like households and firms, are economic units. They enter into bargains from which they derive income and in consequence of which they expend income. Inflows and outflows must always balance *ex post*, a change in any flow item necessarily setting up a simultaneous compensatory change in other flow items. The attempt to reach a preferred balance of flows (in terms of both level and composition) is the function of the heads of government, executive and legislative, who perform the managerial task of coördinating the complex of bargains which compose the flows.

In the case of a governmental unit as with other economic units, the revenue decision involves the amount of and the manner in which revenue shall be raised. It has its "tax line" similar to a firm's product line; income tax, excises, license fees, property, estate, poll, head, and use taxes, special assessments, and so on, offer possibilities of substitution, differential reliance, and innovation—a scope for manipulation by the government to achieve its objectives. Such revenues may be supplemented by borrowing against expectations. The budget decision involves the application of the inflows, in the variety of forms with which everyone is familiar. There is no need to expand here on the possible methods of adjusting inflows and outflows to secure a preferred balance. They differ in form but

259

not in essence from the methods available to business and household units.

The government as an economic unit is a provider of services. It maintains a police force and army, educational establishments, hospitals, roads, public museums and parks, and so on. It is also a means for redistributing income, to the extent that the services received by individuals bear no direct relationship to the payments they make to the government. The nature of the services performed changes over the years, with changing conceptions of the functions of government. Unemployment compensation and old age pensions are now paid out of the public treasury, although such a practice would have been frowned on by many only a quarter of a century ago.

SOVEREIGNTY

The government is something more than an economic unit, however. It holds a coercive power over others which goes by the name of sovereignty. Sovereignty is the power of making decisions which take precedence over decisions made by others, where there is any conflict. The necessity for sovereignty lies in the necessity for some decision binding on all; whether war shall be waged, who shall issue currency, whether public services shall be provided, under what conditions unemployment shall be compensated, and so on, are matters about which people may have divergent opinions but about which not much can be done without agreement. Agreement cannot always (or often) be achieved by consensus, however, but only through coercion. The power of sovereignty thus rests on the power of coercion.[1] Under penalties of fine or imprisonment, the

[1] Sovereignty is thus obviously nothing confined to states. Any organized government (of labor unions, businesses, trade associations, and so on) necessarily has—within the scope of its competence—sovereignty in the sense of power to coerce agreement. Limitations on sovereignty do not negate the fact of sovereignty within the permissive zone: even the sovereignty of states is limited, as in the United States by constitution. The sovereignty of states is distinguished from that of infrastate governments only in the fact that its permissive zone extends to areas where the sovereignty of the lesser jurisdictions is, by definition, limited.

governmental unit can determine by fiat how much of his income each individual shall relinquish to it, can seize property and conscript services in a manner that no other authority can do, and can require compliance with any lawful edict.

The powers of sovereignty are exercised not merely in the provision of services and the redistribution of income, through the income flows of the government; they are also used to redistribute bargaining power in society. By regulating the powers of others to impose costs of agreement and disagreement on those with whom they trade, the government can alter the structure of scarcity and interdependence relationships in the system. Through antitrust legislation, public utility regulation, labor laws, protective tariffs, farm programs, and so on, the government can employ its powers of sovereignty to modify the prevailing system of relative bargaining powers.

The fact that edicts of the sovereign must be lawful to be effective is a reminder, however, that sovereignty is never absolute but always limited, at least by custom and tradition or constitution. But within such limitations and a more fundamental one yet to be mentioned, sovereignty is the denial of discretion to others where the government itself exercises discretion.

There are other limits to the effectiveness of sovereignty than custom or constitution. In the case of any law, there is always the possibility of citizen disobedience or evasion, a possibility which is likely to be made real in those instances where the costs to the offender of disobedience (considering both the penalty involved and the probability of being caught) are less than the cost of conforming to the law. Despite price controls during World War II, black market operations were carried on. In the face of state laws providing for compulsory arbitration, strikes in such industries and states can yet be expected. Prohibition was honored in the breach. Gambling continues in most major cities despite laws to the contrary, and so on.

Sovereignty means the permissive power to coerce agreement, but where the costs of agreement are greater than the costs of disagreement sovereignty is ineffective. Sovereignty thus stands revealed as simply a bargaining power relationship, distinguished only by the special kinds of coercive powers available to the government to increase the other's cost of disagreement on its terms. Sovereignty is limited by the power of dissent retained by the governed. To make its sovereignty effective, a government must sometimes compromise with those to whom a law is designed to apply. As Professor Lloyd Fisher remarked with respect to the administration of agricultural wage rates in California during the war (an administration which was controlled by farm employer groups in their own interests), "If, on balance, the choice which confronted the Office of Economic Stabilization was a program administered to the satisfaction of the growers or no program at all, it may have been the choice of wisdom and not cynicism to have offered the program on the growers' terms. . . . Any program which was firmly opposed by growers would prove virtually impossible of enforcement. The choice [in agriculture] is essentially self-regulation or no regulation at all." [2] Even in Soviet Russia, where authority over the individual is generally assumed to be close to absolute, the government in 1953 was forced to compromise on its farm program in order to secure a greater measure of compliance with its regulations. Peasants who had balked at high taxes and heavy compulsory deliveries by cutting down on production, jeopardizing the supply of food, were appeased by reductions of taxes and forced deliveries, along with other concessions.

If legislation—the exercise of sovereignty—represents a bargaining relationship between those who make laws and those to whom they apply, in the sense that compliance demands a lower cost of agreement than disagreement, this does not require any direct negotiation between the two groups. The process is commonly one of assumption, trial, and learning. Nevertheless, to label the legislative process a form of bargaining is not intended as a figure of speech but as a precise classification.

[2] Lloyd H. Fisher, *The Harvest Labor Market in California* (Cambridge: Harvard University Press, 1953), pp. 136, 138.

Because sovereignty can be employed to modify the structure of relative bargaining powers in the system, the government—the executor of the sovereign power—is something which individuals and groups in a society seek to control for their own advantage. To the extent that they can influence legislation and its administration, they can improve the terms of their bargains and modify to their benefit the flows of income. In the pursuit of this objective, individuals and groups seek to bargain with those who form the government. Citizens and bargaining agents for households and firms bargain with politicians either to have the legislative power used on their behalf or to restrain its use against them.

In the bargaining process which occurs in these political bargaining units, the determinants of bargaining power are those with which we are already familiar—the aspirations and alternatives of the symbionts. The aspirations of those who seek to capture the powers of sovereignty for their own benefit need no elaboration. But what are the aspirations of those who compose the government?

POLITICAL BARGAINING

The politicians are the managers of government, and like their counterparts in industry, they have multiple goals. These include a drive for personal power and the same artist's feel for creative expression that characterizes most leaders, whether in government, business, unionism, or the professions. But power and its creative exercise in the political case commonly find their focus in an ideological conception of society which the political leader would like to translate into reality through his influence in government, through his access to the coercive powers of sovereignty. This embraces such matters as some rough notion of what constitutes political and economic justice and what class within the citizenry should be charged with preserving and advancing the values regarded as characteristic of the kind of society in which the politician would like to live and rear his children.

Such an ideological conception is not always consciously espoused and is not likely to be the product of logical reflection or philosophical introspection as much as of prejudice and belief engendered by family and social background. Thus Professor Stephen K. Bailey characterized a Republican senator from Delaware who had opposed passage of the Employment Act of 1946 in the following terms: "Senator Buck is no 'man of the people,' and except for an occasional play for the Polish vote in Wilmington, he seldom if ever has talked like one. He is a member of one of the ruling families in the American economy; he is at home in the luxurious estates of Newcastle county; he shares the fears of the economic and social class epitomized by the DuPont name [a family into which he married]—the fears of any aristocracy in a revolutionary world." [3] As Professor Bailey has suggested, a person's background gives him an alignment or orientation with certain interests, and a susceptibility to their arguments, a concern for their welfare, and a willingness to appeal for their support.

To pursue his long-run ideological objective (the actual content of which is subject to change over time) requires that the politician maintain himself in office, so that election and reëlection becomes a more immediate objective than the ideological goal. In futherance of political survival he must secure support from his constituency; this demands, as the most proximate objective, bargains with those who are likely to be influential in securing him in office.

In this time stream of a politician's aspirations, running from present bargains for maintenance in office to the achievement of ideological goals, the long-run objective must usually be compromised to secure the proximate and shorter-run goals. To garner votes commonly requires bargains that do violence in some degree to the values which he would foster, and in some instances the notions of what constitutes a good society may in time be molded chiefly by expediency, until reëlection becomes an objective in its own right. Nevertheless, cynicism and disillusionment should not trap us into arguing that politicians are men unmotivated by ideals;

[3] Stephen K. Bailey, *Congress Makes a Law* (New York: Columbia University Press, 1950), p. 193.

a politician will probably sell his soul for votes—will consent to *whatever* bargains are necessary for political victory—no more (and no less) quickly than will another person barter his conscience for wealth or prestige. The effective rationalization is that he will, even so, obtain more of his long-run goal than he would without compromise, than he would if he stood obstinately for principle but shorn of power.

The aspirations of the politician—for a kind of society, for his own political security—dictate the kinds of terms which he offers to his constituents in exchange for their support and determine with what political symbionts he seeks to strike bargains. The aspirations of his constituents in all walks of life, which they seek to achieve by the most promising alternatives available to them, leads them to attempt to employ the instrument of government either to gain their objectives directly from it or to improve their bargaining advantage in relations with others (or, negatively, to prevent its use to improve the bargaining power of their symbionts). These objectives set the terms which they demand from the politician in exchange for their support.

There follows, then, the familiar bargaining process, with the outcome dependent on the relative costs of disagreement and agreement on each other's terms. Such political bargaining more commonly than not involves the process of assumption, trial, and learning that we noted before. Nevertheless, politicians and constituents often do more than react to the conditions each finds in the other. There is the same opportunity for manipulation of bargaining power in the political sphere as in the economic.

We identify three types of bargaining processes which, while also to be found in price relations, are most applicable to political relations. These are: (1) the explicit bargain, in which the terms of politician and constituent are clearly defined and the agreement, if one is reached, is unambiguous, (2) the implicit bargain, in which the terms of agreement are expressly delineated with respect to one of the parties but only implied for the other, and (3) the conjectural bargain, in which the terms offered by both politician and constituents are uncertain and can only be surmised by each.

In all this there is not intended the slightest implication of an economic interpretation for all political behavior. Nor is our interest concerned with all political behavior. We assume that the elements of aspirations and alternatives lead to a bargaining relationship in politics generally, but we are interested only in such political bargaining as affects income flows either directly (through redistribution of income via the political unit's budget) or indirectly (through redistribution of bargaining power via the exercise of sovereignty).

1. Explicit bargaining is perhaps the least common form of bargaining to be found in politics. It requires a known *quid pro quo* between politician and constituent, and thus is suggestive of bribery or intimidation. A company may threaten to cease retaining a lawyer-legislator if he fails to support some wanted measure. An agent for an insurance company may suggest to a medical doctor serving as representative in a state legislature (as actually revealed in congressional investigation) that the agent "would attempt to see that he didn't get any more examinations" if he did not withdraw a bill that was considered inimical to the insurance trade.[4] Perhaps the most frequently encountered form of explicit bargain is where a politician trades support of some measure for an organization's endorsement.

2. Implicit bargains are more frequently encountered. In these some specific action is demanded of one of the parties (usually the politician), while the obligations of the other are at best a gentlemen's understanding, usually only an expectation. It appears that most measures introduced into legislatures are actually drafted by interest groups outside the legislature and are simply sponsored and supported by politicians within the legislature.[5] In at least some of these instances such support is undertaken in the expectation

---

[4] *Investigation of Concentration of Economic Power*, Hearings before the Temporary National Economic Committee, Seventy-sixth Congress, first session (1939), Part 10, pp. 4416–4417.

[5] V. O. Key, *Politics, Parties and Pressure Groups* (New York: The Thomas Y. Crowell Company, 1942), pp. 220–221, citing studies by Harvey Walker.

that it will be rewarded in the next campaign. The expectation is not, however, underwritten by any firm commitment.[6]

It is not only in the field of legislation that such implicit bargaining occurs. Laws do not administer themselves, and the same interest groups which press for passage of a measure may press for its sympathetic administration. Thus the United Mine Workers have not been satisfied with simple passage of federal legislation in the field of mine safety, but have brought pressure on the Interior Department to secure its adequate enforcement. In 1953, the first year of a change of federal administration, the Secretary of Interior entered into an agreement with President Lewis of the Mine Workers and President Moses of the Bituminous Coal Operators' Association, promising a more modern version of a mine safety code, retention of a director of the Bureau of Mines whom he had previously planned to replace, and appointment of a member of the Federal Coal Mine Safety Board of Review favorable to both miners and operators. No explicit concessions were offered by the two groups to the Interior Secretary, but he might reasonably have considered that there was an implied bargain that miners and operators would commend rather than condemn, support rather

---

[6] The congressional hearing referred to in footnote 4 disclosed that a representative of insurance companies had secured the withdrawal of a measure considered harmful to insurance interests by means of an implicit bargain. (*Investigation of Concentration of Economic Power*, Part 10, p. 4775.) Writing to an official of the Association of Life Insurance Companies, he explained:

"You wrote me on February 2nd in regard to [Georgia] Senate Bill No. 21, suggesting some amendments.

"The easiest way to handle this bill is to kill it. I think that has been done. The First National Bank of Valdosta, Ga., is the financial backer of the Hon. Nelson, who introduced the bill. I hand you a copy of a telegram that was sent to Senator Nelson yesterday by this bank, at the instance of one of our agents, Ex-Senator E. E. Dekle, to wit."

The accompanying telegram, signed by the president of the First National Bank read:

"We believe passage of Senate Bill twenty-one detrimental to business interests of Georgia. Hope you will not urge its passage."

The Senator might well have read into such a telegram an implication that financial backing would be withdrawn if the bill were not killed and a hopeful if not completely logical corollary that he might reasonably expect continued assistance if he complied with the expressed wish.

than attack, the Secretary for his administration of the program.

3. The most important form of political bargaining is the conjectural variety. Here both politicians and constituents must choose among alternatives without being sure of the terms of the alternatives. They can only guess and gamble.

The terms which a politician offers to his constituents are the specific attitudes which he promises to adopt toward known legislation and the general attitude which he can be expected to adopt toward unknown legislation. These attitudes will be influenced, as we know, by his assumptions as to what the constituents want of him, but they will also be influenced by his own ideological conception of the kind of society he himself prefers. Political leaders become known as "liberals" or "conservatives," for example, not simply because they expect to catch votes by such attitudes but because such attitudes are consistent with their own ideologies. Constituents, however, cannot be certain of the terms which are being offered them. Sometimes they trust a politician's assurances, other times they are suspicious of his integrity, or again his words and actions appear inconsistent, leaving doubt. They may know very little about the man so that they have an uncertain basis for judgment. Nevertheless, if the constituent is to strike any political bargain at all (that is, to seek to establish a symbiont relationship that will align sovereignty in his own interests), he must choose among the alternatives as best he can, "by faith and faith alone embrace, believing where we cannot prove," in Tennyson's words.

The strength of party allegiance rather than independent choice among rival politicians has often been remarked in the United States, raising the question as to how such behavior conforms to the notion of political bargains and the conception of constituents choosing among alternative politicians on the strength of terms which the latter offer. Party allegiance appears to be characteristic of two types of people: (1) There are those who believe that "politicians are all alike" and who therefore indulge an inherited predisposition toward a party; because the alternatives are regarded as relatively equal, within their structure of aspirations, the choice is reasonable rather than rational. (2) There are, however, others who believe that politicians are bound by a party ideological discipline and who therefore choose by party rather than by person; in this case the choice is rational, but as between conceived party ideologies rather than those of individuals.[7] In both cases, however, bargains are struck in the sense that there are offers of alternative relationships carrying differing costs of agreement and disagreement. The relationsips must always be among people, in this case constituent and politician, and the fact of party affiliation enters as an element influencing the constituents' choice (either reasonably or rationally) among politicians.

On the other side of the bargain, the terms which constituents offer to the politician are their votes and campaign contributions, conditional on the politician's espousal of certain interests or adoption of a general predisposition favorable to those interests. But the politician can never be certain as to what the constituent's conditions are. He is deluged by pressure groups and organizations which purport to speak, as bargaining agents, for blocs of voters, but he can never be sure as to how reliably they represent their memberships. Leaders of labor unions have spoken on political issues as though they spoke for their entire followings, for example, but the evidence is compelling that however influential such leaders may be, they are unable to deliver the vote *en bloc*. The politician must therefore decide as best he can how many votes will be won and how many will be lost by adopting some stand or espousing some general interest and what will be the net effect of accepting the terms of the bargaining agents which profess to speak for groups of voters. In making such a judgment he is forced to estimate the extent to which the conditions demanded by the organized bargaining agents actually appeal to the individual members of his jurisdiction, num-

---

[7] That this latter belief is a significant influence in the making of political bargains is strongly indicated in Richard Centers' interesting study, *The Psychology of Social Classes* (Princeton: Princeton University Press, 1949).

bered by hundreds or thousands or millions, an estimate which is bound to be only a hunch.

In the fall of 1953 when the Secretary of Agriculture was under fire for his opposition to the extension of high, rigid farm price supports, a delegation of several hundred cattlemen, formed into a temporary committee sponsored by the National Farmers Union, descended on Washington, secured several conferences with the Secretary, and sought to change his attitude toward price supports. Failing to do so, they were told by the president of the Farmers Union to carry their fight to Congress. As reported in *The New York Times*, "He called for the cattlemen to 'petition the Government, more and more and more.' He urged them to send leaders to the House Agriculture Committee when it starts its Western tour in Cheyenne, Wyo., Monday to sound out farm sentiment. He bade them to get to know their Representatives and Senators in Congress and tell each one that 'if he wants to stay in Congress he had better listen to the voice of the people instead of a few fat cats who are running with the [meat] packers." [8] The problem facing both the Secretary and legislators was, for how many constituents was this committee of the Farmers Union speaking? How many other voters might be opposed to their demands? What would be the marginal gain or loss of votes by adopting one program or another? Any answers to these questions were necessarily conjectural. The costs of disagreement and agreement on the terms of this bargaining agent could only be surmised.

The conditions attaching to vote or campaign contribution are not often so specific as the expectancy of his support of some identified bill. They are often no more precise than that the politician will "do something" about a bad situation—"do something" to relieve unemployment, hold down prices, prevent serious strikes, provide better schools, increase old age pensions, and so on. Definition of the means is left to the politician, and choice among rivals may hinge upon their relative abilities to convince the electorate that they can "do something."

[8] *The New York Times*, October 28, 1953.

In winning the support of numbers of constituents, the politician must attempt to reconcile the demands of general interest groups with special interest groups. Every individual is a member of a number of classes or groups, each meeting certain of his needs and aspirations. Out of this background of multiple affiliations the individual constituents make multiple demands on the politician, sometimes directly, sometimes through bargaining agents, sometimes only impliedly. Which of these demands is most important to the constituent? Can the politician rely solely on general appeal to those who support some particular governmental philosophy to produce the necessary votes? Or must he also seek to satisfy the narrower interests of numbers of small groups as well? Can he by espousing special interests overcome in the minds of some voters a bias against his broad political platform?

The fact of multiple interests of individual constituents commonly means that the politician must stand for a program which predisposes in his favor a large class of voters (such as the business community or the working class or the liberal element, and so on) but must also establish his beneficent attitude toward specific interests in his jurisdiction, such as companies and trade associations and labor unions and civic organizations and veterans' societies. Attention to such particularized interests is often but by no means always more decisive in winning constituent support than are general principles. (In a time of widespread unemployment, for example, special political favors for a variety of private groups are less likely to be decisive than the stand taken on what the government should do about jobs.) The politician's need for combining attention to parochial and general interests both is shown in this characterization of Senator Barkley of Kentucky: "Barkley has taken pains not to antagonize the main economic interests of his state. He voted for a tariff on coal in 1931, he has fought legislation opposed by the racing people, he has attempted to appease strong tobacco interests like the Burley Tobacco Cooperative, he has dispensed his share of patronage, he has paid close attention to the needs of the railroad workers and United Mine Workers. But on broad national issues his first loyalty has been to his party and to his own liberal philosophy." [9]

The politician must thus guess as to the terms which are sought by more or less specialized or generalized interest groups in his total constituency, and as to their relative strengths. In agreeing with what he conceives to be the terms of one group, he disagrees with another. His cost of agreement on the terms of the former is the votes of the latter that he loses, and his cost of disagreement is the votes within the first group that he would thereby lose. But he can only surmise what the net gain or loss has been.

We have so far been talking of the political bargains between constituents and politicians. In a representative government, however, laws are not made by single politicians but by legislative majorities. In order for any politician to secure the legislative action he desires (either to satisfy personal aspiration or political bargain), he must win the support of enough fellow legislators to create the majority vote he needs. This calls for agreements with them, agreements which must be bargained out. There is no reason to believe that other politicians will espouse precisely the principles he espouses or seek to achieve them by precisely the same means; there is even less basis for expecting them to support, without some further inducement, legislation favoring special interests in someone else's jurisdiction. To gain the support necessary to the program on which the achievement of his objectives (both short and long run) depends, each politician must therefore bargain for the votes of his fellows by making concessions to them, concessions to their ideologies, concessions to the special interests which they espouse. As Professor Bailey has remarked, "In the absence of a widely recognized crisis, legislative policy-making tends to be fought out at the level of largely irresponsible personal and group stratagems and compromises based upon temporary power coalitions of political, administrative, and nongovernmental interests." [10]

[9] Bailey, *op. cit.*, p. 208. It is worth noting too how expedient bargains to maintain office and personal ideological goals both play their part in the characterization of this generally beloved politician.

[10] *Ibid.*, p. 236. I would delete the term "irresponsible" from the passage quoted,

Indeed, political parties can be charged with forwarding political principle or effecting party pledges only because party whips and leaders possess powers of punishing irregularity. Party majorities can be secured, when needed, only if the cost to individual politicians of disagreeing on their party's terms (perhaps loss of patronage or party support for a favored measure) is greater than the cost of agreeing on those terms (perhaps some denial of conscience or the inability to discharge a promise to constituents).

Political relationships, like economic, are thus composed of a number of bargains which are sought in order to achieve a time stream of aspirations. There are bargains between constituents and politicians, and bargains among politicians, without which government would be impossible. The terms of such bargains are often influenced by noneconomic considerations, having to do with aspirations completely unrelated to the flow of income, but their terms also often affect directly the income flows of the community or redistribute the relative bargaining powers affecting income flows, and in these respects political bargains affect economic relationships.

The political bargain is therefore one means of manipulating bargaining power in economic relationships. A National Lead and Zinc Committee descends on Washington to demand relief as a "hardship" case under the "escape clause" of the Reciprocal Trade Agreements Act. The Missouri Automobile Dealers Association urges the state legislature to prevent Detroit manufacturers from overloading dealers with inventory, by enacting provisions for the state licensing of dealers that would render harmless "veiled threats" by the manufacturers to remove franchises if quotas are not kept.

---

however. I fail to see how legislation can be enacted in a representative government without such bargaining processes.

Professor Bailey's remark comes after a detailed examination of the steps leading to final passage, in considerably modified form, of the Full Employment bill [S. 380] in the 1946 Congress. He goes on to say: "Put in its baldest form, the story of S. 380 adds up to the fact that majority sentiment expressed in popular elections for a particular economic policy can be, or frequently is, almost hopelessly splintered by the power struggles of competing political, administrative, and private interests, and is finally pieced together, if at all, only by the most laborious, complicated, and frequently covert coalition strategies."

Small retail establishments unite in supporting price maintenance laws. Distillers seek to extend the period from eight years to twelve years during which aging whiskey stocks are free of excise taxes, to improve their position versus the consuming public as stocks increase. Management groups seek to reduce the bargaining power of unions by restricting the secondary boycott. These are but a few examples of the innumerable situations in which bargainers have sought to modify their power relative to symbionts, in economic transactions.

Merely the threat to resort to use of one's political bargaining power may be influential in determining the relative bargaining powers in a straight economic transaction. In the period of postwar inflation, fear of congressional reaction undoubtedly served to restrain price increases by the large corporations or at a minimum to influence their timing of price increases. Fear of governmental intervention sometimes prompts the settlement of a strike on terms that otherwise would not have been granted. Here the influential symbionts are the buyers of the company's products, who stand to suffer from price increase or withdrawal of supply. Their actual or potential pressure may lie in direct influence brought to bear on governmental agents or a politician's conjecture that they expect him to "do something" about the situation, with his failure to act entailing as a likely cost of his disagreeing on their terms the loss of their support at the polls in the next election.

Political bargains thus constitute, among other things, a means of manipulating relative bargaining power in economic affairs. Because of their value for this purpose, organized groups often seek to improve their political bargaining power by manipulations. We thus encounter the attempted manipulation of political bargaining power to further an attempted manipulation of economic bargaining power. No point would be served by undertaking any extensive examination of the means by which political bargaining power may be manipulated. It will serve our purpose simply to suggest two of the primary methods by which this may be accomplished. The first is by efforts to mold public opinion. To the extent that a pressure group can influence the thinking of other members of the public, it can enlist their support in its interests. The principal objective is to bring others to believe that general interest and special interest coincide. A Taft-Hartley Act can be passed, improving the relative bargaining power of managements in their relations with unions, if public opinion can be mobilized around a wave of strikes (such as occurred in 1945–1946) to support a legislative move to curb the powers of unions. The second principal means of manipulating political bargaining power is through combinations and alliances. One group enlists the support of another, perhaps by accommodating the latter's interests to its own, perhaps through explicit or implied promise of reciprocal support of some measure the latter is promoting.

Political bargaining is, accordingly, a process by which various individuals, groups, and classes seek to have the power of sovereignty exercised on behalf of their interests. But the power of sovereignty itself is limited, as we earlier saw, by the necessity that the cost of agreement on the terms which are promulgated in its name be less than the cost of disagreement on those terms, a requirement which involves another set of bargains. Labor groups maneuver to secure legislation improving their bargaining power with respect to employers, but to secure employer compliance with the legislation its terms must be bargained down to where the government-imposed penalties for disagreement are greater than the costs that are incurred by conforming.

We are now in a position to arrive at several conclusions which relate political bargains and economic bargains.

1. Political bargaining power is a supplement or substitute for economic bargaining power in affecting income flows. In managing one's position of interdependence and scarcity, to achieve one's time stream of aspirations, political as well as economic relations are important. Prices and votes both deal with the terms of bargains, and both are significant to the economist but only in so far as they affect income flows.

2. When bargaining power in economic transactions declines or

is expected to decline for a number of similarly situated individuals (commensals), involving multiple economic units and attributable to some common cause, greater emphasis is placed on political bargains as a means of restoring position. The deterioration of position may affect a particular industry or trade or region, or it may be applicable to a whole class of interests, such as the working class, the managerial class, rentiers.

Shifts in relative bargaining power only slightly affecting income flows are not likely to evoke major political moves, however, since other than economic issues enter into political bargains. The increase in political pressure may be assumed to be functionally related (perhaps even roughly proportional) to the decrease in economic position and to the numbers involved. Economic interests will dominate political bargaining only where aspirations are least satisfied or most threatened because of a deterioration of bargaining power in economic transactions. On the familiar principle of the declining marginal rate of substitution, as economic interests suffer relative to other interests, they will tend to displace other interests in the terms of political bargains. And as larger numbers are involved, their concerted interest makes them a more potent political influence.

3. As economic interests come to dominate the terms of political bargains for a particular group or a class of people, their bargaining power relative to favorably disposed politicians falls, while relative to politicians predisposed unfavorably it rises. The cost of disagreeing with the politicians most likely to assist their specific cause is greater because of their economic exigency, the cost of disagreeing with those who are unlikely to help them on this specific issue is slight, since whatever the coincidence or conflict of views on other issues, other issues have become less important.

4. Where the economic distress of the group or class persists, an opportunity is created for new political leaders to rise to power by the espousal of the interests of the class or group affected. This is equivalent to a producer's seeking to capture a product market through innovation or differentiation, meeting a need previously

inadequately met. The new politicians may be expected to be those whose own political ideologies accord with reforms which purport to remedy the distress of the public whose support is sought, or those whose conjecture of the terms which will capture the constituency is shrewder than the conjecture of the "old guard."

5. Regardless of the extent to which shifts in bargaining power reflected in economic distress have substituted favorable for unfavorable politicians, in individual jurisdictions, as long as sovereignty is shared by a number of legislators, there must be further bargaining within the legislature before sovereignty can be exercised on behalf of those who seek to improve their bargaining power. The larger the number of legislators the more difficult does it become to secure a redistribution of relative bargaining power to the advantage of any group or class, since the more numerous the concessions which must be made to other groups or classes to secure their support. The more representative the government (the more the legislature is a reliable sample of the universe for which it stands) the less likelihood is there of a violent readjustment of relative bargaining power.

6. Any redistribution of bargaining power will be limited by the relative strength of the coercive powers of the government, on the one hand, and the group against whose interests it acts, on the other hand. The redistribution of bargaining power, to be effective, must be moderated to the point where the state's power of imposing a cost of disagreement is greater than the cost of the agreement which the state seeks to impose.

7. If important group interests are involved, with one seeking to improve its command over scarcity goods at the expense of another through political processes, and if the powers of sovereignty are so evenly divided as to prevent political compromise, a stalemate results. The stalemate may not be dangerous; the tension it creates may be tolerable in the short run, and sooner or later some slight political manipulation may lead to some slight compromise which resolves it. At other times, however, a stalemate creates an explosive situation which can even lead to revolution. The rise of Na-

tional Socialism in Germany has been attributed by some students to such a stalemate.[11]

In still other situations, if important group interests are involved, with one seeking to improve its position relative to the other, and if their given relative positions are such that the demanding group feels that it has little to lose by disagreement and the dominant group believes it has everything to lose by agreement, and if the powers of sovereignty are so unevenly divided as to prevent alleviation, so that neither economic nor political bargaining power is effective to remedy an aggravated situation, violence may be the only recourse. It is presumably such a situation which Marx believed to be developing in capitalist countries. Workers, whose deteriorating scarcity position left them with "nothing to lose but your chains," would rise up against masters whose greed inexorably drove them to concentrate wealth in their own hands. That this situation has failed to develop in the capitalist cultures of the United States and Great Britain should not blind us to the possibility of its occurring in other societies, even—perhaps especially—in those which are not capitalist in the Marxian sense. An increase in the level of aspirations may be all that is required to spark explosive unrest in underdeveloped countries lacking representative political institutions. Rising aspirations may make intolerable conditions previously tolerated, at the same time leading to demands which impose a high cost of agreement on those whom the distribution of bargaining power previously favored. To secure agreement it is therefore necessary for the aspirants to increase their symbionts' cost of disagreement. Among the forms of manipulation which may be resorted to, particularly if other means offer little promise, are an attempted violent seizure of the powers of sovereignty.

8. If the analysis of this chapter is valid, then economic and political bargains, in so far as they affect the flows of income, require integration within the same theoretical system. The study of price relations constitutes only a specialization within the field of eco-

[11] Karl Polanyi, *The Great Transformation* (New York: Rinehart & Company, Inc., 1944).

nomics, and not the whole of it. The field of economics is defined by income flows, not prices; prices are simply one aspect of one set of bargains which affect income flows, and they are significant only because of their effect on flows. Votes, too, affect bargaining power, and the terms of bargains, and the flows of income; they become no less than prices a mechanism in the use and allocation of scarce resources. We should now be prepared to make a final conclusion, affecting our set of basic concepts.

Traditionally, economics has been regarded as the discipline which deals with the allocation of scarce resources, while politics is the discipline which treats of the use of power. Recognizing that arbitrary lines of demarcation are necessary to specialization, we may nevertheless question whether lines of specialization are so drawn as to permit the maximum cumulation and integration of knowledge.

In so far as economics (as defined above) has been concerned only or primarily with price transactions, it has chosen an unwisely narrow basis for abstraction. Price is only one element in the bargaining power relationships which determine the allocation of scarce resources, only one determinant of the costs of agreement and disagreement. Moreover, its significance has been overstressed since it is limited to whatever is its effect on income flows, at both the micro and macro levels of analysis.

In so far as politics has been concerned with power relationships, it has chosen as a basis for *specialization* something which permeates scarcity-interdependence relations *generally*. All of economics, for example, is based on power—bargaining power—relationships. If politics is thus defined by power, it necessarily establishes an uncertain area of overlap with economics, and the resulting vagueness sacrifices the discipline of specialization.

Politics embraces more than *certain types* of bargaining power relationships affecting the allocation of resources, but it is obvious that it must include such relationships, just as economics embraces more than the price element of bargaining power relationships affecting the allocation of resources, even though it must include that element.

In the system of concepts which we are developing, then, we shall define *politics* as the process of attaining and retaining control over the management function within a bargaining unit. That function, it will be recalled, is the *coördination* of the bargains among all those who compose the unit, with its two conditions that for all on whom the unit depends cost of agreement must be less than the cost of disagreement and that aggregate outflows must be covered by aggregate inflows. The advantage of control over the management function lies in the fact that the necessary integration of bargains can be sought in ways which are more acceptable to those exercising control, and which permit a maximum of initiative through the residual powers accruing to management after the terms of the coördinated bargains have been satisfied.

The political process thus permeates society, just as does the economic process. Politics and economics are not separate departments of social activity, separated in that facultative manner once identified by such terms as "economic man" and "political man," but are different ways of looking at people in the totality of their activity. Just as psychologists and sociologists have now agreed that their common concern is people in the totality of their activity, and that the basis for their separate disciplines lies in the approach rather than in a separate subject matter, so too may economists and political scientists work with overlapping data but from specialized points of view.

Control of the management function is sought within a variety of bargaining units ranging from the household to the "omnipotent" state. The bargains which are struck embrace other elements than scarce resources, including matters of status and prestige, ethics and morals, physical security, anything, in fact, which is included in the aspiration patterns of those who compose the group. The management of the corporation has its economic aspects, just as does the management of the state (which we call government), and the management of the corporation has its political aspects, just as does the management of the state. The interest of the student of politics is in how the distribution and use of bargaining power affects control of the coördinating function, while the interest of the student of economics is in how the distribution and use of bargaining power affects the allocation of scarce resources. Each is only part of the total picture, each must rely on the other in its analyses, but the focus of theoretical interest differs.

In our system of concepts, then, we need add nothing new to provide for the influence of government on the pattern of resource use. Government is simply management, within the framework of a defined bargaining unit.[12] We need only be made aware of the fact that the concepts which we have already developed permit us to integrate those "political" considerations which are usually relegated to related but discrete analyses.

[12] There may be those who would object that the citizen-government relationship is fundamentally different from the worker-management relationship, in that the former permits no alternative while the latter has many. The position adopted here denies such a contention. Instead, it adopts the view that each relationship has its own set of alternatives, though some relationships have more and better alternatives than others. It is not true that the citizen-government relationship has no alternatives. At a minimum, a citizen may migrate or escape to another country or accept the penalties of civil disobedience. Admittedly these are limited alternatives—but economists have long been used to recognizing that the alternatives for some buyer-seller relationships are better than for others. But equally important, as has been argued in an earlier chapter, the larger an organization becomes the more does it transform external competition into internal competition. The more comprehensive the organization, the fewer are the alternatives external to it but the greater the possibility of alternative internal alignments designed to secure control over the unit itself. "Monopoly" based on combination or alliance is thus not a means for escaping competition but only for changing its form. We shall observe the significance of this in a later chapter.

CHAPTER 15

Income Flows: The Role of the Banking System

MONEY permits the complex exchange of goods and services among millions of households, business firms, and government units, allowing A to dispose of his services or goods to B but to be repaid by products made by X, Y, and Z. The use of money for this purpose does not now require, as it once did, the accompanying transport of any gold or silver coins or even of greenback currency. A check written on the purchaser's bank and sent through the mails does the trick. The amount of the check is deducted from the purchaser's account, and when the check is deposited by the seller, is credited to his account. A bookkeeping transaction has taken place, with the check serving merely as a chit from one bookkeeper to another advising him what change should be made in the books which he is keeping. The changes in the entries on the books of the banks draw down the claims remaining to the buyer and add to the claims accruing to the supplier.

We may envision all the transactions transpiring between the millions of economic units in the United States as based upon such bookkeeping entries. Each of these units is integrated into an economy-wide bookkeeping system, in which his purchases appear as debits to his account and his sales as credits. The banks of the nation are the keepers of these accounts. No gold changes hands, greenbacks rarely are offered in these transactions. One bank simply makes an entry in the receiver's account and another bank makes an entry in the seller's account.

The most important function which the banking system performs is that of keeping this record of transactions among economic units, as indicated by the checks which are presented for recording. In so doing it ties one unit in with all other units, becoming the chief mechanism for the flows of income. A bank is principally the legally authorized keeper of the record of transactions involving its customers. No other function which it performs is nearly so important as this one.

The business of keeping transaction records for the economy is a complicated one. Let us examine how the system works, carrying the analysis through principally in terms of business units. On any day millions of individuals are depositing checks with their banks, for credit to their account, which they have received for the sale of goods or services. But each of these checks represents not only a credit for the depositor but a liability for the person or firm that wrote the check. The amount of each check must therefore be charged as a debit to the account of the one writing the check before the bookkeeping process is complete. The check which is deposited as a credit must be returned to the bank on which drawn so that it can be entered in the appropriate account as a debit. The check, as we have seen, is simply a chit which conveys instructions to the bookkeeping banks as to how the transaction is to be recorded.

In some instances the accounts of both the person receiving and the person writing the check are carried in the same bank. The retailer who rents his store and the realty company which is his landlord may both have accounts in the same local bank. In these instances the bank can simply credit one of its accounts and debit the other. The bookkeeping is complete, and the check is returned to the one who wrote it for his own records. But in many more instances the check writer and the check receiver carry accounts in different banks, so that when the latter deposits his check with his bank, for credit to his account, that bank must then forward the check to another bank for debiting. Often, however, the two banks involved are located in the same community. To facilitate the return of checks, banks in most cities have organized clearinghouses, in which all checks received by local banks are sorted and returned to the appropriate local banks for debiting. If the check is drawn on a bank outside the local community, however, some further procedure is needed.

Most national banks and a number of state banks in the United States are members of the Federal Reserve System, which has twelve regional offices, also called banks. These Federal Reserve banks are often referred to as "bankers' banks," since their dealings are directly with the commercial banks rather than with the public. Each of the twelve Federal Reserve banks operates a clearinghouse for its region. Hence, when checks cannot be exchanged by banks in their own communities, through their local clearinghouse, they are forwarded to the Federal Reserve bank for clearance there. The regional clearinghouse sorts the checks forwarded to it and returns to the banks in its own region all those checks which must be debited to accounts in these banks.

There still remain checks which must be returned to banks in other regions, however. In these cases one Federal Reserve bank forwards to each of the other regional Federal Reserve banks all those checks drawn on banks in the latter's region. The Federal Reserve bank which receives such a shipment then sorts them for return to the appropriate banks in its region, where they are finally debited. The bookkeeping process is complete.

Each day, then, the accounts of millions of individuals and business firms are being credited with the amount of checks which they have received and deposited on that day and are being debited with checks which they wrote on previous days and which have been returned to their banks. These debits and credits to individual accounts are posted at least once a day and in some of the larger banks as often as three times a day. The process of posting reveals how each individual account stands—in technical terminology, it reveals the deposit balance. If a larger amount is credited than is debited, obviously the deposit balance increases. If checks for a larger sum have been written than have been received, the deposit balance declines.

This process by which checks written are balanced off against checks received, to determine the deposit balance, is sometimes called "offsetting" or "clearing." If the sum credited at the time of posting was always just equal to the sum debited, then the deposit balance would always remain the same. It would be theoretically possible for an individual firm—even of the size of the American Telephone and Telegraph Co., or Standard Oil of New Jersey—to operate with a checking account (that is, a deposit balance) of no more than $1, if it could always be sure that its debits and credits would offset in the posting process. Millions of dollars of operations could be carried on, on the basis of that $1 balance which would serve only to keep the account alive, if the checks charged against it were always balanced by the checks it deposited, each time the bank posted.

There is seldom such perfect synchronization of payments and receipts, however, and consequently the deposit balance of a firm fluctuates as on one day checks deposited exceed checks debited and on another day the reverse is true. Nevertheless, a substantial proportion of checks written and received do offset each other in this manner, within the account of an individual or firm; they are balanced off, at the time of posting, by such intra-account clearing. Table 1 (pp. 286–287), which shows the debits and credits to one business firm's account over a period of a month, indicates that for this firm over two-thirds of the volume of checks debited to its account were offset at the time of bank posting by checks which were being simultaneously credited to its account. On 7 of the 20 days in which checks were debited to the account the deposit balance did not decline at all, due to offsets.[1]

[1] Charles A. Dice and Philip Schaffner, "A Neglected Component of the Money Supply," *American Economic Review*, vol. 29 (1939), pp. 514–516. The conception of the banking process which is presented in this chapter derives almost wholly from the lectures of Professor Dice in his graduate seminar on money and banking at Ohio State University, though I do not commit him to all that is said here.

TABLE 1. INTRA-ACCOUNT CLEARING IN A BUSINESS FIRM'S BANK ACCOUNT

Date	Debits	Credits	Offset[a]	Nonoffset	Initial[b] Balance	Nonoffset ÷ Initial Balance (percent)
February 1	$ 437.50	–	–	$ 437.50	$ 591.37	73.98
2	–	–	–	–	153.87	–
3	19.21	–	–	19.21	153.87	12.48
4	6.14	–	–	6.14	134.66	4.56
5	197.55	$1,000.00	$ 197.55	–	128.52	–
6[c]						
7	2,802.42	4,000.00	2,802.42	–	930.97	–
8	4,931.79	3,500.00	3,500.00	1,431.79	2,128.55	67.27
9	92.81	–	–	92.81	696.76	13.32
10	30.48	205.76	30.48	–	603.95	–
11	284.60	–	–	284.60	779.23	36.52
12[c]						
13[c]						
14	197.90	513.52	197.90	–	494.63	–

[a] The offset data are inexact in so far as the computations are based on the assumption of only one posting at the end of each day, whereas this bank also conducts a morning posting of debits. Since there is no method of allocating check deposits between the morning and afternoon postings, the exact amount of offsetting cannot be determined. This defect in the data, however, is compensated to the extent that check deposits are distributed throughout the day in about the same proportions as checks received against the account.

[b] Whereas bank records show the deposit balance as of the end of each day, the table has been arranged to show the balance as of the beginning of each working day. This procedure facilitates the computation of the percentage of the deposit balance utilized each day.

[c] Legal holiday. *Note*: A dash indicates a zero amount in the column for the day concerned.

SOURCE: Bank ledger, as presented by Dice and Schaffner, *loc. cit.*

286

Table 1. Intra-Account Clearing in a Business Firm's Bank Account (*Continued*)

Date	Debits	Credits	Offset[a]	Nonoffset	Initial[b] Balance	Nonoffset ÷ Initial Balance (percent)
15	—	—	—	—	810.25	—
16	465.22	—	—	465.22	810.25	57.42
17	17.82	—	—	17.82	345.03	5.16
18	29.70	—	—	29.70	327.21	9.08
19	21.78	—	—	21.78	297.51	7.32
20[c]						
21	465.66	3,000.00	465.66	—	275.73	—
22[c]						
23	4,288.03	5,000.00	4,288.03	—	2,810.07	—
24	2,184.02	500.00	500.00	1,684.02	3,522.04	47.81
25	636.57	—	—	636.57	1,838.02	34.63
26	432.97	750.99	432.97	—	1,201.45	—
27[c]						
28	904.70	—	—	904.70	1,519.47	59.54
Total	$18,446.87	$18,470.27	$12,415.01	$6,031.86	—	—

Intra-account clearing is facilitated by business practices of settling claims at particular times of the month, so that the greatest volume of checks will be written and received within the space of perhaps a week, a large proportion of the debits and credits offsetting each other at the time of bank postings. To the extent that a firm expands its operations concurrently with other business firms, so that it receives more checks as well as writes more checks, intra-account clearing permits it to increase its expenditures without first increasing its bank account. The amount of current business transacted in the American economy, as reflected in the volume of checks written, thus bears no fixed relationship to the size of deposit balances. With balances of the same magnitude, the business community can increase its activity without definable limit as long as the expansion is general and synchronization is perfect. All make more payments but all receive more payments, so that the chits which record the transactions balance each other off. Even without perfect synchronization, it is possible for current business operations to expand, at least in some degree, without increasing business needs for operating funds.

A relatively small deposit balance may thus support a substantial volume of payments by a firm, provided the flow of receipts matches the flow of payments reasonably well. But these two flows do not always proceed at the same rate, and there occur intervals when the debits to an account continue to accrue without any offsetting credits. The credits may come later, in bunches rather than in a smooth stream; if posting took place monthly, intra-account clearing would perhaps still be possible. But since posting occurs at least once a day, debits to an account without offsetting credits must be met out of the deposit balance, which must be kept large enough to provide for contingencies of this sort. Similarly, when a business wishes to expand its output it requires some immediate additional expenditure, at least for wages, but usually does not receive a compensating return until after the sale of product has been completed. In these instances the debits to the firm's account will increase, without any currently offsetting increase in credits, so that its deposit balance will be drawn down.

Although English banking practice is to permit overdrafts (that is, the deposit balance may be negative under certain circumstances), in this country an account holder is always required to maintain a positive account balance. If the debits to a firm's account threaten to exceed the deposit balance, then some action must be taken. A positive deposit balance is the condition which the firm must meet if it is to maintain its integration with the economy-wide bookkeeping system which is so essential to its operations. To replenish its balance the firm may follow either of two courses of action: it may dispose of some of its assets, or it may incur debt. The proceeds can then be used to replenish its deposit balance. For short-term operations its principal means of disposing of assets is by selling securities or liquidating inventories, and its principal means of incurring debt is by negotiating a loan with its bank. Here enters a bank's second chief function.

The business firm which wishes to tide itself over a period when the debits to its account, after all intra-account clearing has taken place, exceed its deposit balance, can ask the bank for a short-term loan. The bank investigates the nature of the firm's operations and if it is satisfied that the prospects are good that within the period of the loan the firm's credits will be sufficient to meet all debits and also repay the bank, the loan is arranged. The loan, too, is a bookkeeping transaction. The bank simply enters as a credit in the firm's account the amount of the loan, thereby increasing the firm's deposit balance sufficiently to meet the debits which will be charged against it. If the bank's judgment as to the firm's prospects has been a sound one, ultimately the firm will obtain receipts from its operations adequate not only to meet all business debits but to repay the bank loan. The loan is repaid by a check drawn on its account, which thus wipes out that portion of the deposit balance which was advanced by the bank.

The commercial-loan function of a bank is thus designed to balance the leads and lags of a firm's operating receipts and expenditures, as these affect the firm's deposit balance. When debits and credits in the firm's account do not offset each other, and the balance is insufficient to make up for an excess of debits, the bank in effect guarantees the difference to the firm's creditors by making a deposit in the firm's account, holding the firm's debt for the time being. This service relieves the firm of the need for trying to secure credit from its own suppliers, who may be unable to advance such credit or uncertain of the desirability of doing so.

The commercial-loan function of the banking system thus places on it the task of determining which businesses among those applying to it for credits are likely to be successful in obtaining buyers for their goods at prices which will allow, over a period of time, their expenditures to be matched by their receipts. For those firms which are not in a position to maintain their deposit balances by other means, it is the bank's judgment of their business position which determines (for some) whether they remain in business and (for others) whether they can expand their operations. And the bank's judgment is based upon the firm's prospects of regaining a position, within a short run, where any excess of debits over credits in its account, at times of posting, is nonrecurring and sustainable on the strength of an adequate deposit balance. The frequency of bank postings acts as a continuous check on the liquidity and solvency of business firms.

What permits banks to extend credit to business firms in this fashion? Alternatively, we might ask what restrains banks from making loans without limit. If credit is only an accounting entry, what harm can come to the bank if the loan is not repaid?

If banks could lend without restraint, then obviously the claims on goods could mount without limit. Demand for all goods would exceed the supply at current prices, and prices would have to rise to choke off some portion of demand. Inflationary pressures would be perpetual. To avoid this situation, limitations on bank extension of credit must be built into the economy-wide bookkeeping system. These operate chiefly through the central bank, in the United

States the Federal Reserve System, whose clearinghouse functions we have already briefly encountered.

In the first place, each commercial bank, with all its customers' accounts, is viewed as a single unit. On any day it receives (its customers collectively receive) a sum of credits in the form of checks drawn on other banks' customers. It also has presented (against its customers' accounts) a sum of debits, in the form of checks which have been returned to it by other banks on behalf of their customers. On any day these two sums may conceivably balance each other, so that credits on other banks' accounts are equal to debits to its own accounts. This corresponds to the intra-account clearing in the case of its customers' individual accounts. But as in their case it rarely happens that the credits and debits exactly balance each other at the time of posting, so too in the case of the bank it is seldom that the two sums are the same on any given day, at the time of the interbank clearing operations previously described. And just as the individual customer must have a deposit balance on which to draw when debits exceed credits, so too must the individual bank have the equivalent of a deposit balance on which to draw when the debits to its accounts exceed the credits.

This deposit balance for the bank itself is customarily maintained at the Federal Reserve bank in the particular region,[2] and is known as a "reserve balance." And each bank must defend its reserve balance in the same manner that its own customers are required to defend their deposit balances. In the latter case, as we have seen, the only requirement is that customers maintain a positive balance. A more rigorous condition applies to the banks themselves, however—they must maintain a reserve account equal to a given percentage of their customers' deposit balances. The percentage is fixed by the Federal Reserve Board of Governors, operating within a discretionary grant of authority by Congress. Any sums in excess of the required percentage are then known as "excess" reserves.

[2] Nonmembers of the Federal Reserve System carry such accounts at member banks, called "correspondents," who thus integrate them with the system.

In order for a bank to make a loan, therefore, it must have *excess* reserves at least equal to the fixed percentage of the deposit which it creates by the loan. If banks are obligated to keep in their reserve accounts an amount equal to 10 percent of customers' balances, for example, then if a bank wants to lend a firm $1000, it must be prepared to add $100 to its legal reserve requirement, which in effect means that it must have $100 of excess reserves before it can extend such business credit. If a bank does not have such excess reserves and still wishes to make the loan (perhaps because the firm is a good customer, which should be accommodated if at all possible), then it must—just as its customers must do when they have to replenish their deposit balances—either sell some of its assets or incur debt, using the proceeds to build up its reserve balance by the required amount.

The sale of assets may take the form of disposing of bonds which it has purchased for its own investment portfolio. Banks hold large quantities of government securities, for example, and they can if they wish sell enough of these in the open bond market to obtain the necessary funds. It may, alternatively, go into debt to the Federal Reserve bank; the most common method is by "rediscounting" some of the business I.O.U.'s which it holds—that is, obtaining a bookkeeping credit from the Federal Reserve bank by using its own claims against its business customers as collateral. When the claims mature and it collects from its business borrowers, it can then write a check to the order of the Federal Reserve bank, which reduces its own obligation. However it accomplishes the replenishment of its reserve balance, that balance must be maintained at least equal to the required percentage of all its own customers' deposit balances, including the balances which are created by whatever loans it makes.

This is not the whole of the story, however. As we have seen, on any day that the total debits charged to the bank's customers, collectively, exceed the sum of their credits, the bank must make up the difference out of its reserve account. That is, whenever in the interbank clearing process debits exceed credits for any bank, it must be prepared to see its reserve balance drawn down. If it possesses no excess reserves at the time when this occurs, it must either sell assets, borrow from the Federal Reserve bank, or call in some of its own loans. Consequently, when a bank makes a loan to one of its customers, allowing the latter to write more checks on it, it is likely to increase the amount of debits which will be presented against it in the clearing process. Unless others of its customers are simultaneously receiving a greater volume of checks from noncustomer business firms, without themselves expanding their volume of expenditures, or unless others of its customers are restricting their expenditures while continuing to receive the same volume of checks, the lending bank will be faced with a drain on its reserves.[3] The amount which it can lend at any one time is thus limited to the amount of its excess reserves. The latter is drawn down as the former is utilized.

We have said that when a bank makes a loan to one of its customers, allowing the latter to write more checks, it is likely to increase the amount of debits which will be presented against it in the clearing process. There is one circumstance under which this is not the case, however. If the checks which are written by the bank's borrowing customer are drawn in favor of others of the same bank's customers, then the bank can simply shift credit from the one account to the other accounts. Its reserve balance is thereby unaffected. If a bank could be sure that all its loans would come back to it as new deposits, it could expand its loans from lendable funds by a multiple based on the reserve requirement. If the requirement is a 10 percent reserve against all customer deposit balances, then it could lend 10 times the amount of its excess reserves, the excess reserves serving as the legally required 10 percent of the deposit balances which the bank creates. As the borrowers drew

[3] As the borrowing firm writes checks and draws down its deposit account, this of course diminishes the amount of reserves which the bank must retain against its deposits—diminishes it by the legal reserve requirement. But there is concurrently an increase in the amount of debits which will be presented against the bank in the interbank clearing process, and this increase is greater in amount than the decrease in reserve requirements occasioned by the reduction in its customers' deposit balances.

down their balances by writing checks, the same checks would be re-deposited by other customers, so that the amount of deposit balances would remain the same as far as these operations were concerned. The reserve requirement would continue to be met. An individual bank, then, can extend a volume of credit greater than its excess reserves to the extent that it can expect the resulting checks to come back home for redeposit.

This same possibility of a multiple expansion of credit out of lendable funds exists *for the banking system as a whole*, though not for individual banks, even when checks do not come back for rede-posit to the same bank on which they are drawn. If a bank extends a thousand dollars of credit out of its excess reserves, an unfavorable balance in the interbank clearing process may cause it to have debited to it the whole of that amount. The banks whose customers receive the checks written by the borrower will present those checks for clearance, and the lending bank may thus find itself $1000 short when the regional Federal Reserve bank totals up all the credits and debits for the individual banks in its region in the clearing process. That amount will then be deducted from the bank's reserve balance. But the same $1000 must be credited to the reserve balances of those banks presenting the checks on behalf of their customers.

Of this increase in their reserve balances, only the legally re-quired proportion (say 10 percent) must be retained as a compul-sory reserve. The other $900 would then become excess reserves, on the basis of which those banks could extend credit. The process then could repeat itself. Those banks, if extending $900 of credit, must be prepared to have that sum deducted from their reserve bal-ances, and this will be added to the reserve accounts of other banks, who must retain the legal requirement against these increased de-posits but are free to lend the remainder.

If there are enough good loan risks, then, the banking system as a whole could expand deposits on the basis of excess reserves by some multiple (determined by the legal reserve requirement), even though the checks drawn on the strength of such loans did not return to the same bank on which they were drawn. There would be a "spilling over" from one bank to another, until ultimately the original $1000 increase in credit, resulting from one bank's loan, had found its way into the reserve accounts of a number of banks to be held as a legally required reserve against the deposits resulting from the total number of loans. The original increase in credit of $1000 might then lead—if the banks had enough good borrowing prospects and assuming a 10 percent reserve requirement—to a total increase in credit of $10,000.

A good deal of flexibility is thus built into the credit system, allowing a substantial increase in credit when business conditions warrant. But the possible credit expansion is limited. A bank cannot create deposits by loans without any restraint. That restraint is provided by the reserve requirement, which puts a ceiling on the volume of loans which a bank may make, limiting the amount of credit which it may enter in the "books of the economy" on behalf of its customers.

Let us summarize the several ways in which the flexibility of the credit system is achieved. First, if the business customers of one bank are in step with general business activity, the bookkeeping system permits them to expand operations without resort to loan operations. The check-clearing or offsetting process allows them to write a greater volume of checks on the strength of their existing deposit balance provided they can be reasonably sure that their own receipts will simultaneously be expanding. Intra-account clearing permits such action. The debits and credits will offset each other at the time of posting, at least in some degree.

Second, to the extent that intra-account check clearance is imperfect and there are leads and lags between debits and credits, businesses may rebuild their balances by selling assets or incurring debt. The most important source of short-term credit is the banks, which become the community's agents for judging whether a firm's operations are likely to be successful (whether its services will find sufficient takers at the prices it is asking). Where the judgment is favorable, banks can extend credit—but not without limit.

They are capable of expanding loans out of excess reserves by some multiplier which is determined by the legal reserve requirement.

This loan-expansion process works in two ways: (1) through intrabank clearing, where the debits to the loan account are offset by new deposits credited to another account within the bank, so that use of the loan involves no change in the deposit balances of the bank's customers and hence no change in legal reserve requirements. Excess reserves here become the basis for multiple loan expansion by a single bank; (2) through interbank clearing, the "spilling-over" process, where the debit to the lending bank's reserve balance gives rise to credits to other banks' reserve balances, becoming the basis for loan expansion by them, with the process continuing as long as these additions to the reserve accounts are greater than the legally required reserves. The intrabank and interbank clearing processes operate concurrently, and between them they permit the expansion of credit by a multiple which is the reciprocal of the reserve requirement.[4]

[4] In this chapter we seek to obtain an understanding of the functions of the banking system which are relevant to a theory of income flows based on a distribution of bargaining power. In so doing we necessarily abstract from the considerable detail which customarily is included in descriptions of the banking mechanism. We carry through the analysis in terms of a bookkeeping process, since this goes to the heart of the important integrating function which the banks perform. It should be pointed out, however, that when a bank accepts a deposit, it does more than make an entry in the depositor's account. It incurs a liability for that account—a liability in the sense that it guarantees, to the extent of its resources, that the checks written on that account will be honored in the clearing process—that is, will be made good out of its reserve balance if not offset by other checks. This guarantee is underwritten by the bank's assets and expectations, which can be sold or borrowed against to provide the needed reserve. At the same time the deposit becomes an asset for it, in the sense that it adds to the bank's own reserves and becomes the basis for loan expansion, on which it earns interest and profit. Loans when made become guaranteed deposits, in the same sense, with the customer's debt acting as the bank's asset.

If the bank's judgment in making loans is faulty, however, so that credits extended by it are not repaid, then its reserves will be drawn down not only at the time that the borrowers write checks on the deposits created for them by the bank but at the time when the original depositors write checks on their accounts. The consequence may be to precipitate a crisis in the bank, since its reserves must be maintained at a given level by law. To rebuild its depleted reserves it may be forced to call in other loans, liquidate investments, seek new

So far we have been talking as though the banks' lending function was directed only to the supply of business's credit needs. Actually, business loans after World War II constituted less than one-fourth of total commercial bank loans. Table 2 (pp. 298–299) shows the amounts of credit extended by commercial banks to various other groups, over a period of years, and reveals that the federal government has been the heaviest borrower in recent years. The principle underlying such credit transactions is the same as in the case of business loans, however. The government frequently has need for additional credit because its inflow of receipts is insufficient to offset its outflow of payments, and consequently its balance at the banks must be replenished from time to time by borrowing.[5]

Government bonds sold to the banks are simply the equivalent of businessmen's notes, except that some series are redeemable only over longer periods but are more easily sold by the banks if it becomes necessary for them to add to their reserve accounts. The deposits which the banks set up for the government, in exchange for its bonds, must have the legally required reserve held against them. Withdrawals from such deposits by the government draw down the banks' reserves, just as the checks written by a business borrower do.

When banks make loans to others than business and the government, the bookkeeping nature of the transaction remains unchanged. A credit is entered in the borrower's account, against the bank's excess reserves, and the debt is written off when the borrower accumu-

capital. If unsuccessful in these respects the bank would fail. It is to forestall such crises that periodic bank examinations are required by state and federal governments. Thus there stand behind the deposits which a bank accepts or creates, as guarantee that the checks drawn on these accounts will be accepted by others, the assets of the bank, including the loans which it makes. Underlying the whole bookkeeping structure is thus a structure of assets, the soundness of which determines the soundness of the system.

[5] Actually the federal government issues checks drawn not upon the commercial banks but upon the Federal Reserve banks, with which it keeps accounts. It uses the commercial banks as depositories for funds to be transferred to its Federal Reserve accounts as needed. But if it is unable to transfer the sums which it requires, it then can borrow—giving its bonds as surety—from the commercial banks to build up its deposit balances with them, for transfer as needed.

TABLE 2. LOANS AND INVESTMENTS AT ALL COMMERCIAL BANKS AND SELECTED DATES [a]

In billions of dollars

Type of Loan or Investment	1914	1920	1930	1935	1940	1945	1951
Total loans and investments	17.3	36.9	49.4	34.8	41.2	114.6	126.0
Loans, total	13.4	28.6	35.0	15.0	17.4	23.7	54.8 [b]
Business [c]	7.1	15.7	15.8	6.8	7.9 [d]	9.3	26.8
Consumer					1.9	1.2	7.7
All other					2.0	2.0	4.3
Real estate	1.8	3.1	6.0	3.5	4.4	4.5	14.1
Security [e]	4.5	9.8	13.2	4.7	1.2	6.8	2.6
Investments, total	3.9	8.4	14.4	19.8	23.8	90.9	71.2
U.S. government securities	0.8	3.6	4.9	12.8	16.6	84.1	58.5
State and local government securities	0.6	1.0	2.2	2.7	3.6	3.8	8.5
All other	2.5	3.8	7.3	4.3	3.6	3.0	4.2

[a] Data are as of end of June. For years prior to 1951, they are taken from a preliminary tabulation of a revised series of banking statistics.
[b] Figures for various loan items for 1951 data are shown gross (i.e., before deduction of valuation reserves); they do not add to the total and are not entirely comparable with prior figures. Total loans continue to be shown net.
[c] Includes agricultural loans.
[d] Estimated.
[e] Prior to 1940, includes loans secured by collateral other than securities.

298

TABLE 2. LOANS AND INVESTMENTS AT ALL COMMERCIAL BANKS AND SELECTED DATES (*Continued*)

Percentage distribution

Type of Loan or Investment	1914	1920	1930	1935	1940	1945	1951
Total loans and investments	100.0	100.0	100.0	100.0	100.0	100.0	100.0
Loans, total	77.5	77.3	70.9	43.1	42.2	20.7	43.5
Business	} 41.0	} 42.2	} 32.0	19.5	19.2	8.1	21.2
Consumer					4.6	1.1	6.1
All other					4.8	1.7	3.4
Real estate	10.5	8.4	12.2	10.1	10.7	3.9	11.1
Security	26.0	26.5	26.7	13.5	2.9	5.9	2.1
Investments, total	22.5	22.7	29.1	56.9	57.8	79.3	56.5
U.S. government securities	4.6	9.7	9.9	36.8	40.3	73.4	46.4
State and local government securities	3.5	2.7	4.4	7.8	8.8	3.3	6.8
All other	14.4	10.3	14.8	12.3	8.7	2.6	3.3

SOURCE: *Monetary Policy and Management of the Public Debt*, Part I, Joint Committee on the Economic Report (Eighty-second Congress, second session, 1952), p. 530.

299

lates in his account an equal amount which can be credited to the bank. In the case of nonbusiness as well as business loans, the process is one of bookkeeping, within the institutional structure of the banking system.

Not simply bank credit but all forms of credit are part of this bookkeeping system. The use of customer charge accounts by department stores, installment-plan purchases, the sale of bonds by business firms, all these and other forms of financing are methods by which one spending unit accepts a debit to its account so that a credit may be entered on another's account. Customarily in such transactions some asset—a promissory note, a specific claim on property—accrues to the one who lends his credit, as security that the borrower will at some agreed time in the future accept a debit so that the lender will regain his credit.

Where does coin and currency enter into the pecuniary transactions of the economy? Till this point our description would suggest that all sales and purchases were effected by checks, despite the fact that all of us daily make purchases by small change and bills. Currency is, in fact, simply one aspect—relatively unimportant—of the bookkeeping process. The Federal Reserve has estimated that more than 90 percent of the nation's business is transacted by checks, as many as seven billion of which may be written in a year's time, totaling the staggering sum of over two trillion dollars. Currency takes care of the rest of the transactions. It provides another method of bookkeeping. As one writer has suggested, "it keeps the moneyflow accounts . . . in much the same way as poker chips serve as a substitute for a scorepad; transactors whose score is improving get in the chips, others get out of chips. When our monetary and banking system is operating properly [an individual or firm] can convert any part of his score in currency into a score in bank deposits, or conversely, as suits his convenience." [6]

Shifting currency around when we buy and sell performs the same function as shifting bookkeeping entries when we buy and

[6] Morris A. Copeland, *A Study of Moneyflows in the United States* (New York: National Bureau of Economic Research, 1952), p. 233.

sell. It is a peripheral means of effecting transactions, employed instead of checks primarily in two situations: (1) when small amounts are involved in face-to-face transactions, so that it is easier and cheaper to hand over currency rather than write a check and the danger of carrying such sums on one's person is limited; (2) when transactions involve payment by an individual whose credit standing cannot be assumed, so that a check is less to be trusted; these are usually isolated, single nonrecurring transactions. There are other situations in which currency carries advantages over checks, but none sufficient to make currency anything more than a relatively minor aspect of the whole economy-wide bookkeeping system—a facilitating device which makes the system more workable.

The integration of our economy thus rests on an accounting system, and the banking system serves as the principal keeper of the books. Even those individuals who themselves have no accounts with banks are tied into the system, through individuals who do carry accounts (just as banks which are not part of the Federal Reserve System are tied into it through relations with banks which are members of the system). The worker who receives his wages in currency and makes all his expenditures out of currency and who never visits a bank is nevertheless dependent for his wages on a business unit which is integrated with all other business units through the accounts of the banks.

We have described the banking system as integrating the books of the country's economic units, serving as a mechanism for transmitting flows of income among the units. We have also seen that banks extend credit to economic units to enable them to maintain their place in this system of integrated accounts. If a firm's deposit balance is insufficient to accommodate the daily discrepancies between inflows and outflows, it can seek a loan to increase its deposit balance to the required level. This borrower-lender relationship, like all other relationships involving flows of funds, is a bargaining relationship. Whether the loan is made and if so on what terms is a consequence of the relative costs of agreement and disagreement to bank and borrower on each other's terms. We shall not examine in detail the influences which make these costs what they are, but we shall note certain of the more important ones.

For the borrowing firm, the cost of agreeing to the bank's terms is not only the interest charge which it must pay but also the risks it runs in obligating itself for the repayment of the principal within the time period specified. While we may assume that the prospects for ultimate repayment of the loan are a consideration relevant to other bargains than that with the bank and concern a decision which must be made even before the bank is approached for a loan, the question of *how soon* the loan must be repaid is part of the terms to be negotiated with the bank. If interest rate and the time term are the chief costs of agreement, the costs of disagreement are the profits which must be foregone, the market position and growth potential which must be sacrificed, and the greater risks which must be accepted if an equally favorable loan cannot be arranged elsewhere or if no loan can be arranged.

From the side of the lending bank, the costs of agreement are any risks of nonpayment attached to the loan, the risks of illiquidity during the term of the loan, and the possible loss of a more profitable loan or the disappointment of a preferred customer when its lendable funds are inadequate to accommodate all who would borrow. The costs of disagreement are the possible loss of an interest-earning asset, affecting the bank's own profit and market position and growth.

The borrower-lender bargain is thus influenced by a number of variables, a change in any one of which may affect whether any bargain is struck and if so on what terms. The interest rate, the time allowed for repayment, the assets of the firm and bank, expectations of the borrowing firm and business generally, the availability of alternative borrowers to the bank and of alternative lenders to the firm—these are among the major influences determining the costs of agreement and disagreement of each.

It is sometimes suggested that the interest rate serves as the common denominator for all these costs, that, for example, the rate can rise as necessary to allow for a longer repayment period, poorer expectations, low assets, and absence of alternative lending agents. It is true that the rate might have to rise to astronomical levels in some instances, but there would always be *some* interest rate at which the loan would be tendered, a rate at which the bank's cost of agreement would fall below its cost of disagreement.[7] At such a level it would be unlikely that the would-be borrower would accept the loan, but this would simply be his response to the rate of interest.

Whatever the logical consistency of this approach, it lacks conceptual reliability. There is abundant evidence that interest rates commonly move within a fairly narrow range and that relative bargaining powers of borrower and lender are revealed as much through the availability of loans as through rates. When banks are faced with large excess reserves, they will tend to shave interest rates more than if their reserves were smaller, but they will, at the same time, make loans at the going rate carrying greater risk. "When interest rates are stiffening, bankers show a tendency to shrink the number of clients entitled to the prime rate [the rate charged on loans made to their highest rated customers]. Conversely, they expand the number of such favored borrowers when any pronounced slump in the demand for bank loans starts developing."[8]

An important determinant of the bank's cost of agreement on the borrower's terms, then, and hence an important determinant of relative bargaining powers, is the size of lendable reserves. This is something which lies partially within the control of the central bank, the Federal Reserve Board. By adjusting the legal reserve requirement, by modifying the rediscount rate at which banks can borrow to replenish reserves, and by open-market operations in government securities which put money into or take it out of bank reserves, the Federal Reserve can influence the level of the banks' excess reserves. As it does so, it alters the relative bargaining powers of lenders and borrowers. With greater excess reserves,

[7] This is the same type of argument which seeks to reduce all job satisfactions to a pecuniary base, on the premise that there would always be *some* wage rate at which a worker would be willing to forego the job satisfaction he seeks.

[8] *Business Week*, January 16, 1954, p. 46.

the banks' cost of agreement falls, lowering interest rates and increasing the availability of credit. With reduced reserves, the reverse transpires.

There is no guarantee that the shifts in the distribution of bargaining power caused by the Board's actions will be sufficient to affect whether bargains are made, however. In times of depression, business expectations may be so pessimistic that at no terms which a bank felt able to offer would firms seek loans. In boom times, expectations may be so optimistic that only at rates so high that they may entail unacceptable consequences (such as so severe a restriction on the availability of business loans as to jeopardize continuity in some instances and needed growth in others, or interest rates so high as to limit new construction undesirably, which because it undertakes long-term loans is more susceptible to interest rate changes) would the demand for loans slacken.

The action which the Federal Reserve Board undertakes is itself a function of bargains, but involving a political rather than a price component. Its members are presidential appointees not subject to removal except on charges, so that—except in the act of appointment—they are less susceptible to the same types of administrative pressures to conform as if their position was dependent on a politician's approval. Nevertheless, they are subject to demands being made on them—by the federal administration as it seeks to fulfill its political bargains, by the business community as it seeks to improve its position, by the member banks in their own interests. The costs of agreement and disagreement on such terms as are demanded may involve in part such considerations as desire to retain office and authority (hence appraisal of where political influence lies) and desire not to offend individuals or groups whose friendship is valued, but they are influenced too by ideological aspirations of the sort referred to in the preceding chapter, including the desire to foster a preferred kind of society or to satisfy the interests of the class group to which it is preferred to entrust the control of society.

The policies which are adopted are thus products of the personal aspirations of those in authority and the alternative courses of action demanded (explicitly, implicitly, or conjecturally) by groups whose bargaining power and income flows stand to be affected. The so-called "accord" of March 4, 1951, between the Federal Reserve Board and the Treasury is but one outstanding example of such policy bargains.[9]

[9] A detailed recital of the events leading up to this accord was given by Secretary of the Treasury Snyder before the Joint Committee on the Economic Report, and is reproduced in *Monetary Policy and the Management of the Public Debt* (1952), Eighty-second Congress, second session, Part 1, pp. 50–74. Its perusal reveals the nature of the negotiations between these two agencies over the period July, 1945–March, 1951. "Most of the differences were worked out in a genuine spirit of give-and-take." It is impossible to summarize here the story of that period, but some notion of the nature of the give-and-take can be suggested for the Korean war period. The Treasury was anxious to maintain a strong market for government issues, so that it might be ready for all eventualities, and suggested that inflationary pressures be restrained by tax measures rather than by monetary controls. While concurring in the advocacy of tax measures, "the Federal Reserve also felt that great reliance should be placed on traditional measures of general credit restraint which involved a declining securities market and increase in interest rates. . . . The differences between the two agencies on the necessity for stability in the Government security market became serious in connection with the Treasury's September–October refunding operation." Federal Reserve action on the rediscount rate at that time permitted the short-term rates on outstanding issues "to reach levels inconsistent with the rate on the refunding offering of the Treasury," resulting in "a significant financing failure for the Federal Government." After further differences between those two arms of government, a meeting was held between the President, the Chairman of the Board of Governors of the Federal Reserve Board, and the Secretary of the Treasury, in which the Chairman "assured the President that he need not be concerned about the 2½ percent long-term rate on Government securities."
"About this time a series of conferences was held between the Treasury, the Chairman of the Board of Governors, the Chairman of the two banking committees in Congress, and the Chairman of the Joint Committee on the Economic Report. It was generally agreed between the parties involved that there should be no change in the existing situation in the Government security market, and no Congressional hearings held on differences between the Treasury and the Federal Reserve, for a short period while I was in the hospital recuperating from an eye operation.
"Shortly after these meetings, however, a change in the Federal Reserve attitude began to be apparent; and the Chairman of the Board informed the Treasury that, as of February 19 [1951], the Federal Reserve was no longer willing to maintain the existing situation in the Government security market. It was evident that some new agreement had to be reached. . . . Representatives of the Treasury and the Federal Reserve were designated, therefore, to work out a way in which differences could be compromised. The result was the accord announced jointly by the Treasury and the Federal Reserve in a statement released for publication on March 4, 1951."
The terms of the accord are given on pp. 75–76 of the reference cited above.

In summary, the income flows of the economic units of society are transmitted by the banking system, as keeper of the accounts of the economy. The integration of an economic unit into this accounting system requires maintenance of a deposit balance (or a link to another unit maintaining a deposit balance) which is adequate to offset any temporary lead of outflows over inflows. Where deposit balances are inadequate for this purpose, assets may be liquidated or credit negotiated to supply the deficiency. Another important function of banks is to provide such credit, the terms depending on the relative bargaining powers of borrower and lender. These bargaining powers are themselves subject to the influence of the central bank, which possesses the power to increase or decrease the supply of lendable funds, in line with policies which at any moment are also the product of bargains, in this case between the Federal Reserve, the federal government, and others whose economic position leads them to make demands (sometimes only implied or conjectured) and to exert influence for action on their behalf.

CHAPTER 16

From Micro to Macro

IN the preceding pages we have seen how individuals follow patterns of aspirations which are broadly defined by the culture and more narrowly defined by comparisons with the achievements of others, comparisons having varying degrees of compulsiveness. Those aspirations having an economic component are pursued within a framework of scarcity and interdependence, involving both commensal and symbiotic (competitive and coöperative) relationships. These personal relationships center in three principal types of economic units—the household, the firm, and the government. The aspirations of the individual and the objectives of the economic units through which he pursues his aspirations are ongoing, requiring an ongoing stream of income for their realization. The stream of income of these micro units is fed by numerous bargains, which are significant to the economist only for their impact on the streams of real and money income. The terms of these bargains are the result of relative bargaining powers.

In each economic unit there must be a revenue decision and a budget decision. The revenue decision involves the management—through bargains—of the position of scarcity and interdependence in the achievement of the inflow of income. The budget decision involves the management—again through bargains—of the position of scarcity and interdependence in directing the outflow of income. Since the revenue and budget decisions are interrelated, the prime responsibility of management—in the household, firm, or governmental unit—is to coördinate the numerous bargains so that inflows and outflows balance at a preferred level and with a preferred composition.

The economic relationships of individuals and economic units and the income flows between them thus depend on their relative bargaining power. Bargaining power in turn depends on the distribution of aspirations and alternatives in society. Potentially, any change in the distribution of aspirations or alternatives leads to changes in relative bargaining power, and through changes in the terms of bargains, to changes in the flows of income. Shifts in bargaining power may also be traced to changes in the effects of past and future on one's present position, through changes in the asset position or the expectations of individuals or units. (These time effects are themselves reflections of past and expected future distributions of aspirations and alternatives in the economy.)

A change in aspirations or alternatives can arise within any economic unit in the system. Such a change may be attributable to some event or expected event within the unit itself which affects its bargaining power in relationships with other units, or it may be attributable to some actual or expected event in another unit, to which there are commensal or symbiotic ties.

We have already traced, in an earlier chapter, the kinds of changes in aspirations and alternatives which may occur. It will be recalled that there are four possible changes in aspirations: (1) A greater or lesser coincidence between personal and cultural objectives (whether one continues to prefer a house in a community which has come to emphasize apartment living; whether one turns to a life of contemplation in a culture which continues to emphasize material accumulation). (2) A voluntary movement along the comparative-achievement scale (the acceptance of a new social group as the standard by which to judge the satisfactoriness of the quality of goods and services which are consumed; the identification of a new occupational group by which the satisfactoriness of one's own remuneration is judged). (3) A change in the timing of one's plans (the postponement of achieving one's graduate degree by another year; the deferring of the purchase of a new car because the old one is operating so well). (4) Changes in personal inclination (the preference for one model over another, within the same quality bracket; the choice of one job over another because of the kind of associates). Since aspirations are balanced against each other in a preferred *pattern* (which is the equivalent to the economist of what the integrated personality is to the psychologist), it is unlikely that a change in any single aspect of that pattern will leave the rest of the pattern unaffected. Except for relatively minor decisions (where changes in personal inclinations approach the level of reasonable choices, involving choices among alternatives that contribute neither more nor less to the achievement of one's objectives, at the given degree of specificity), we can expect that the modification of any single goal will affect goals which are necessarily closely related.

Changes in alternatives are also of four general types: (1) innovation; (2) imitation; (3) discovery (involving chiefly supplemental supplies of known natural resources); and (4) changes in the population composition. These four types of changes have their effect either in the quality or the number of the alternatives available.

In all the above cases of change, the effect is to modify the desirability of the alternatives which others offer to the individual or unit, or to modify the desirability of the alternative which the individual or unit offers to others. Similar effects are produced by changes in assets and expectations. Both of these influences of the movement of time modify the degree of risk attaching to any bargain. As in the case of changes in aspirations and alternatives, changes in assets and expectations can occur at any point in the network of symbiotic and commensal relations. All such modifications become of interest to the economist whenever they induce a change in the direction and magnitude of the flows of income. Moreover, changes in income flows themselves induce further shifts in relative bargaining power.

Some change in the distribution of aspirations and alternatives, assets and expectations, is always occurring. The passage of time guarantees that some individuals will be accumulating experience and skills, thereby becoming better alternatives to others, that some will be losing physical and mental vigor, thereby becoming less desirable alternatives, that the number of individuals in the population will be changing, that inventions will be occurring, that aspiration patterns will be undergoing refinement and adjustment.

There is, of course, no guarantee that any given change will shift bargaining powers so as to affect the flows of income. The potential effect may not become actual. Workers at the X Company may find that they are falling behind in the local wage structure, and to satisfy their proximate goal of maintaining a particular relative position in the local wage hierarchy they ask their employer for a raise, which he resists. The workers' cost of agreement on the employer's terms is a loss of aspiration (comparative achievement), their cost of disagreement depends on the alternatives to their present job, alternatives—which if actually present, in the form of job openings—are improved because of the wage increases attaching to them. The employer's cost of agreement on his workers' terms may be the likely failure to achieve his projected balance, though perhaps not by an amount proportionate to the increase in his wage bill if he anticipates that he can renegotiate or manipulate other bargains. His cost of disagreement is the possible loss of workers, depending on their alternatives, and the possible loss of morale if they stay, affecting perhaps not only productivity but the climate of the work society in which he himself must live. Probabilities must be estimated of whether these costs would actually eventuate. We cannot say, without knowledge of the workers' and employer's actual calculations, whether their relative bargaining powers have actually shifted, or whether the potential influence on income flows has been realized (whether higher wages are paid and the workers remain on the job, whether the same wages are paid and the workers stay on the job, whether the same wages are paid and the workers leave but are replaced by others at no increase, or whether they can be replaced only by others at an increase in rates). But with respect to the whole complicated network of symbiotic and commensal relations, we can be all but sure that at any moment in time *some* changes in aspirations and alternatives, assets and expectations, are *actually* affecting the distribution of relative bargaining powers and the flows of income through the system.

Wherever income flows are modified, a chain or wave of effects is set in motion. The initial impact is but the beginning of a series of repercussions without discernible end. Suppose, for example, that a change in cultural tastes reduces the desirability of the alternatives which some occupational group constitutes to others. We may assume that their potential loss of bargaining power results in an actual reduction in the income flow to them. But this restriction on their income increases their bargaining power as buyers relative to retailers, landlords, churches and schools, and so on. The reduction in the flow of income to *these* groups similarly modifies *their* bargaining power in transactions with others, and these others in turn are affected, transmitting the effect to still others, and so on and on, the chain of effects stretching out with no final link evident. Or suppose that a household, pursuing aspirations involving comparative achievement, moves into a higher-quality bracket on the consumption scale. Its bargaining power relative to goods previously in its budget now rises, relative to the goods now desired declines. We may assume these shifts in bargaining power to be translated into shifts in the flow of income, with less flowing to the sellers of lower-quality items, more to the sellers of higher-quality items. These in turn will find their relative bargaining powers affected by the changes in their incomes, transmitting these effects to still others, with waves of effects rolling on and on, raising receipts in one succession of effects, reducing them in another. Moreover, since aspirations tend to be organized into a pattern, a movement along the consumer quality scale with respect to only one item (rather than the whole standard of living) is likely to influence the household's attitude toward related items in the household budget; the purchase of new furniture moves the housewife to aspire to new draperies to set them off, a better suit emphasizes the need for higher quality shoes or coat. A gradual movement along the quality spectrum may be initiated in this manner—a slide rather than a step. Shifts in relative bargaining power with respect to certain kinds of consumer-retailer relationships may thus arise subtly, being transmitted into income effects which fan out and cumulate, with expenditures declining in certain directions and increasing in others, and in all directions setting in motion a sequence of income effects.

There is no point in further illustration. It should be noted, however, that shifts in the magnitude and direction of flows of income through the complex of symbiotic relationships may arise from changes not only in the aspirations and alternatives of people at any point in the system, but from variations in assets and expectations. The accumulation or disbursement of liquid assets, or the accumulation and usage of stocks (particularly of durable goods) affects the flow of income out of one unit and into other units. Expectations of favorable or adverse future bargaining positions likewise influence a unit's inflows and outflows (especially in the decision as to whether or not to apply liquid assets in the present).

The process by which the changes in an individual's or unit's relative bargaining position are translated into income effects which are transmitted with chain reaction through the web of economic relationships which comprises an economy, we shall call the multiplier effect. This is the same term which Keynes applied to the cumulating effects of a change in aggregate expenditures (in his system, those of an investment nature), but the process is similar and the term equally relevant to the system of interpersonal relations. Any change in a unit's relative bargaining power potentially affects its income flows, and to the extent the potential effect becomes actual, it initiates the multiplier effect. (a) If a unit increases its net outflow of income (as may be attributed to a change in aspirations and may be facilitated by an expenditure of greater effort, an improvement in the quality of the alternative it constitutes to others, or the application of its assets), its expanding outflows will accrue as additions to the inflows of others, who in turn may be expected to increase their outflows, and so on. (b) If a unit reduces its net outflows (due perhaps to a change in the time scale of its aspirations or enforced by a deterioration of its position as an alternative to others or militated by its pessimistic expectations), its contracting expenditures will reduce the income of other units, who may be expected to reduce their outflows, and so on. (c) If the unit maintains its inflows and outflows at a constant level but shifts their source and direction, this will mean an increase in the inflows for certain others and a reduction in the inflows of different groups, with each of these transmitting the income effect to others.

We can conceive of the nation's economy as consisting of a vast number of economic units, related to each other commensally and symbiotically, whose symbiotic connections are concretely evidenced in a complicated set of interrelated accounts, one for each unit, showing its inflows and outflows as a form of double-entry bookkeeping. An entry in A's account must appear in two columns; in the receipts column it represents either an expenditure or loan by another unit (Z) or the application of its own assets; in the payments column it represents either a disbursement to another unit (B) or an increase in its own assets. Z's expenditure and B's receipt must be matched by compensating entries in their own system of accounts, revealing expenditures by Y and receipts by C, and so on.

Any change in the size or direction of the entries in any account must find its way into another account, and through it to another and another and yet another account, except as this multiplier effect is short-circuited at any stage by a compensating change in a unit's own asset position. By drawing on its own assets or borrowing another's assets, a unit may maintain its pattern of outflows even though its inflows have been reduced. By adding to its assets it may maintain its pattern of outflows even though inflows have been increased. As we have already seen, the banking system actually maintains a set of accounts for the economy conforming to this conception. It debits and credits to the accounts of an enormous number of units, and even those not themselves maintaining accounts with the banks are tied into the system through those who do. Leads and lags of inflows over outflows may be offset by changes in the deposit balance (asset position); the balance can be drawn down or allowed to increase, though a normal outflow pattern is continued.

Any economic unit is thus subject to multiplier effects from changes in income flows in other units, resulting from a change in their relative bargaining position. But the multiplier effects to which it is subject are several, and it is possible for the several effects to cancel each other out, leaving the unit's total income flows unaffected. If one symbiotic relationship is broken, withdrawing a source of income, another may be substituted for it, replacing the income lost. Thus a firm makes some new customers and loses some old customers, and in the process the balance of inflows and outflows may be unaffected.

Where such a result occurs, we may say that the income effects of changes in relative bargaining power in the system have been offset, as far as their impact on the individual unit is concerned. The income effects of one changed bargaining relationship have been offset by the income effects of another changed bargaining relationship, leaving the unit's total income flows unchanged. In the economy-wide network of economic relationships, then, it is possible to conceive of constant shifts of bargaining power among individuals, the net effect of which, however, is to leave each economic unit with the same magnitude of inflows and outflows, even though the directions of the micro flows have changed. This result is possible due to offsetting bargains (more precisely, due to offsetting income effects of changes in bargaining relationships).

Instead of regarding the income effect of shifts in bargaining power from the viewpoint of the individual unit, however, we may regard it from the viewpoint of the economy as a whole. In this case the multiplier effect of changes in bargaining power within the system may leave the system's total income flows unaffected, even though individual units may be unevenly affected. One firm has a net loss of customer trade but another firm enjoys a net gain, so that the flows of the economy as a whole remain at the same level, even though for the units involved they vary. Here the income effects of changed bargaining relations are offset from the viewpoint of the system as a whole, even though nonoffset from the standpoint of the affected units. The flows of the units which compose this system may thus fluctuate but the aggregate flows remain the same, revealing a redistribution of income among the units.

As long as income effects are offset, we are free to describe the changes in bargaining power relations as random. From the viewpoint of the individual unit, the substitution of certain relationships for others is a consequence of purely random changes in the bargaining power of actual or potential symbionts. Similarly, from the viewpoint of the system, the substitution or partial substitution of one unit for another unit, as the focus of individual symbiotic relations, may be regarded as the consequence of purely unpatterned changes in bargaining power. Regardless of whether such change is attributable to changes in aspirations or alternatives, assets or expectations, as long as the effects on one unit are offset by the effects on other units, we can look upon such modifications as random. They may result from wholly purposive and carefully planned actions on the part of the individual units, but because such purpose and planning can arise at any point in the system and do arise at many points, and where they do lead simply to substitution of one unit's bargaining advantage over another, the shift can properly be considered random.

When income effects are nonoffset over time, however, we can regard the change as nonrandom. From the viewpoint of the individual unit, a continued decline or a continued rise in the level of its income flows must be attributed not to some erratic redistribution of bargaining powers in the system, but to some more patterned change in the aspirations, alternatives, assets, or expectations of itself or its symbionts. Similarly, from the viewpoint of the economy as a whole, a continued decline or a continued rise in aggregate flows cannot be considered as the effect of random redistribution of income among the component units, but as a consequence of more general influences operating on aspirations or alternatives, assets or expectations, throughout the system.

The significant difference between multiplier effects at the micro (unit) and the macro (aggregative) levels is that the former can be offset within some larger system (at a higher level of integration), while the latter cannot. The multiplier effects on one unit can be offset by the multiplier effects on another unit, leaving the aggregate flows unaffected. Here nonoffset changes at the level of the individual unit are offset at the level of the economy. But the multiplier effects of changes in aggregate income flows in the economy at large cannot be offset by other multiplier effects within some larger system.[1]

These relationships are precisely similar to those we encountered in analyzing the check-clearing functions of individual banks and the banking system. Checks which are not offset at the level of the individual bank, and which therefore give rise to changes in the size of its reserves, may be offset at the local, regional, or national level by changes in the opposite direction on the part of other banks or regions. It is only in the event that changes in the accounts held in individual banks are not offset by changes in accounts held in other banks, it is only when the amounts of money flows from the individual banks are moving in the same direction, either up or down, that we experience fluctuations in the total volume of expenditures.

To repeat: multiplier effects at the micro level can be offset within some larger system, and when so offset they imply only random income effects from the larger viewpoint, and from the larger viewpoint they can be ignored. But at the macro level which *constitutes* the system with which one is concerned there can be no offsetting, and changes in aspirations and alternatives which lead to

---

[1] Except at a world-economy level, where the income effects of the several national units can conceivably offset each other. We disregard this possibility here to simplify discussion, though a more complete analysis would take it into account. But even in such a more elaborated analysis, it would then be necessary to say that the multiplier effects of changes in the aggregate income flow in the world-economy unit could not be offset by multiplier effects from other similar units.

changes in (aggregate) income have general (nonrandom) effects which *must* be viewed as *generally* desirable or undesirable from the viewpoint of the system as a whole.

It is the fact that changes in bargaining power relations within the system can lead to changes in income flows among the units which are not offset at any more inclusive (macro) level that gives rise to the economic problem of fluctuations in national income. If all shifts in bargaining power led to income effects which offset each other at the macro level, we would have only a problem of allocation. It was because classical economics dealt only with real income flows in a static setting that it could indeed confine its systematic theorizing to the allocation question. But once the element of time is admitted, inescapably producing changes in aspirations and alternatives, assets and expectations, a redistribution of bargaining powers and income flows follows. And when such changes are general rather than random, nonoffsetting bargains at the macro level produce multiplier effects leading to fluctuations in aggregate income.

By fluctuations in aggregate income we shall mean any changes in total flows (in real or money terms) which are attributable to nonoffsetting bargains. And we shall now inquire as to the influences which give rise to such shifts in relative bargaining power as lead to fluctuations of income upward or downward. We shall concern ourselves only with secular and cyclical influences.[2]

[2] We are interested only in nonoffsetting bargains which produce a *patterned* effect. One can conceive of spasmodic and unpatterned nonoffsetting bargains which give rise to irregular and quite meaningless fluctuations. We shall disregard these. We shall also disregard here certain patterned effects which, for more specific purposes, might be usefully examined, such as seasonal and diurnal.

Some question may be raised as to why what is commonly referred to as "trend" is here regarded as "secular fluctuation." First, a constant rate of increase or decrease in income would be purely accidental; the discontinuities in the underlying distribution of scarcities and interdependencies provide no ground for expecting a smooth rise or fall over time. In view of such discontinuous influences on income, we are justified in regarding secular trend as the equivalent of long-term upward fluctuations or downward fluctuations. But second and more important, trends can be called such only because of arbitrarily delimited time spans. Just as the recovery and prosperity phases of a cycle might be called an upward trend if the total period of observation were limited to the span of the cycle and we were concerned

It is beyond the purpose of this work to lay out in any detail the nature of the generating influences which, by affecting the position of scarcity and interdependence of numbers of similarly situated economic units, modify the distribution of bargaining power within the economy and potentially influence the terms of bargains and the magnitude and direction of the micro income flows, and—to the extent they are nonoffset at the macro level—give rise to fluctuations in aggregate income. We shall identify the major influences, however.

SECULAR INFLUENCES

Secular influences on the direction and magnitude of nonoffsetting bargains include the long-run forces operating on a culture's aspirations and alternatives. "Long-run" is used here in a historical rather than an economic sense.

Secular changes in aspiration patterns embrace such matters as the degree of acceptance or rejection of materialistic attitudes, and basic shifts in the nature of material wants. In their most fundamental form, such changes are reflections of the historical epochs which go by such names as the Reformation and the Renaissance, but less sweepingly they may also be due to cross-cultural fertilization. Rising levels of aspirations lead individuals to increase outflows, either by drawing on assets, or by borrowing against the future, or by greater present effort to expand inflows. However ac-

---

with isolating some epicyclical movements, so may secular movements appear as cyclical if related to some more comprehensive span of time. In view of these considerations there seems to be warranty for viewing such movements as simply a form of income fluctuation resulting from nonoffsetting bargains which are attributable to particular kinds of influences. But if this terminology is found disturbing, the effect can be avoided by substituting the word "movement." I have not done so here because "fluctuations" appears to be more widely used to describe the aggregate movements which, along with the study of "allocations," compose the study of economics.

Finally, it should be noted that by cyclical fluctuations no regularity of movement is implied but simply cumulative rises and falls of income around the secular income movement.

complished, the result is a shift in relative bargaining power in favor of sellers, increasing expenditures and giving rise to nonoffsetting bargains which expand aggregate income. Declining levels of material aspiration would lead to a contrary result.

Such general influences on people's goals are facilitated by the process of coercive comparison. Aspiration is a social phenomenon, and an individual's aspirations are influenced by his social setting. Satisfaction with the goals which one has set for himself depends in great measure on the comparative achievement of others within a social group. As material wants and the level of their fulfillment increase for some individuals, particularly those exercising leadership roles, the effect is to draw along both aspirations and accomplishments of others, whose comparative achievement influences still others, and so on, until the advance in the level of aspirations is quite general.

Not only secular changes in consumer wants but in producer goals as well can influence aggregate income. The expansion mindedness of business firms has the same effect as a rising rate of household aspirations. The rise of the modern corporation in particular has given new scope for the ambitious producer; and business expansion, sought as a proximate goal, necessitates increased inflows, which are in part stimulated through the devices of advertising and product differentiation, which are calculated to improve the seller's bargaining power relative to buyers by altering the latter's aspirations and increasing their expenditures. In no other country has the art of advertising been raised to a level of such importance as in the United States, whose citizens have been satirized throughout the world for their material wants, and whose *per capita* income has risen at a faster long-run rate than the incomes of other countries. Business expansion and advertising and consumer wants and rising income are all parts of a pattern of changing aspirations (changing in both level and nature) which give rise to nonoffsetting bargains inducing a long-run upward movement of aggregate income.

Secular changes in alternatives involve principally (1) changes in the practice of scientific and engineering techniques, affecting the possibility of producing certain alternatives at all and of producing others better or more cheaply; (2) changes in the size of the population, affecting the numbers of those who stand as alternatives to others in various capacities; and (3) changes in the availability of natural resources, through both discovery of fresh resources in settled areas and the opening up of new areas for exploitation. Changes in any of these alternatives redistribute bargaining power as between buyers and sellers.

1. A general increase in productivity can be expected to drive product prices downward in some measure and to increase the returns to sellers of such products in some measure (the measure in each case depending on the bargaining position of sellers in various circumstances). In either event, the real income of both household and business units, generally, increases either through income retained by buyers as prices fall or through income retained by sellers as prices fall by less than the productivity savings. The exceptions to this generally favorable influence are those alternatives whose relative bargaining power has been weakened through a comparative reduction in the quality of the services they offer—for example, workers whose services can be more cheaply or more satisfactorily performed by machinery. These adverse income effects partially offset the favorable income effects. But as long as those whose services have been displaced or partly displaced by superior alternatives continue to be employed elsewhere (even if at lower levels of remuneration), the increases in income in some units are greater than the declines in income in other units, revealing nonoffsetting bargains which drive aggregate income upward.

The increases in income *must*, however, find their way into new bargains for this result to be achieved. The shift in bargaining power as between buyers and sellers encourages such an outcome, since falling prices and rising incomes (whether in real or money terms) improve the bargaining power of sellers relative to buyers.

An increase in real consumption can thus be expected in response to both price and income elasticity.

With secular improvement in productivity, the increasing purchases of goods (whether for consumption or investment) can be expected to continue at least to the point where the originally existing general level of material aspirations has been achieved—but at that point, unless aspirations adjust upward, the bargaining power of buyers relative to sellers rises promptly and sufficiently to foreclose any additional bargains: the lack of unsatisfied aspirations means a zero cost of disagreement on the terms of any new bargains. Thus, unless the original level of material aspirations is pitched so high as to be unattainable even in the long run (a situation which is psychologically unrealistic, since it implies no proximate goals in a time stream of aspirations), a continuing increase in the level of aspirations is necessary to a continued increase in aggregate real income. That is, past some point demand becomes completely price and income inelastic in the absence of a rise in the level of material aspirations.[3]

2. An increase in population (in the absence of other changes in alternatives) raises the bargaining power of sellers of subsistence goods and lowers the bargaining power of sellers of less essential goods which were formerly bought by the households affected. This redistribution of bargaining powers leads only to offsetting income effects, however, leaving aggregate income unaffected. We

[3] If productivity increases past this point the consequence is a stable level of aggregate real income but a declining level of aggregate money income. There is a continuing redistribution of income from those whom productivity changes render poorer alternatives to all others, with the latter failing to respond to price declines and increased inflows except as necessary to restore a level of achievement previously attained but lost through prior adverse productivity effects. Thus certain skilled employees may find their bargaining power weakened and their incomes reduced by new machinery. The increased incomes of groups favorably affected are, however, not spent, since their aspirations are already satisfied. The loss of income to the skilled employees affected is only temporary, however, since in succeeding years different groups will be similarly adversely affected, and as prices fall and the incomes of others rise, the skilled employees first affected will restore their former level of achievement. The gain from productivity will come wholly in the form of increased self-employment, that is, "leisure."

can be sure, however, that barring other changes the bargaining power of sellers of labor services will fall relative to buyers of such services.[4] The resulting general fall in the rates for labor can be expected to drive product prices downward in some measure and to increase the returns to nonlabor sellers in some measure (the measure in each case depending on the bargaining position of sellers in various circumstances). In either event the real income of both business units and households deriving income from non-labor sources increases, either through income retained as buyers as prices fall or through income retained as sellers as prices fall by less than the labor-cost savings. Whether the income of individual households relying on the sale of labor for income will fall depends on whether they modify their revenue decision by allocating the time of additional members of the household to remunerative work. (Thus the wage rate of the principal breadwinner may fall but the household's income be sustained or actually rise if the wife or an older child is induced to seek employment.) Even where this is not the case, the household's real income falls by less than its money income to the extent that lower wage rates are reflected in lower prices.

In any event, whatever dampening income effects there may be on labor-oriented households only partially offset the expansive multiplier effects on other units: if the additions to the labor force from the increasing population are employed, aggregate real income must continue to rise. But the expanding incomes of the favored units must find their way into new bargains for this result to be achieved. As in the case of productivity changes, this outcome can be initially expected since rising incomes improve the bargaining power of sellers relative to buyers, inducing increased expenditures. An increase in real consumption can thus be expected in response to both price and income elasticity.

With continued growth in the size of the population, such in-

[4] This decline in labor's bargaining power in the distribution of the firm's receipts would of course occur only on the assumption that there has been no change in the number of other alternatives. The actual redistribution of bargaining power would depend on the relative rates of change of all the alternatives.

creasing expenditures (whether for consumption or investment) can be expected to continue to the point where (1) the increasing population gives rise to a labor force which, if fully utilized and applied to a given technology and given resources, would push production past the range of practical output due to diminishing returns; at that point the bargaining power of buyers of labor rises to shut off any further bargains; or (2) where the originally existing level of aspirations has been achieved, at which point (unless aspirations adjust upward) the bargaining power of such buyers relative to sellers rises promptly and sufficiently to foreclose any additional bargains.

Thus, unless there is a continuing increase in productivity or the availability of other resources to avoid the limitations of point (1), and a continuing increase in the level of aspirations to avoid the limitations of point (2), at some point the demand for labor services and goods becomes completely price and income inelastic, and further increases in aggregate real income are forestalled.

3. Changes in the availability of natural resources involve an analysis similar to that applying to changes in the size of population, except that the bargaining power of those depending for income on the sale of labor rises relative to the bargaining power of those depending for income on the resources whose availability has increased.

A long-run increase in aggregate income thus relies on (1) an increase in the level of aspirations and (2) an increase in the number and quality of the alternatives. What general shifts in bargaining power are reflected in these conditions?

First, over the long run these two conditions are not independent of each other, allowing a reliance on one to the exclusion of the other to achieve a rising aggregate real income. The rate of increase in real income depends on the relative rates of increase in aspirations *and* alternatives. Each is permissive of the other: a rise in aspirations permits a concomitant increase in the number and productivity of the alternatives to eventuate in rising real income, and an increase in alternatives permits a concomitant rise in aspirations to be translated into an addition to real income. It is the net effect on relative bargaining powers of the *concomitant* movements in aspirations and the various alternatives that is decisive of the net impact on aggregate income. We may expect that changes in the level of aspirations, in the size of the population and labor force, in the availability of other resources, and in productivity are occurring simultaneously and continuously—but at different rates. It is the total effect of these changes on the bargaining positions of buyers and sellers that is important. It is the similarities and differences in the rates of change of these determinants that count.

In the long run the alternatives which are significant are, as we have just noted, the elements entering into the production functions of the producing units—labor and materials and the manner of their combination. This is in contrast to shorter runs, when finished goods themselves likewise stand as alternatives confronting the consumer. Hence, in the long run any change in the number or quality of the alternatives directly affects producing units such as governments and firms, as buyers of the factors of production. Such producing units, standing as intermediary between primary resources and final consumer, may be regarded as *secondary sellers*. Individuals supplying labor and materials are the *primary sellers*, whose bargaining relationship is with the firm as buyer; the firm in turn, as secondary seller, is in a bargaining relationship with consumers as buyers.

Let us initially assume a stable composition of the population. An increase in alternatives (labor now excluded) increases the bargaining power of the buyers of such alternatives, who are the secondary sellers. Similarly, an increase in aspirations likewise shifts bargaining power in favor of the secondary sellers, who supply the goods and services satisfying material aspirations.

Any increase in the level of aspirations and in the quantity or quality of alternatives (labor still excluded) thus creates a bargaining power relationship favorable to secondary sellers. Since it is these conditions which also support a rising aggregate income, then it is the long-run maintenance of a distribution of bargaining power favorable to secondary sellers (the producing units, whether business firms or governments) that supports a rising aggregate income.

An increase in population which also increases the quantity of labor can have a similar favorable effect on aggregate income, as we have already seen. But there may be further consequences differentiating this effect from an increase in the nonlabor alternatives. First, as we have also seen, past some point of increase in population *per capita* real income may decline even though aggregate income continues to rise, as the contribution of the additional members of the population is less than is required to maintain them at the formerly existing standard. Second, the resulting shift of bargaining power in favor of the nonlabor units, if carried far, may result in such a concentration of income as to preclude any *general* increase in achievement and aspirations; at the same time, the material objectives of the relatively small number whose incomes have risen may not expand fast enough to insure the *total* expenditure of those swollen incomes or their offsetting equivalent, either in consumption or investment, which is necessary if aggregate income is not to decline.

As long as population does not outrun other resources, however, and as long as the general aspiration for material wants continues to rise sufficiently, any increment of revenue—to whomever accruing—will be used, whether for consumption or investment,[5] thus utilizing the potential production of any increase in the number or productivity of the alternatives. This does not by any means imply, however, that we can *expect* the demand for material goods to be so continuously and ubiquitously buoyant. Aspirations may rise

[5] The relative rates of change in the numbers and productivity of the alternatives influence the distribution of bargaining power and income in the budget decision of the firm. If the supply of labor is plentiful relative to the supply of entrepreneurial or managerial talent, this influences the distribution of income favorably to the latter. In the light of our conclusions concerning the aspirations of management, this is likely to mean increased investment, particularly in those periods when in the society at large aspirations are outrunning alternatives. It is the differential rates of change in the alternatives that determine the allocation of resources over the long pull, deciding *whose* aspirations are most realized at any one time.

over time—but jerkily, by fits and starts, leaving pools of unemployed, failing to utilize all the alternatives available, and providing a secular increase in income far below what would have been possible.

If the increase in alternatives comes primarily from other sources than rising population (that is, if the increase in output is more than proportionate to the increase in population), then past some stage, which may be rather quickly reached, further increases in aggregate income *depend* on innovations which open up new forms of consumption, thereby inducing new forms of investment. If an increase in the primary resources satisfies subsistence needs, these resources may be used to satisfy ever less pressing aspirations, and indeed *must* be so used if there is to be a secularly rising income. The general level of aspirations must rise to induce agreements which absorb an increasing number of increasingly productive alternatives, agreements whose nonoffsetting income effects lead to higher levels of aggregate income. It is the *persistence* of a strong income elasticity in the face of an increasing number of alternatives, maintaining the distribution of bargaining power favorably to secondary sellers generally (that is, producing units, whether firms or government units), which supports a secularly rising national income.

CYCLICAL INFLUENCES

Short-run and discontinuous changes in aspirations are chiefly responsible for cyclical fluctuations in aggregate income. Short-run changes in the number and effectiveness of the alternatives determine primarily what proportion of the change in aggregate income is in real terms and what proportion in money terms.

Cyclical shifts in aspirations, *because* cyclical (that is, because they involve a *return* to a former position), cannot be regarded as some permanent shift in the whole level or structure of aspirations, even though influencing them. Such short-run changes involve a resetting of the proximate goals. This may and quite likely does involve some shift in the whole time stream of aspirations, since proximate goals both influence and reflect intermediate objectives and long-run aims (that is, since the present affects the future). But it is also possible that the change in proximate goals involves only a temporary modification dictated by expediency, or a substitution of immediate goals having no effect on long-run aims, or an adjustment of timing unrelated to an adjustment of objectives. It seems probable that most cyclical fluctuations are actually a composite of both such effects, with changes in proximate goals—originally made without conscious expectation of affecting the whole time stream of aspirations—nevertheless having some modifying influence.

The cyclical changes in immediate objectives are characterized by being unexpected and self-adjusting. By the latter is meant only that they are anchored to the long-run trends, with real income fluctuating above and below the level which the secular (historical) forces would lead one to expect. If there were not this anchor to the long-run forces, we would have to deny the influence of any but the immediate past on the present.[6]

Among the short-run changes in objectives which have the effect of inducing nonoffsetting income effects, either downward or upward, there are some which embody general, others collective, and still others vicarious consumer goals.

General short-run changes in material wants primarily take the form of major innovations requiring extensive investment for their exploitation, involving bargains which are offsetting only to a limited degree. The rise of the automobile industry beginning in the 1920's is an obvious example; it required an enormous capital accumulation which, once completed, however, could be maintained with proportionately smaller replacement expenditures. The initial increase in expenditures through investment was thus a temporary

[6] Even secular forces are subject to fluctuation if the time span is long enough, as has been said before. But such secular change itself requires its explanation in the past: we must either conceive of an even longer-run trend to which the secular is anchored, or incorporate into the secular trend those very forces which give rise to its change.

phenomenon—a bubble above the normal trend line. The investment bargains in the innovating industry may be partly offset—but only partly—by a decline in investment bargains (the rate of replacement) of some industry or industries for which it stands as alternative.

Because the timing and effect of innovations are not continuous —even though a culture may continuously encourage innovation— temporary fluctuations due to variations in the magnitude of the effects and to irregularities in their rate of introduction are inescapable. Such effects are not wholly offset by a falling off of capital expenditures in the declining industries.

Like effects are produced by a concentration of demand in point of time (as following a war), when the pressure to provide for deferred consumption leads to an increase in productive facilities which stimulates nonoffsetting investment bargains. As the concentrated demand is satisfied, however, only a replacement rate for capital equipment is required, so that income fluctuates back downward.[7]

Collective short-run changes in material objectives relate primarily to expenditures for defense and war, while vicarious changes are illustrated by public expenditures (through charitable donations or tax contribution) for the relief of victims of major disasters.

The effect of all such changes in proximate objectives (both of consumers and producers) is to modify the bargaining power of the secondary sellers (business firms or governmental units) relative to their buyers. A general increase in the bargaining power of such units (or at least general enough to produce nonoffsetting bargains), without any manipulation by the sellers, implies an increase in consumption or investment demand. It is equivalent to a rightward shift in the demand curves, and generates an increase in aggregate income. But sellers may also stimulate the same result by manipulating relative bargaining power to their advantage, evoking a demand

[7] Professor David McCord Wright has analyzed these general short-run changes in material wants at some length in *Economics of Disturbance* (New York: The Macmillan Company, 1947).

response by lowering the cost of agreement or raising the cost of disagreement. This may involve a rightward movement along the
existing demand curves, an application of the standard concept of
price elasticity, but such manipulation may be also achieved by
changing other variables than price. It is the shift of bargaining
power to the advantage of secondary sellers, relative to their buyers,
that is necessary for an increase in aggregate income, whether arising autonomously or manipulated by the sellers. Let us observe the
principal ways in which such a shift in bargaining powers may
emerge.

1. There may be an increase in the proximate goals themselves,
collective, vicarious, general, along the lines discussed above.

2. A general and abnormal increase in the income of buyers will
raise the relative bargaining power of sellers. Such an increase in
money income may be attributable to the multiplier effects of an
abrupt increase in demand, or to the creation by governments of
claims to goods; an increase in real income can arise from lowered
product prices due to a short-run increase in the number or quality
of alternatives, as through a sudden spurt in productivity in the
early stages of production of a new (and major) product.

3. An increase in the liquid assets of buyers, whose proximate
goals are, however, unfulfilled, favors sellers.[8] Even a constant rate
of saving, if savings are allowed to accumulate, leads to an increase
in liquid assets which improves the bargaining position of selling
firms. Well-heeled households are conducive to an expansion of

[8] The influences of time on the distribution of bargaining power will be recalled from an earlier chapter: an increase in assets, the fruits of the past, increases
the bargaining power of sellers relative to buyers, since expenditures involve less
risk to a standard of living; expected changes in relative bargaining power, the
effect of an anticipated future, affect relative bargaining power in the same direction as would similar present changes. These influences are less operative in the
long run than in the short run, and we have ignored them in our previous discussion of secular changes. In the long run liquid assets find their way into real
assets, and real assets must be replaced, but in the short run liquid assets may
accumulate or decumulate, and the durability of assets may be significant. With
respect to long-run changes affecting the distribution of bargaining power, the
present importance and the probability of expectations so diminish as to modify
bargaining relations only slightly, but the effect of short-run expectations is significant for present relationships, and probabilities seem more calculable.

consumption, and well-heeled businesses are conducive to an expansion of investment.

4. Sellers benefit by buyers' expectations of those conditions which make for a further shift in bargaining power favorable to sellers. Buyers may anticipate an increase in their incomes, attributable to the increased general demand for services or goods. Buyers may expect that an increase in the general demand for goods will further raise prices, making it advantageous to buy now items which can be stored for the future (an inventory buildup). An expectation of lower prices in the future for those things which must be purchased currently and cannot be stored will turn bargaining power in favor of sellers generally, by promising a higher real income in the future.

A short-run increase in the proximate goals or in their achievement will thus expand aggregate real income, provided it is accompanied by a short-run increase in the number of alternatives or a more effective employment of the existing alternatives.

Aggregate income may move downward cyclically for reasons the reverse of those mentioned above. There may be a temporary satiation of the proximate material goals. This is notably true when a war is brought to a close or a disarmament pact curtails defense expenditures. An increase in real assets or inventories may raise the bargaining power of buyers relative to sellers of goods of those types, curtailing further purchases: if a new or expanding industry has been selling durable goods (whether consumer or capital) at a fast rate of increase, it can expect to encounter a leveling off in demand at existing prices as the market becomes satiated. The income formerly allocated to such expenditures may be diverted to savings, leading to multiplier effects which, if not offset by some increase in proximate goals leading to new expenditures elsewhere, will drive aggregate income downward. A decline in buyers' income (perhaps in money income in consequence of multiplier effects of a decline in demand, perhaps in real income in consequence of a rise in prices due to a decline in alternatives) will shift bargaining power adversely to secondary sellers, with dampening effects on total income. Expectations of conditions making for a further shift of bargaining power in favor of buyers will have similar repercussions—expectations of declining income; expectations of a declining general demand for items which can be postponed to the future, when prices will be lower; expectations of higher prices in the future for items which must be purchased currently for consumption (and in anticipation of which careful present budgeting will permit greater precautionary savings); expectations of declining assets (as are common in any depression).

It is the *net* effect of changes in all these influences which is determinative of the short-run shifts in bargaining power as between secondary sellers and their buyers. It is the *net* effect of

1. changes in demand (proximate goals), general, collective, or vicarious;

2. changes in the number and quality of alternatives (affecting the potential for sellers' manipulation of prices);

3. changes in buyers' incomes (households, businesses, and governmental units alike);

4. changes in the level and composition of assets;

5. changes in expectations with respect to all the above variables.

Of all these influences, however, it is the first—changes in the proximate material goals (demand)—which is the most effective. The initiation and the termination of a war, the initiation or completion of a public works program, the creation of new wants (as currently for color television and household air conditioning) the income effects of which are not wholly offset by declining expenditures for other items, or conditions making for the temporary satiation of demand at current and prospective prices for important durable goods such as housing and home appliances and automobiles, and the abundance or lack of prospect of expanding demand to stimulate further investment—these are the prime influences on short-run fluctuations in aggregate income.

A word more should be said about the effects of cyclical changes in the number and quality of alternatives, however.

First, such changes—when related to the rate of change of current demand—determine the extent to which aggregate income changes are in real or in money terms.

1. (a) If demand (the rate of attempted achievement of proximate goals) increases faster than the increase in alternatives, this leads to a larger increase in money income than in real income. (There are more bargains, and these are at higher prices.) (b) If demand falls faster than the fall in alternatives, this leads to a greater decrease in money income than in real income. (There are fewer bargains, and these are at lower prices.) [9]

2. (a) If demand increases equally with alternatives, money and real income rise together. (There are more bargains at stable prices.) (b) If demand falls equally with alternatives, money and real income fall together. (There are fewer bargains at stable prices.)

3. (a) If demand increases more slowly than alternatives, this leads to a smaller increase in money than in real income. (There are more bargains but at lower prices. (b) If demand declines more slowly than alternatives, this leads to a smaller decline in money than in real income. (There are fewer bargains but at higher prices.)

Second, these relative changes in the rates of increase or decrease of demand and alternatives affect not only the levels of real and money income but also the distribution of income. If we regard the secondary seller as the unit of entrepreneurial activity (firm or governmental unit), represented by management as the coördinator of bargains, its bargains as seller are with the purchasers of its goods or services. Its bargains as buyer are internal, consisting of the allocations of the budget decision. Here the firm, as represented by management, faces those whom we have designated primary sellers (labor and the controllers of other resources).

Any increase in demand affects the secondary seller favorably, as a collectivity, but how the accruing revenues are allocated in the

[9] Case 1(a) also covers the situation where demand rises and alternatives decrease, though in this case money income may either fall but by less than the fall in real income or rise as real income falls—in either case there is a fall of real income relative to money income. Case 1(b) covers the situation where demand falls and alternatives increase.

budget decision depends on the bargaining powers of primary sellers relative to management. This distribution of bargaining powers is affected by any change in the number or quality of the participants and their alternatives. Similarly, any decline in demand reacts adversely on the firm as secondary seller, but how the adverse effects are felt depends on the relative bargaining power of the firm's management and the primary sellers with whom it deals.

In the three sets of cases of relative movements of demand and alternatives which we distinguished above, the effects of the changes on the firm as secondary seller and on the alternatives as primary sellers are as follows:

	Increases in demand	*Decreases in demand*
Case 1.	(a) Favorable to secondary sellers, favorable to primary sellers	(b) Unfavorable to secondary sellers, unfavorable to primary sellers
Case 2.	(a) Favorable to secondary sellers, primary sellers unaffected	(b) Unfavorable to secondary sellers, primary sellers unaffected
Case 3.	(a) Favorable to secondary sellers, unfavorable to primary sellers	(b) Unfavorable to secondary sellers, favorable to primary sellers

It is only in those cases where the shift in bargaining power is favorable to secondary sellers (that is, to entrepreneurial activity by firms and governmental units, represented by their managements) that aggregate income can be expected to rise. But in these cases the position of certain of the primary sellers (labor, for example) may improve, deteriorate, or remain unchanged. Demand for goods and services may increase, adding to business revenues, but how the increment to revenues is distributed will depend on concomitant changes in the relative bargaining power of the partners in production. These movements in relative bargaining power may be attributable to changes in the number or quality of the participants and their alternatives, as we have seen, but they may also be attributable to manipulations of bargaining power undertaken by some group of commensals (workers, through labor unions, for example), manipulations which are likely to have pre-dominantly short-run effects.[10]

Cyclical fluctuations in income are above all else, then, a function of fluctuating demand which affects the bargaining position of secondary sellers favorably or adversely. It is the temporary surges and recessions of material wants (from whatever source, as long as sufficiently generalized in the culture), increasing or diminishing the bargaining power of secondary sellers vis-a-vis their buyers, that is the dominant consideration. Any temporary effect lessening the buyers' cost of agreement or increasing their cost of disagreement leads to temporary upward movements in aggregate income, and vice versa. The short-run shifts in the number and productiveness of the alternatives determine chiefly whether the fluctuations initiated on the demand side take the form of changes in money or real income.

Many volumes have been written identifying the causes of business cycles. Numerous theories have been offered to explain cyclical income fluctuations. As in the case of explanations of the pricing behavior of firms, it is quite possible that such explanations may all have their element of validity. There is no reason to believe that there is some *single* path to the nonoffsetting income effects of changes in bargaining power, any more than there is some single method by which producers set prices. It seems reasonable to believe that the specific causes of modifications in the bargaining power of secondary sellers relative to their buyers, at an historical moment, must vary in kind and degree, and the immediate reaction effects of such changes likewise can be expected to vary. It is possible that the extent of our generalizations as to the causes of such movements may, therefore, be that when the *net* effect of changes in aspirations and alternatives is to affect adversely the bargaining

---

[10] The reason for expecting primarily short-run effects from the manipulation of bargaining power is that the manipulation of one group will in time evoke reactions from those adversely affected, and there is no reason for believing that such retaliatory response will be less effective. In the historical long run it is the underlying real forces affecting bargaining power, which we have identified above, that can be expected to have the primary influence.

power of secondary sellers, generally, relative to buyers, this will (on a probability basis, considering the number of sellers and buyers involved) lead to downward fluctuations in income, and vice versa. The depth or height of the movement would then depend on the intensity and extent of the particular, identifiable, perhaps unique influences (or conjunction of influences) operating on the costs of agreement and disagreement of buyers and sellers.

The economist is concerned with two central problems: (1) The allocation and distribution problem deals with the level of individual satisfactions. Focus is on the micro relationships, and the analysis is carried through in terms of relatives—the relationship of price to price, or consumption standards coercively compared, or the relative satisfactions of two jobs. (2) The problem of fluctuations in the level of income, which deals with the aggregate level of achievement. Focus here is on the macro relationships, and the analysis is carried through in terms of absolute levels of total income in a time series.

The individual and the aggregate, micro and macro, are related through the multiplier effect of bargains. The whole is not a simple sum of individual actions, except in a purely arithmetical *ex post* sense. But in any analytical sense, individual actions are influenced by the multiplier effects of the total (that is, of *all other*) relationships. The individual's action can be taken in response to his own bargaining power position, but his action (micro activity) does not actually lie wholly within his control. It depends on the offsetting effects of all the bargains which are concurrently being struck by others (a macro phenomenon). In Keynes's familiar example, the effort of a given individual to save something out of his income depends for its success on the bargains of others: if they too try to save, the result (*ex post*) is a decline in income which makes the planned saving impossible.

From the aggregative point of view, it makes no difference whether, in the complex of bargains, one unit substitutes for another in part or in whole, so that the multiplier effects of one set of bargains are offset by the multiplier effects of other bargains, leaving the aggregate unaffected. These offsetting effects may be regarded as random. But when the distribution of bargaining power in the system is influenced not randomly but specifically and generally, then nonoffsetting income effects emerge, leading to fluctuations in the aggregate level of income. The general bargaining-power modifications which appear of strategic importance are those affecting the position of the secondary sellers—those who stand as middleman, broker, and entrepreneur between those who control the primary resources of the economy (whom we designated as primary sellers) and the buyers of goods and services, both consumption and investment. Anything which affects the bargaining-power relationship *generally* between secondary sellers and their buyers affects the level of aggregate income.

A redistribution of bargaining power adverse to secondary sellers insures a decline in aggregate income, and vice versa. We cannot deductively determine the magnitude of the income movement, however. That depends on the magnitude of the nonoffsetting income effects, which cannot be deductively calculated but must be empirically estimated. We can, however, relying on the law of large numbers, legitimately seek to deduce the direction of movement. When general influences on aspirations, income, assets, or expectations make themselves felt, so that bargaining power moves, let us say, in favor of secondary sellers, then on a probability basis we can safely assume that *some* new bargains will be made, since buyers will now more readily concede sellers' terms, and that the multiplier effect of such nonoffsetting bargains will be to increase aggregate income. The reverse is equally true.

The same bargaining power concept is thus used to explain both allocations and fluctuations. It is relative bargaining powers, subject to manipulation, which determine the distribution and allocation of income at any moment of time. It is modifications in relative bargaining powers which determine the fluctuations in income over time.

CHAPTER 17

Bargaining Power and Equilibrium

EQUILIBRIUM in economic analysis refers to a position of balanced forces or pressures; it is a state of affairs offering no inducement to change the system of relationships which any individual has established with others. The concept of equilibrium implies no belief or expectation that conditions (in particular, tastes, technology, and the level and quality of population) will remain "given," but that for the situation existing at any moment there is some set of relations which if it could be established would represent the best that anyone could do under the circumstances. This conception of equilibrium amounts to saying that if such a state of balance could be reached, there would be no change in the system of economic relationships as long as there were no change in the conditions giving rise to those relationships.

Once the element of time is introduced into the analysis, then this static notion of equilibrium loses much of its analytical usefulness. Time necessarily produces change in the underlying conditions. The pattern of population growth changes; knowledge increases and with it there are changes in people's wants and their methods of satisfying them; governments and governors succeed each other; wars are fought or anticipated; in at least these respects the underlying conditions which determine economic relationships are constantly undergoing change. A concern for the pattern of relationships which would be established if there were no change becomes peculiarly pointless once change is admitted as continuous. Certainly within the framework of analysis developed in this volume, we can expect continuing modifications in people's aspirations and alternatives, thereby modifying relative bargaining powers. The consequences are, first, an action effect, as people are induced to substitute new agreements for old agreements, and then a reaction effect, as those who are unsatisfied with their bargaining power position or whose bargaining power has been adversely affected seek to improve their positions by the variety of manipulations available to them, including combinations and alliances with others. Whenever aspirations are thwarted or spurred, whenever the alternatives for their satisfaction become inferior or superior, the system of bargaining power relationships is altered, and action and reaction effects are unavoidable.

The recognition of time and the admission of change do not, however, imply an absence of all stabilizing influences on the system of relationships. It is possible to accept constant change, involving continuing inducements to effect new relationships, and yet conceive of limits within which the effects of such changes are confined, of controls preventing extremes in both the allocation and fluctuation of income. Within the limits so defined, change could be incessant and yet the situation could be regarded as stable. But whenever some movement took the system of relationships outside of those limits, reaction effects might be induced which would restore the system to its position of continuing change within limits. It is this conception of equilibrium that is here adopted. And in this chapter we are specifically interested in whether there are reaction effects to changes in the distribution of bargaining power which do impose limitations (1) on the concentration of incomes, and (2) on the amplitude of fluctuations in income.

To aid discussion let us briefly define the concepts which are relevant, concepts with which we are already familiar. In Figure 3 the circle represents the *organizational unit* (here depicted as a business firm). The management of that unit or firm enters into numerous bargains—on the selling side, bargains with households, with other business units to which it supplies parts or finished goods, or with governmental units which it may also provide with goods and materials; on the buying side, bargains with workers, with materials suppliers, with capital suppliers, and so on. Each of these bargains is made within its own *bargaining unit*. The unit for the bargain

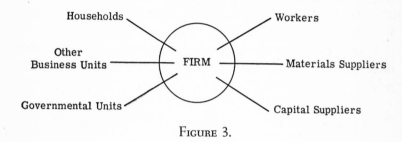

FIGURE 3.

with workers may be one embracing not only this firm but several business rivals and all the employees of those firms (a comprehensive multiemployer unit), while the units in which the terms for its materials are set may be simple firm-to-firm units. The firm is the focal accounting point for all these bargains.

The direct bargaining relationships in which the firm through its management is sometimes involved as buyer and sometimes as seller we refer to, as economists have always referred to them, as *exchange relationships*.

The coördination of all the buying and selling bargains into a complex of bargains satisfying the conditions of a going concern is what we refer to as the managerial function and identify as the political process. Management coördinates all the bargains (struck in whatever bargaining unit) which affect the revenue and budget decisions of the organizational unit, a process which requires adjustment of one exchange relation to satisfy the terms of another, which necessitates sacrificing certain symbionts in order to meet the terms demanded by others considered more important to the continuity of the unit under its present management. This process of coördination is never ended but continues daily.

The managerial powers are exercised or sought by individuals (1) who see in them a means of better achieving their aspirations, chiefly through the residual powers of the office, and (2) who have the support of others who believe themselves to be in an advantageous bargaining relationship to those whom they support. The relationships which are engendered by the desire to be management or to be advantageously related to management we call *political relationships*.

These are the concepts most relevant to the question of whether there is an equilibrium range within which income flows are channeled.

LIMITS ON THE CONCENTRATION OF INCOME

We are interested here in limits on the accumulation of income in the hands of particular economic units (say a corporation or the members of a given union) or in the hands of a class of economic agents (say property owners or labor). We shall distinguish two broad categories of reactions imposing limits on the concentration of income—those occurring in the exchange relationship itself and those occurring in the political relationships of the economic unit which is aggrandizing its income. Within each of these two principal categories we shall identify two types of reaction effects—the automatic and the manipulated.

Reactions in the Exchange Relationship

1. Automatic reactions. This first class of restraints is one which has been long familiar to economists. The availability of alternatives is the primary limitation on the concentration of income; indeed, it has received almost exclusive consideration in economic analysis. If income accumulates in some units because the latter is exacting a high price for its goods or services, past some price two results

may be expected which act as a brake on its powers of income accumulation.

First, at some price the symbionts' cost of agreement becomes greater than their cost of disagreement, and they accept alternatives which while less desirable on the quality basis are preferable because of their lower prices. Inferior goods become better alternatives because their prices become relatively lower. In the case of buyers who exact hard terms from sellers, such action increases the relative attractiveness of the alternatives facing the sellers. In either buying or selling transactions, one cannot say in advance what the effect of an exaction of better terms will be, but where the terms are directed to a number of symbionts (as, for example, a price quoted to all the customers or a wage to all the employees of a firm), then *any* exaction can be expected to have *some* consequences. The failure of a firm to grant a wage increase or a price reduction, at a time when other firms are improving their offers, may lead some (even if seldom all) of its employees and customers to desert it for agreements elsewhere.

Depending on the coerciveness of the comparisons between workers as to wage rates and working conditions, and between consumers as to standards of living, any deterioration of their relative position may be expected to create or increase a *disposition* to turn to alternatives holding more promise of satisfying the social pressures felt. This disposition will become effective when the opportunity presents itself. A firm's wage action which weakens its bargaining power in the labor market may not induce its employees to take up an active search for alternative jobs, but it is likely to create in them a greater receptiveness to openings which come to their attention. If position 1, in the table below, represents the initial wage offers of three firms, and if at these rates the bargaining power of firm A was adequate to hold its employees (in the light of the relative steadiness of employment and congeniality of work associates and the aspiration patterns of what may be a more easily satisfied group of workers), then at position 2, A's bargaining power may be less effective. The fact that firm B has now matched the rate of firm C, leaving A's workers more clearly isolated as the low-paid employee group, is likely to create a disposition among at

	Firm A	Firm B	Firm C
Position 1	$1.00	$1.10	$1.20
Position 2	$1.00	$1.20	$1.20

least some of A's men to take jobs at B or C when the chance appears. Once B and C become real alternatives (firms with job openings), the cost of agreeing with A on the terms which it offers will rise, and the relative shift in bargaining power between the three firms will cause *some* movement of workers to B and C. The interfirm structure of wage relationships cannot be too far modified without also modifying employment relationships.

Thus at some indefinite but sure point the exactions of a superior bargaining position create their own limit. The bargaining power of the unit weakens as the cost of agreement on its terms rises relative to its alternatives. One limit of concentration of income occurs, then, where the comparative achievement which the bargain makes possible to the symbiont fails to represent any advantage over alternative bargains.

There is a second respect in which the existence of alternatives sets a limit to the concentration of income. The success of some unit (as indicated by its income stream) is likely to induce others to provide alternatives not presently available in order to cash in on the former's good fortune, thus limiting its bargaining power. Or the inventiveness and initiative of those comprising some unit perhaps not now a direct competitor are likely to result in an unexpected and superior alternative, again restraining an intrenched firm's bargaining power. These are the cases of imitation and innovation.

Imitation places a long-run downward pressure on prices, as firms are driven to reduce their terms as a means of improving their bargaining position relative to a growing number of competitors. Innovation relies on a quality advantage which more than offsets an initial price disadvantage to a sufficient number of buyers to make the venture profitable. Successful innovation is always succeeded by imitation, so that the long-run effects are both reduced prices and superior goods. This continuing process of innovation and imitation (which Schumpeter labeled the process of creative destruction) acts as an effective limit to the possibility of the concentration of income in particular economic units. The bargaining advantages which any enjoy at the moment are always subject to deterioration through the introduction by others of superior goods or the reduction by others of the price of existing lines of products, as these others seek to better their own bargaining position.

To some extent the threat of competition from alternatives can be reduced by combination or alliance. The economic unit, by merging with its commensal rivals or by buying them out or by effecting an understanding with them, may be able to control the principal alternatives to the goods or services which it provides, bolstering its bargaining position by making its symbionts' cost of disagreement higher. The common managerial aspiration for the growth of the organization and an increase in its share of the market may be served by amalgamation with commensals and an increase in symbionts' cost of disagreement no less than by intenser competition based on lowering its symbionts' cost of agreement.

But if an economic unit achieves an increasing concentration of income in its hands by its powers of controlling the alternatives (by monopolizing, in the broad sense), it faces new limits to such concentration.

2. Manipulations in the exchange relationship. The power of an economic combine may be met by countercombination, which imposes on the aggrandizing unit a higher cost of disagreement. Giant packinghouses are met by farmer marketing coöperatives, for example. There is no need for elaborating here on a line of discussion which has been made familiar in previous chapters. The effectiveness of any group in making use of the counterweapons of combination and alliance depends largely on how successful they may be in securing agreement among themselves, as commensals. If combination so strengthens their position vis-a-vis the unit which opposes

them, then even those members of the combination which must sacrifice something to achieve a working relationship with their fellows will gain more by sharing in the expanded power of the group as a whole. The more inclusive the countercombination (inclusive, that is, of alternatives which are important to the opposing symbiont), the greater is their combined strength.

REACTIONS IN THE POLITICAL RELATIONSHIP

1. *Automatic reactions.* In addition to the limitation on bargaining power imposed by countercombination, a unit which seeks to accumulate income in its hands by swallowing up or joining with the effective alternatives to the relationship which it offers is faced with limitations arising out of its political relationships. By political relationships, it will be recalled, we mean those arising out of the effort to control the management function for one's own advantage.

As we have seen in a previous chapter, the participants in an organizational unit are tied together by a complex of bargains, the characteristics of which are two: (1) that for all participants the cost of agreement is less than the cost of disagreement, and (2) that the aggregate outflow of the unit must equal the aggregate inflow (plus changes in assets or liabilities). Each individual in the organization strives through his part in this complex of bargains to achieve his aspirations, which in turn requires each individual to seek a measure of bargaining power *within* the unit adequate for this purpose. Factional disputes and policy conflicts within an organization reflect the struggle for control over the organization along lines which are expected to advance the interests of the particular participant.

As an organization grows, it incorporates within itself conflicts which previously were external to it. The larger the number of bargainers within the unit, the more difficult becomes management's job of coördinating all bargains to achieve a complex satisfying the two conditions given above. Because for more and more individuals the means of satisfying their aspirations lie in what terms they can effect *within* the organization, and because the larger the organization, the fewer the alternatives available to the participants (the fewer the number of other organizations to which they can turn), the internecine struggle for position, prestige, remuneration, and security become intenser, cliques develop, policy fights become bitter, the stakes are higher. The unit is subjected to internal strains lacking in a smaller organization.

However much they are concealed by the machinelike operation of bureaucratic procedures, the large organization always harbors smoldering feuds, resentful groups, ambitious cliques, office politicians who are in continuing conflict with each other over the fruits which each shall derive from coöperation with the others, making the managerial function of coördinating all bargains more and more difficult. At some point for some of the individual participants and perhaps for their coteries the cost of agreement on the terms which are all that can be offered (if the demands of others in stronger positions are to be satisfied), becomes greater than the cost of disagreement. Over time the large organization can be expected to breed its own competitors by failing to satisfy the demands of some of its own members and thereby forcing their separation into an independent unit or their alliance with a rival. The persistence of the inducement to combination and merger is equalled only by the persistence of the inducement to separation and disunity.

Nor need it be argued that every large organization faces its sure disintegration in order to conceive of such internal limits to the continuing concentration of income. It is enough that past some point size imposes an increasing difficulty of effecting bargains with one participant or set of participants that are compatible with the interests of others,[1] and the power to act boldly and to take large

---

[1] This is perhaps as good a place as any to suggest that the coercive comparisons which set the proximate goals of most individuals relate not only to commensals—though it has been that which has been stressed in the earlier chapters—but to symbiont classes as well. The disputes between management and labor sometimes involve not only comparisons between what workers in this plant are getting relative to workers in comparable plants, but also how much workers' wages have in-

risks diminishes. More individuals must be brought in on decisions, and the more cautious (whose terms must be met in some degree if their participation is to continue) act as weights on those who would move with daring. Management's residual powers—on which initiative largely depends—are dissipated in making concessions to assure the continuity of the enterprise under present management. This increasing sluggishness that comes with size sets an internal limit to expansion of the unit and the concentration of income in its hands.

2. Manipulations in the political relationships. The political relationship occurs not only at the level of the firm, in the struggle for control over or advantageous relationship to corporate management, but at the governmental level, where the bargains which are coördinated apply to all and the going concern is the community itself. Those whose income position has worsened relative to others are in a position to seek remedial action not only through the micro unit of the firm but at the macro unit of government. At the latter level, as in the former, they seek to control for their benefit the coördination of bargains among all the factions of the society. By transferring the competition from the smaller unit, in which their power may be weak and the weapons of manipulation limited, to the larger unit, where support can be won from other similarly situated or from sympathetic groups and where sheer numbers count, importunate groups may improve their position. They can employ political pressure to restrict the power of a symbiont rival, as through regulatory legislation, or to gain some advantage for themselves, as through subsidy.

From our previous analysis it will be recalled that those whose economic position is deteriorating (as through the concentration of income in the hands of others) have their bargaining power

---

creased relative to management salaries, or why it is fair for management to set up pension programs for itself but none for the workers, or whether stockholders are not entitled to some higher dividend rate before a wage increase is granted, and so on. These symbiont rivalries are important but probably less urgent than the commensal rivalries, since in the latter case the basis for any inequality of return seems less arguable.

increased relative to those government officials or candidates who are opposed to their interests, while candidates or officials who are willing to fight on their behalf are in a stronger position to capture their support. Issues which are less immediate or extraneous to self-interest (international relations, internal subversion, government economy) recede in importance, while issues which bear directly on economic welfare eclipse all other considerations (unemployment programs, relief from oppressive taxation, control of inflation). The politicians whose stand on the self-interest issues most favors the cause of those who consider themselves economically depressed will be strengthened in their efforts to capture the management of the government. If political action embraces enough individuals to threaten defeat to governments which do *not* act in support of their interests, state support will be more assured than if the opposing interests appear capable of defeating governments which *do* act in support of the petitioning group.

There are thus political relationships affecting the bargaining power at the level of the firm as well as at the level of government. We can view the former as an internal conflict for control over the management function, that is, within the unit itself, and the latter as an external conflict for control over the management function, occurring within a unit larger than the firm itself and threatening those whose bargaining power has permitted them to capture for their own advantage the management of that firm.

If one set up a continuum representing the relative proportions of external and internal conflict of an economic unit, such proportions could be roughly measured by the percent of the total group or society excluded and included within the particular unit.

External _____ Internal

conflict   conflict

       0——percent of total group within unit——100

As one moves from a small organization embracing few members of the total group to a large organization involving almost all of the total group, he moves from a situation where most of the conflicts facing the unit are external to it to a situation where most of the conflicts facing the unit are internal. But except at the two extremes, both forms of conflict are always present and operate as checks upon the concentration of power and income within the hands of any segment of the whole.

It thus appears unlikely, for political reasons, that bargaining power can be greatly concentrated for long in the hands of any group. If the group is large (even a majority, say all workers), the scarcity relationship inescapably existing between them is likely to cause the formation of internal alliances and combinations (perhaps external as well) for competitive purposes, disintegrating the group. (Factional splits within unions sometimes have this origin.) If the group is small, it is likely that steps will be taken to neutralize or reduce its power by the larger numbers who are affected adversely by that power. (A good deal of regulatory legislation would appear to be so explained.)

There are, then, several limits to the concentration of income within a society. We have identified these limits as imposed, in the exchange relationship, by the alternatives to the goods or services provided by the unit in whose hands income is accumulating. At some point the exactions on which the income accumulation is based impose a cost of agreement higher than is acceptable to symbionts in the light of existing alternatives. Where alternatives exist, there is a limit to the price which the particular unit's bargaining power will sustain. But in addition, existing alternatives are not the only threat to a strong bargaining position. Innovation, which may come from any quarter, provides new and better alternatives than those theretofore available, and imitation drives the price down over time as rivals bid for symbionts. The exchange relationship may also be affected by the device of countercombination and counteralliance in the direct transaction.

Still other limits to income accumulation are imposed in the form of political restraints. If an economic unit seeks to embrace its principal rivals, controlling its alternatives, it must still face the threat of disintegration and conservatism that comes from the managerial necessity of building a complex of bargains satisfactory to the larger and larger number of participants. This is the internal restraint on income accumulation. But in addition, those whose economic position is weakened by the monopolizing unit can seek influence over a higher level of management—the government—to curb the unit's power or bolster their own through political manipulations of power.

These limits to the concentration of income are not predictably certain, nor are they logically inevitable. We can only say that while the incomes of individual units will rise and fall with the redistribution of bargaining power arising from changes in aspirations and alternatives, there is an unmeasured probability that no one unit or class of units, no factor or class of factors, can continue to concentrate income in its possession without inducing a reaction effect which will prevent further increase in the rate of accumulation.

LIMITS ON THE FLUCTUATION OF AGGREGATE INCOME

We turn now to limits on the fluctuation of aggregate income. No implication is intended, however, that a stable aggregate income is desirable. It is more likely that an upward rising total real income would be viewed as preferable, and with an increasing population would indeed be necessary if *per capita* income was to be maintained. Nor are employment fluctuations identical with income fluctuations, even though they are likely to be associated. We are interested only in whether there are controls built into the system of social relationships preventing aggregate income from rising or falling beyond certain limits. These limits, if reached, could then be counted on to produce reaction effects—a redistribution of bargaining power—such as to halt or reverse the direction of income movement.

The cumulative nature of income fluctuations has been suggested in the preceding chapter. The multiplier effect of nonoffsetting bargains is responsible for such cumulation. If inflow expectations of some units are disappointed, outflows are reduced by those units, leading to reduced inflows for still other units, and so on in a downward movement. The fact that some units whose inflows are reduced may draw on assets to sustain outlays does not alter the probability, when we are dealing with large numbers, that the general income effect will be downward. Similarly, if the inflow expectations of some units appear unusually bright or are surpassed in fact, their outflows will be increased, leading to increased inflows for still other units, and so on in an upward movement. And again the possibility that some units whose inflows are increased will add to savings does not affect the probability, when we are dealing with large numbers of units, that the general income movement will be upward. The question which we face, then, is whether there are reactions which may be expected to bring a halt to such cumulative income movements or even to reverse their directions.

REACTIONS IN THE EXCHANGE RELATIONSHIP

One limit on upward income fluctuations, imposed by the direct actions of economic units, has its origin in the fact that, for units operating above a subsistence level, wants can be satiable in the short run. Aspirations entertained at a given point in the time stream can be sufficiently satisfied, at given income levels and with the existing means of satisfaction, so that the distribution of bargaining power turns against secondary sellers, particularly the sellers of durable goods. Barring a general lift in the standards of living and the introduction of new goods and types of services, the demand for houses, household appliances, automobiles, and investment goods becomes stabilized at some level, requiring only a given output for new and replacement sales instead of the rising output previously needed. The deceleration effect is primarily felt in the investment goods industry and its suppliers, and it is transmitted by them through multiplier effects to the rest of the economy.

At times, however, the slackening of demand relates not simply to rates of increase but to actual levels of output and is then felt by the producers of consumers' durables themselves, who transmit the income effect to their suppliers. As Professor Wright has shown, this latter situation is likely to arise following major innovations, which make former equipment obsolete, provoking a fast rate of replacement which cannot be sustained once the innovation has been widespreadly introduced and the pace of basic modifications has slackened.

This satiation effect does not rely entirely on the dissemination of the fruits of innovation, however. With rising incomes, family units can sometimes achieve the material position to which they immediately aspire (in their time stream of aspirations) sufficiently to reduce the effectiveness of their demand. It is not that they are unable to adjust to higher living standards, but that the adjustment takes time. The newly achieved position must be experienced for a while before new goals are set or before a person or unit defines, in terms of new proximate goals, his new position in the time stream of his aspirations. The standards of the group with which comparisons are made may have to rise generally before dissatisfaction with new achievements reaches the stage of imposing new immediate material objectives. If people could be induced to change their consumer habits readily, so that they stood ready to buy a new home every five years, a new automobile every year, discard their wardrobes annually, until the productive capacity of the economy expanded to permit this level of satisfaction, and then could be persuaded to change homes every two years, automobiles semiannually, and wardrobes monthly, and so on, this convenient adjustment of consumer wants would always guarantee the full use of increasingly productive resources.

The notion of insatiable wants which characterized classical economics is at best a long-run phenomenon (as befitted a long-run theory). If, in the short run and with rising incomes, the standards of people in a given social grouping become reasonably well met— within their experience—it may take time for the more adventurous and imaginative in that group to establish new standards acting as goals for the others. The discontinuity of innovations is a further factor permitting the relative satisfaction with one's current level of achievement. Lacking new instruments for the satisfaction of new wants, people may be reasonably content with their existing standard of living, particularly if it represents an advance over a previous standard in accordance with their own time stream of aspirations.

A period of steadily rising income is thus likely to effect its own termination as the relative satisfaction by economic units with the level of their achievement eventually turns the bargaining power relationship against secondary sellers. This is the pause in the upward movement of income which is sometimes popularly referred to as the period during which people "digest" their gains. But income fluctuations downward are also influenced by past experience and present expectations concerning consumption standards. Aggregate income cannot continue to decline indefinitely for the simple reason that people's consumption standards are not infinitely repressible. At some point expenditures by those still possessing the necessary income or assets cannot be further curtailed without cutting below a minimum culturally conditioned standard, so that inflows to other units are maintained and the downward spiral is halted. Minimum culturally conditioned standards of living can be maintained only by a greater proportionate expenditure out of smaller incomes (a reduced level of savings) or by the use of assets, either course of action serving to short-circuit the income effects of non-offsetting bargains and to maintain the level of aggregate expenditures on which aggregate income depends. This is the point of Keynesian equilibrium, where the reduced amount of total saving in the system is no greater than the reduced amount of total investment, so that total expenditures (consumption plus investment) are sustained. The income effects of all bargains are then offsetting.

Time has its effect in still another way. Periods of rising levels of aggregate income, generally indicative of a shift in bargaining power in favor of secondary sellers, are normally associated with rising prices, while falling income is associated with declining prices. These price movements are themselves reflective of the redistribution of bargaining power which has taken place and of efforts made to profit from it or to overcome its adverse effects. They are linked with inflationary and deflationary movements—shifts in money income which are nonproportional to shifts in real income. Aside from the question of whether there are limits to fluctuations in real income, we may, then, also be interested in whether limits exist to the fluctuation of money income.

If prices rise, this puts more income into the hands of sellers and encourages further expenditures by them, leading to further price increases. But past some point price rises discourage purchases, not simply in the gradual and equilibrating manner envisioned by price theory but in a much more general and abrupt fashion. This effect is due to the fact that at some level prices become so un-related to past (experienced) values that expectations of such price levels continuing are shaken, at least temporarily; intelligence and common sense are insulted that prices of such a magnitude should be asked. The buyers' cost of agreement on such terms rises, par-ticularly in the case of durable goods, while their cost of disagree-ment falls if they entertain expectations that such prices cannot be maintained.

The same is true, in reverse, of price declines. As bargaining power turns in favor of buyers and against secondary sellers, prices decline, putting less income into the hands of sellers and reducing money outlays by them, putting further downward pressure on prices, and so on in cumulative fashion. But somewhere in this path of descent, the price declines encourage additional purchases, and again not simply in the equilibrating manner conceived by price theory but because prices appear to be so unrelated to past (experienced) values as to suggest more generally that such low terms will not long be offered and that expenditures now will con-stitute an effective arbitrage in time.

Thus the time stream itself, which has created memories of past price associations, refuses to permit some present associations to be entertained as realistic. It is only when this tie to realism breaks down that the fantasy of a runaway inflation can emerge, with values having no anchor to any experience in a past more remote than the last transaction.

REACTIONS IN THE POLITICAL RELATIONSHIP

Limits on aggregate income fluctuations also operate through political channels. At some point the generality of adverse effects occasioned by the loss of real income through either depression or inflation can be expected to stimulate a political reaction. This line of discussion has become so prominent in labor economics that its more general significance is probably now recognized. It has been argued that when unemployment mounts, the pressures of labor unions on the government to institute some kind of a full employment program will be irresistible, and that in the politico-economic climate generated by this necessity for continuing full employment unions will be able to press for wage increases which are certain to create inflationary price movements. It has also been argued, however, that continuing inflation will not be tolerated by the public at large but will evoke pressures for government restraints on price movements. Professor Reder has indeed constructed a model which involves the retention of office by a political party favorable to labor unions until the unions' wage demands have pushed prices beyond a tolerable rate of increase, at which point the opposition party is voted into office, restraining unions and prices by devices which may in time (through the resulting redistribution of bargaining power) create unemployment. When unemployment and declining aggregate income reach a level which elicits a strong support of the party pledged to full employment, there occurs a new transfer of political power, with the cycle repeating itself.[2]

Such indirect limits on aggregate income fluctuations operate with no precision or certainty. They do, however, create a *probability* of a reaction to shifts in bargaining power whose nonoffsetting effects lead to prosperity and depression, and such reaction effects constitute *probable* limits to the income effects which induce them. It would seem reasonable to conclude that any recession or

[2] Melvin W. Reder, "The General Level of Money Wages," in Industrial Relations Research Association, *Proceedings of the Third Annual Meeting* (1950), pp. 186–202.

inflation from which there is a readjustment without *any* government intervention would be a mild one indeed. Through monetary or fiscal policy or through administrative or legislative actions modifying the costs of agreement and disagreement of private parties on each other's terms, the members of government enter into political bargains which set limits to income movements.

If one is prepared to consider the whole structure of bargaining relationships dealing with the use and distribution of scarce resources, the political as well as the economic, it becomes evident that a Keynesian equilibrium at *much* less than full employment is not a true equilibrium. It is inconceivable that a situation giving rise to substantial unemployment would be allowed to persist by those adversely affected, that it would fail to give rise to pressures for change which would work themselves out through political coalitions or combinations and other forms of manipulation, redistributing bargaining power in such a manner as to force the level of aggregate income (and employment) back within the limits of an equilibrium range. Such an equilibrium range is of necessity more shadowy and imprecise than an equilibrium point, but the loss of deductive certainty is counterbalanced by the gain of empirical probability.

The boundaries of that equilibrium range, it has been suggested here, are imposed by limits on the concentration and fluctuation of aggregate income in both the exchange and political relationships. Any redistribution of bargaining power is considered to produce reaction effects—behavioral responses designed to restore lost position.

The limits on the concentration of income are set by the fact that alternatives automatically become more attractive as the terms of some bargain become more exacting, and the success of the accumulating unit or units induces innovation and imitation, reducing the price of the original good or service and the prospect of income concentration based on its exploitation. These direct effects may be partially forestalled if the aggrandizing unit achieves a combination with its principal alternatives, but in this event countercombination in the direct (exchange) relationship may be effective. In addition, there are political restraints on the concentration of income, internally in the increasing difficulty of an increasingly comprehensive unit to compose the conflicts which are internal to its organization, and externally through political action to weaken the position of the giant or to strengthen the bargaining power of those opposing it.

Limits on the fluctuation of aggregate income are provided by the continuity of consumption patterns (with the aspirations of social groups based on their own past experiences and on changes— which are scarcely mercurial—in the comparisons which are coercive on them) and by the continuity of price expectations (with the responses of buyers conditioned by the realism of the terms of bargains in the light of past experience). Other limits on the fluctuation of aggregate income are found in political actions alternating between support of full employment and opposition to price inflation.

In sum, with a shift in the distribution of bargaining power there is always a potential effect on the allocation of income and on its aggregate level. But if such effects become actual and cumulative, reaction effects can be expected which set limits (admittedly quantitatively imprecise, even if not undefinable) on the concentration and fluctuation of income flows. There is no ground for predicting the behavior of any given economic unit, any more than the physicist can predict the behavior of any atom. It is only the probability, based on observations of large numbers, that permits us to generalize as to actions and reactions under given conditions.

This notion of a range of equilibrium is more compatible with dynamic than with static analysis. The essence of a dynamic model is perhaps better stated as a controlled disequilibrium—never a position where there is no tendency for movement, but always a position where the movement arises out of previous partially determining events and is controlled within limits by the existence of a system of relationships which gives it meaning and a measure of predictability, based on probability.

CHAPTER 18

Summary and Final Remarks

IN the preceding chapters we have attempted to construct a system of concepts which explains the economic process.

1. In our system of concepts, we begin with "economic" aspirations, which relate to satisfactions found through the use of scarce resources and through the work process itself. The latter is significant since it affects the former—the desire for income for consumption is balanced against the accompanying alternative work satisfactions and opportunities for self-employment. Aspirations relate to a person's life span, in a time stream which embodies proximate goals, intermediate objectives, and ultimate ends. Proximate goals are set for the individual by the comparison of his achievements with the achievements of others in some group or groups which are homogeneous in some cultural respect. Probable gains in the realization of aspirations must be balanced against probable risks in the determination of courses of actions, and decisions as to the need for and methods of obtaining income (the revenue decision) interact with decisions as to the amount and kinds of expenditures that should be made (the budget decision).

By aspirations, then, we mean a time stream of multiple objectives giving rise to interacting revenue and budget decisions, largely influenced by cultural forces so that classes of uniformities are statistically discernible.

2. Aspirations can be achieved only through competition with

others in a world where scarcity of resources does not allow the satisfaction of everyone's material desires. But aspirations can also be obtained only through coöperation with others in a world where specialization has led to interdependence. The terms of coöperation, which resolve simultaneously the scarcity and interdependence conditions, must be arrived at by a bargaining process, and the nature of the resolution depends on the relative bargaining powers of those who are party to the agreement.

Bargaining power is the capacity to effect agreement on one's own terms. It is defined by the other's inducement to agree on the terms which one offers, which in turn depends on his cost of disagreement on those terms relative to his cost of agreement. Price is only one element affecting those costs. The basic determinants of the costs of disagreement and agreement are the aspirations and alternatives of the individual, which jointly establish how much is given up by failing to effect this particular relationship and how much must be given up by effecting it. The network of commensal and symbiotic relations, arising out of scarcity and interdependence, which in turn are attributable to aspirations and alternatives, thus builds a web of bargaining relations. In the bargaining relationships the bargaining power of one must be laid alongside the bargaining power of the other party or parties, since bargaining power is only a relative matter. For whichever party the inducement to agree is stronger, bargaining power is weaker. But bargaining power is susceptible to manipulation by any of a variety of devices which affect the aspirations and alternatives of those with whom the bargain is sought.

3. The use of resources involves a flow through time, so that the economic problem of allocation (no less than of fluctuations in aggregate levels of resource use) is a matter of income flows, though at the micro level. The only significance of price is the effect on bargains, and the only significance of bargains is their effect on income flows.

4. Income flows focus in organizational units, chief among which are households, firms, and governmental units. The flow of income

into the unit is the resultant of its revenue decision, which involves its determination of the use of its time, its use of its assets, its borrowing against the future. The flow of outcome out of the unit is the resultant of its budget decision, which involves the allocation of its funds among the members who are competing for a share in it, as well as to savings and investment. The revenue and budget flows (income and outgo) must always be equal *ex post* and are planned to be equal *ex ante*.

5. The revenue and budget decisions represent a complex of bargains. The function of management, in any economic unit, is to coördinate the mass of bargains so that they equate inflow and outflow at a level and with a composition that provides for everyone on whom that result depends a cost of agreement lower than the cost of disagreement. Whatever discretion and income remain unallocated after all bargains have been coördinated accrue to management as a basis for managerial initiative and achievement. To maintain the balance at a preferred level management must continually manipulate and renegotiate bargains.

6. The exchange relationship is the bargain struck directly between management (in any unit) and some economic symbiont. The political relationship is the bargain struck with any other individuals, groups, or agents to retain or obtain some measure of control over the coördinating function itself. Both relationships affect the flows of income at the micro level, and both relationships are subject to manipulation. Political bargains may be struck within the unit itself (between cliques or factions within a large corporation, for example), or they may be sought within a larger unit whose management (a government, for example) coördinates bargains among symbionts who include the smaller unit (a corporation, for example).

The politician who seeks votes and the citizen who casts his vote are both offering terms (though frequently only implicit or conjectural) which impose costs of disagreement and agreement on each other and which may include political commitments directly affecting the flow of funds or indirectly affecting them by modifying the distribution of bargaining power in the system. Political bargains cannot be excluded from economic analysis because they are political but only because (or, more correctly, only *if*) they do not affect the size and direction of the flows of income.[1]

7. Shifts in aspirations and alternatives affect the flows of income among the many units within the economic system. As the flow of income to any unit increases or diminishes, it has a multiplier effect on other units. But at the macro level these multiplier effects may cancel out, leaving the aggregate flow unaffected. It is only in the case of the multiplier effects of income movements which are not offset that aggregate income is affected.

8. The shifts in micro income movements are the resultant of shifts in relative bargaining power, which if offset can be regarded as random in nature, while if nonoffset must be regarded as more specific and widespread. Over the historic long run, nonrandom changes are associated with concomitant movements in aspirations and alternatives, such as the spread of materialism and the drive for business success, increases in productivity and population. Such movements improve the bargaining position of the managers of productive activity (principally in firms and government units) relative to those from whom they obtain revenues and relative to those to whom they disburse revenues, expanding their residual discretion and encouraging the exercise of initiative. In the short run, nonrandom shifts in bargaining power are associated chiefly with changes in the proximate goals of economic units, contingent upon such events as the instigation or cessation of wars, the rise of major innovations or the temporary satiation of wants which are coercively experienced (the "felt necessities" of the time, within a particular social grouping). Short-run changes in the quality or quantity of alternatives affect chiefly whether there is a dispropor-

---

[1] I fear that some will object that I have pushed the concept of bargains so far as to include any decision whose consequences are taken into account when it is made. I do not intend to be so inclusive. The only decisions which I include as bargains are those (1) which affect income flows, and (2) which are affected by demands made by others which impose costs if agreed to and costs if disagreed to.

tionate movement between aggregate money income and aggregate real income.

9. If we define equilibrium as a range within which there is constant change, but movements outside of which are subjected to influences forcing their reversal, then there are equilibrium restraints on the concentration of income in the hands of a limited number of economic units and on the amplitude of the fluctuations of aggregate income. These limits are imposed in both the exchange and the political relationships.

Limits to the concentration of income arise from the automatic increase in the attractiveness of alternative relationships when the cost of agreement with certain symbionts rises, from the automatic inducement to others to imitate or innovate in the area where reward is most promising, and from countercombination—all these in the direct exchange relationship. Political restraints arise from the difficulty of managing an increasing complex of bargains (where concentration depends on merger or expansion), and from political action within the larger unit of government. The more distressed the condition of any class or group within the society, the stronger the bargaining position of any politicians who offer terms promising relief of distress. The imminent threat of the demagogue is in fact an effective restraint on power accumulation and income concentration.

Limits on the fluctuation of aggregate income are imposed by the stability and continuity of people's aspiration patterns, which lead to temporary and partial satiation of demand, on the one hand, and to refusal to accept further sacrifice of previous achievements, on the other hand. Political restraints on the amplitude of income fluctuation are to be found in popular support for full employment, on the one hand, and for inflationary controls, on the other—terms which politicians might with some reason decide they could reject only if willing to sacrifice the symbiont relationship (more bluntly, concede defeat).

10. None of the above deduced conclusions can be stated with

certainty. The test of the reliability of the concepts on which they are based lies in the *probability* of the deduced event. In the scientific discipline, the deductions from concepts demand logical certainty, which is the equivalent of a mathematical exercise, but conceptual reliability rests on empirically ascertained probabilities.

What advantages are to be found in this system of analysis? Three will be suggested.

1. It includes relationships affecting the use of scarce resources which are often omitted from equilibrium (systematic) analysis. As long as price remains the theoretical nexus for economic relationshps this rules out of the picture the tax relationship between the individual and his government, since this is not a product of the market. It ignores the impressive system of social security which has been built up, omits any consideration of the imposition of antitrust policies on business firms, skips over labor legislation, leaves unexplained the tremendous foreign-aid programs following World War II, disregards the numerous forms of public utility regulation. All these areas of investigation find their orphan's home within departments of economics, it is true, but they remain unassimilated into general economic theory. In particular, the relationship of the political bargain to resource flows has been neglected. And this in the face of the fact that, as Professor Alexander Gray has pointed out, today more than at any time since the days of mercantilism has practically every economic problem become a political problem.

2. It deëmphasizes price and focuses on income flows, at the micro level, thus permitting the integration of micro and macro analysis. Price falls into perspective as only one manipulable variable affecting relative bargaining powers and thereby income flows. Flows assume their proper importance in view of the emphasis on the time element. The integrated bundle of aspirations extends over time and is achieved and protected over time, and this compels primary consideration of flows. Flows are affected by bargains, and bargains are influenced by prices, but it is the income stream, not price, which is the theoretical nexus for economic relationships.

3. It abandons maximization, which relies on the certainty of deductive logic used in conjunction with the concepts of a static system. It replaces maximization with the notion of a balance of culturally conditioned objectives, the material aspects of which are realizable through the income stream and the empirical reliability of which is tested by statistical probability. Maximization loses its relevance since there is no specific unit of time within which income can be maximized, and there is no justification for carving time into artificially discrete units for theoretical use. Logical certainty ceases to be a test once chance, uncertainty, and novelty are accepted, leaving probability analysis as the more significant test of the concepts from which logical deductions are made.

What are the policy implications of this system of analysis? An answer to this question may be made on two planes.

1. The analysis may suggest methods of meeting particular problems. If, for example, the problem is to forestall downward fluctuations of aggregate real income, it would seem clear that this result can be obtained by anything that sustains aggregate demand. If the problem is to forestall upward rises in aggregate money income at a time when the alternatives are fully employed, it is clear that this result depends on a reduction of aggregate demand. Such problems can then be broken down further into an examination of the conditions under which, below full employment, new bargains will not be offset and foregone bargains will be offset, or the conditions under which, above full employment, new bargains will be offset and foregone bargains will not be offset. Unorthodox (as well as orthodox) methods of achieving these results may then suggest themselves—such as governmental insuring of private investment (in the case of depression) or compulsory saving (in the case of inflation, as in World War II).

2. At a somewhat more fundamental level, however, policies are a matter of aspirations—designed to achieve an objective—and thus of relative bargaining powers. A policy constitutes the terms offered by some to achieve their objectives, and it will be accepted only when the cost of agreement of those whose approval is needed is

less than their cost of disagreement. Policy proposals have no chance of acceptance unless they recommend themselves to some party with sufficient bargaining power to secure their adoption. They make an impact only when they suggest the means for someone's accomplishing his objectives who has sufficient bargaining power to secure the adoption of this means. They will be modified to purify them of anything which runs counter to this purpose, and to some extent they will be defiled with concessions designed only to induce the necessary others to agree on these terms. The only hope of the disinterested scholar who recommends policy in the *public* interest is that some *special* interest group (and perhaps one that he despises) will find something in his proposal that it will want to foster for its own, not the public's gain.

A final comment relates to the emphasis on the *system* of relations which has characterized this book. The viewpoint adopted has been that an understanding of any class of economic relationships (labor relations, for example) is possible only within an understanding of the larger system of relationships. The micro and macro analyses are both necessary to illumine the whole problem, just as a study of both individuals and societies is necessary to explain the conduct of people.

The total structure of relationships in a society—the web of symbiotic and commensal relations—depends, however, on a general acceptability of the individual relationships, since this is the condition necessary for the preservation of an orderliness sufficient to permit the drafting of generalizations concerning economic behavior. At the same time such a system must extend some permissiveness of change, with sanctioned methods of exercising relative bargaining powers to alter positions, since any who would seek to freeze an existing system of relationships would find themselves protecting something of remarkable fragility. (The system must be viable, to use the term commonly employed.) A system thus controls the limits of change at the same time that it offers inducements to change within those limits. It is this systematic aspect of the aggre-